YAN-KIT'S
CLASSIC CHINESE
COOKBOOK

YAN-KIT'S
CLASSIC CHINESE COOKBOOK

Yan-kit So

DORLING KINDERSLEY
LONDON • NEW YORK • SYDNEY • MOSCOW

A DORLING KINDERSLEY BOOK

To my son, Hugo E. Martin

Editor Fiona MacIntyre
Art Editor Sue Story
Managing Editor Amy Carroll

First published in Great Britain in 1984 by
Dorling Kindersley Limited,
9 Henrietta Street, London WC2E 8PS

Second Impression 1984

First published as a Dorling Kindersley paperback 1998

Visit us on the World Wide Web at http://www.dk.com

A CIP catalogue record for this book is available from
the British Library

ISBN 0-7513-0563-4

Printed and bound in Singapore
by Star Standard Industries (Pte.) Ltd.

CONTENTS

Note Monosodium glutamate (MSG) is a white crystalline substance which adds a meaty sweetness to food. It is used widely in Chinese restaurants, but as some people react badly to it I do not use it in home cooking, nor have I used it in this book.

INTRODUCTION

My interest in food is inherited from my father. Although he did not cook himself, he always asked mother to see to it that what was on the table was correct, right down to the last detail: for him, stir-fried dishes had to have "wok fragrance", sugar was to be used very sparingly in marinades; chicken was not to be overcooked lest the flesh became tough; fish for steaming was to be bought live from the market and abalone was to be well seasoned with oyster sauce. Like children in other Chinese families, my brothers, sisters and I joined the grown-ups for dinner from the age of four or five, picking with chopsticks from the dishes served in the centre of the table so it isn't surprising that what has stayed in my mind is delicious well-prepared dishes, seasoned to father's liking, rather than fish-finger nursery food.

From those early childhood days in Hong Kong I also remember father taking us to restaurants where we had delicate hot tid-bits, *dimsum*, or to the boating restaurants in Aberdeen for special seafood. Every year, during the month following Chinese New Year, his *Hong* or import-export trading company, would give a banquet to which our whole family as well as those who worked for him would go. At these banquets the menu would follow a prescribed procedure: two small, hot seasonal dishes followed by shark's fin, either as a soup or braised in a sauce, next a chicken with crispy red skin to augur another prosperous year, then a duck or perhaps succulent pigeons, followed by another soup – turtle or something else equally exotic – then one or two more stir-fried dishes and lastly a whole steamed fish, the pronunciation of which is the same as the word "surplus" which can signify abundant wealth.

Having taken good food for granted, like so many other Chinese, I did not think seriously about it until I became a frugal post-graduate student at the University of London. Short of cash but nonetheless hungry, haunted by the tastes of both home cooked and restaurant dishes, I began to try my own hand at cooking Chinese food. To my delight, I found I was adept at it. One dish led to another, and soon I found that I had become an enthusiast, cooking with zest and satisfying not only my own palate but many others'.

This amateurish approach took a marked turn some ten years ago when I spent a long summer with my young son in Waterford, Connecticut. There I used to entertain my American family and friends with Chinese dishes, and I remember their surprise that the tiny Niantic scallops could be so succulently tender, simply stir-fried; that the Cherrystone clams, delicious served on the half-shell New England style, could make one's mouth

water equally, if not more, when cooked in black bean sauce with garlic, and that sea bass and blue fish could be so refreshing steamed with slices of ginger and seasoned with a little soy sauce. They were equally enthusiastic about the strips of pork I roasted then brushed over with a little honey, and with ox tongue braised slowly in soy sauce and sherry. On my part, I found cooking remedial, relaxing and rewarding. The seed of this book was sown then.

Since that time, I have worked with different Chinese chefs in Hong Kong and London, been to China and Taiwan to sample different regional cuisines, entertained at home, and taught and demonstrated Chinese cookery both privately and publicly. The invaluable reactions of friends and students led to much pondering over food and cookery in general, and Chinese food and cookery in particular. I discovered that many people who are very enthusiastic about Chinese food are, unfortunately, in awe of Chinese cookery. They claim it is time-consuming, fiddly and generally incomprehensible. But since every form of cooking takes a certain amount of time and involves some technique, however trivial, the first two points are irrelevant. On the third point, I strongly believe that Chinese cookery can be as comprehensive as any other, and this book is an expression of that belief. How? Firstly, by taking each recipe and breaking down the method into clear steps, and by giving precise explanation (and in many cases an illustration) of how and why certain methods or techniques are used. Secondly, by illustrating every recipe to show what the dish should look like, and thirdly by describing and illustrating any special Chinese ingredients so that they can be properly selected. Above all, by presenting a fair sample of classic dishes, my aim has been to enable every cook to achieve the desired authentic effect.

WHAT MAKES FOOD CHINESE

Whatever the arguments about the greatness of Chinese cuisine, it is undeniable that certain features make the food look Chinese, smell Chinese and taste Chinese.

One feature, unique to Chinese cooking, is the technique of stir-frying. Here, a small amount of oil is poured into a heated wok and a few condiments are added to "arouse the wok" and lend fragrance to the main ingredients which are rapidly stirred and cooked in a short time.

This very rapid cooking technique requires specially prepared ingredients. In Chinese cooking the ingredients are cut up into uniformly small pieces so that they will both absorb the taste of the seasonings that they are marinaded in, and retain their freshness, juiciness and, in many cases, crispness.

Another speciality of Chinese cuisine is its use of dried products. Before the invention of canning and deep-freezing, drying was the Chinese way of preserving food. But even though canning has become a Chinese industry and frozen food products are now exported abroad, dried products are still widely used and are very often more expensive than corresponding fresh ones. This is because the dried products, when reconstituted, add an extra dimension to the taste and richness of the finished dish. For instance, the flavour and fragrance that dried Chinese mushrooms so miraculously lend to other ingredients are beyond the capabilities of fresh mushrooms. The same can also be said of dried scallops, dried oysters, dried shrimps and dried abalone, one of the most exotic ingredients in Chinese cuisine.

Nowhere in other cuisines is there such a pronounced emphasis on texture. Exotic ingredients like shark's fin, bird's nest, edible jellyfish or duck's feet, and everyday ones such as cloud ears, bamboo shoots or cellophane noodles, often have little taste, yet the Chinese go to any amount of trouble preparing them, combining them with other ingredients to lend them taste. Why? Nutrition apart, it is the texture, whether crisp, elastic or slippery, that they provide that makes them invaluable. Emphasis on texture is also apparent at a more basic level: leaf vegetables, whether boiled or stir-fried, must retain their crispness; noodles must be served *al dente*.

REGIONAL CHINESE COOKING

China is a vast country and as such is exposed to extremes of both geography and climate. This naturally results in the growth of different agricultural products, so it is little wonder that cuisines vary from province to province. Even though there has never been an agreed view on the subject, many cookbooks divide Chinese cuisines into eight main streams: Peking, Shantung, Kiangsu, Anhwei, Kwangtung, Fukien, Szechwan and Hunan; others analyze the sub-regional cuisines within some of these provinces. However, I follow the practice of broadly carving the Chinese gastronomic map into four main regions: Peking, or Northern, Shanghai or Eastern, Canton or Southern and Szechwan or Western.

One may well ask what constitutes regional

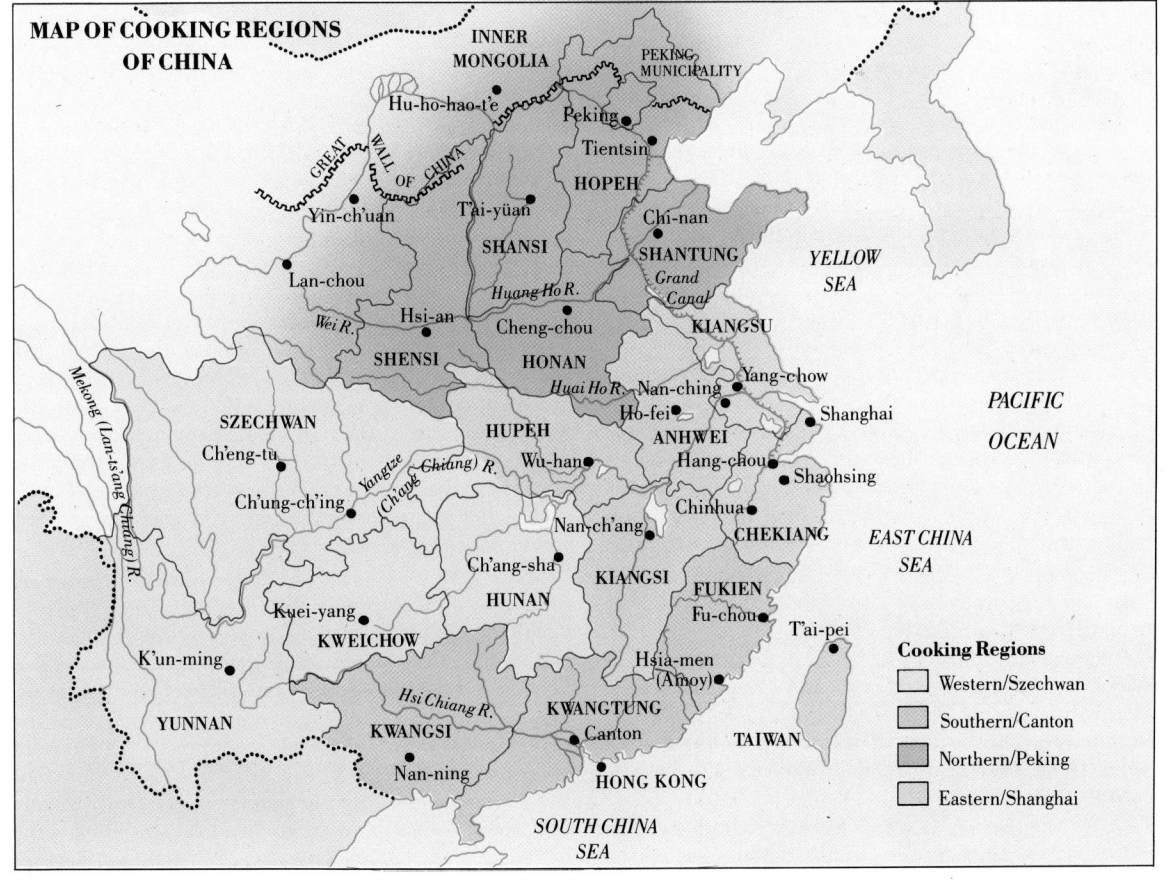

MAP OF COOKING REGIONS OF CHINA

Cooking Regions
- Western/Szechwan
- Southern/Canton
- Northern/Peking
- Eastern/Shanghai

differences since there are basic national characteristics underlining all of the regional cuisines. The main cooking methods – boiling, steaming, braising, sautéing, deep-frying and stir-frying – are used by all Chinese, the wok is the national cooking utensil, and soy sauce is a ubiquitous and indispensable seasoning. The differences are subtle, and are related to climate, to local produce, to the mixing and use of different condiments, to the emphasis on a certain technique, and to the manner of presentation.

PEKING OR NORTHERN CUISINE

This is the largest area, embracing Inner Mongolia, Hopei, Honan, Shantung, Shansi and Shensi provinces. Although Shantung has a more temperate climate, the overall climate of the area is very harsh; Peking itself suffers from extreme heat in the summer and extreme cold in the winter, and in the Spring suffers from periodic sand storms, blown in from the Gobi desert.

Wheat, millet, sorghum, peanuts, corn and soy beans are the main crops and Tientsin cabbage, better known as Chinese leaf or Chinese celery cabbage, cucumber, and celery are the main vegetables grown. Noodles, steamed breads and buns are a more popular staple than rice and, unlike the Southern Chinese who habitually eat their noodles in soup, Northern Chinese eat them on the dry side, seasoned with a sauce.

Food from Inner Mongolia and Shantung forms the backbone of Northern cuisine. The Mongolian influence is reflected in the many lamb dishes eaten, the most famous of which are Mongolian fire pot and lamb slices barbecued on a spit. In fact, mutton here is eaten and cooked in more ways than in any other region in China. Besides bringing refined dishes to the capital, Shantung chefs left their imprint on Peking cuisine with their liking for raw garlic and leeks.

Peking cuisine may be considered plain and robust, but since the nineteenth century it has exported one dish that has captivated the imagination of the whole world: Peking duck. The duck is fattened specially for the table, roasted in a special oven, then pancakes and a special sauce are made to accompany it. In Peking, the duck can be an all-in-one meal, in which the head, tongue and feet are served as separate courses alongside the more familiar crispy skin and meat.

SHANGHAI OR EASTERN CUISINE

This area, based around the Yangtze delta area which covers Kiangsu, Chekiang and Anhwei provinces, is temperate in climate and its fertile land, traversed by many rivers and ponds, is a rich agricultural area growing both wheat and rice, and yielding much fish and seafood.

Taken as a whole, Eastern cuisine is rich, decorative and rather on the sweet side; unlike Peking food, garlic is used sparingly, if at all. Although Shanghai is the name used to identify the Eastern school there are other culinary centres, represented by the main cities of the area – Hangchow, Yangchow, Suchow and Wuhsi for example. The area as a whole is renowned for certain products and dishes: the specially cured *Chinhua* ham, with its pinkish red flesh and succulently savoury-sweet taste, the rich dark Chinkiang vinegar and the amber coloured Shaohsing rice wine. Classic dishes include Crisp stir-fried shrimp, Eel cooked in oil, Yangchow fried rice, Lion's head and fish from the West Lake with a sweet and sour sauce.

One special cooking technique originating from the region has been adopted nationally. This is *hung-shao*, or the red-braising method of cooking, whereby the ingredients, (mainly meat, poultry and fish), are cooked slowly in an aromatic mixture of thick dark soy sauce and rice wine. When, at the end of cooking, the sauce is reduced while being spooned over the main ingredient, the resulting sauce is both rich and fragrant.

Shanghai cuisine is the least known outside China. Its oiliness and sweetness are perhaps less appealing to the Western palate and, because it is decorative, it tends to be labour intensive. Moreover, it depends largely on fresh local produce – the famous Shanghai crabs, studded with yellow roe in the autumn, have no counter-part elsewhere, and for the delicate taste of the famous West Lake fish one *has* to go to Hangchow.

SZECHWAN OR WESTERN CUISINE

Western cuisine is represented by the provinces of Szechwan, Hunan and Yunnan, and of these Szechwan is the most influential. A land of precipitous mountains and the Yangtze gorges, and home of the pandas, Szechwan is the most populous province in China. Fortunately it is also known as one of China's rice bowls. Very humid and rainy in the summer but mild in the winter, the temperate climate is suitable for agricultural growth almost all year round. With good irrigation, the Szechwan basin in the east of the province grows rice, wheat, rape seed, corn and bamboo shoots; citrus fruits, especially tangerines, and mushrooms are also grown. A special spice, Szechwan peppercorns, and a preserved vegetable are two special products.

Many people, when they first encounter Szechwan food, find it highly seasoned and spicily hot. Fresh and dried red chilli are evident, providing the fiery result. But, in fact, the sophistication of Szechwan cooking goes far beyond this apparent over-spiciness. Often in the same dish, the full spectrum of tastes can be experienced: salty, sweet, vinegary and hot. Rather than overpowering the taste buds, the Szechwanese claim that the chilli pepper is only a harbinger awakening them and that once stimulated, they will be able to appreciate the full range of tastes and aftertastes.

A street market where the Chinese go everyday to buy fresh vegetables. On display are some of their favourites: Chinese white cabbage, Tientsin cabbage, flowering cabbage and Chinese broccoli.

Special Szechwanese dishes are Hot and sour soup, Fragrant and crispy duck, Twice-cooked pork and a range of fish fragrant dishes.

In terms of cookery techniques, Szechwan dishes often employ multiple processes; for example its famous smoked duck which is first marinated, then smoked, steamed and finally deep-fried.

CANTONESE OR SOUTHERN CUISINE

Centred in the provinces of Kwantung and Fukien, the climate of this area is sub-tropical, with heavy rainfalls between May and September; the coast is subject to typhoons. The Pearl River delta of Kwangtung and the coastal plains of Fukien are rich agricultural areas. Rice crops are harvested twice a year, and rice is the staple eaten twice a day. Sweet potato, corn, taro and wheat are also cultivated. There are many pig and poultry farms, and fish ponds. Vegetables, especially green leafy vegetables, abound. Tropical fruits, oranges, bananas, peaches, pineapples and juicy lychees are plentiful. High quality tea is a special product of Fukien, while all along the coast fish and seafood – crabs, crayfish, prawns, scallops, clams – are plentiful. This wealth of ingredients has helped to make Cantonese cooking the most versatile and varied of Chinese cuisines.

Cantonese food is not highly seasoned. Instead, a harmonious blending of different flavours is sought in order to bring out the best of the ingredients. However, this does mean that it often relies upon fresh ingredients and when they are not available and substitutes have to be used the results can taste insipid.

Whilst they are adept at all Chinese culinary techniques, Cantonese cooks are at their most skilful when they stir-fry dishes. If red-braised dishes are an Eastern contribution to Chinese gastronomy, then Southern stir-fried dishes reign supreme nation-wide. Their "wok-fragrance", a term used to describe the aroma so desirable in stir-fried dishes, is matchless.

Dimsum, hot hor d'oeuvres of pastry cases stuffed with a mixture of delicacies such as pork, beef or seafood, bamboo shoots or mushroom, steamed, sautéed or deep-fried, is another Cantonese speciality. There are, of course, *dimsum* in all the other regional cuisines, but none can beat the Cantonese for variety. Because of the time, labour and special skill called for to make *dimsum*, they are more of a treat to be enjoyed at restaurants than at home.

WHAT IS A TYPICAL CHINESE MEAL?

To the Chinese, a meal constitutes rice or another grain, with a few dishes. The number of dishes accompanying the rice depends on the number of people sharing the meal, but a family of six may have three or four dishes at dinner, and perhaps one less at lunch. Obviously the more the dishes, the more festive and special the occasion. Whatever the number of dishes, they should be well balanced so that in one meal a variety of ingredients, including meat, seafood and vegetables, are eaten, and different cooking methods appreciated.

LAYING THE TABLE

As a Chinese meal is a communal affair, a round table is usually used, being more conducive to sharing of the dishes. For each place setting you need one rice bowl, a matching saucer and a pair of chopsticks. As the name so aptly suggests, the rice bowl is for the rice, the saucer underneath is for food taken from the communal dishes before you eat them, or for the bones you gently spit out. The chopsticks are placed vertically to the right side of the bowl and saucer – the Chinese do not seem to have made concession to left-handers!

The basic table setting is a rice bowl, saucer and chopsticks. On occasion you may also need a soup spoon and small dish for sauces.

HOW TO SERVE A MEAL

On a day-to-day basis, all the dishes are served together in the centre of the table (with extra rice kept warm for second or third helpings). There is no specific order for eating the dishes, so one may have a mouthful of chicken followed by another of bean curd, followed by yet another of fish. However, for more formal occasions, the dishes are served individually. The sequence of order varies from place to place, but generally one or two seasonal "delicacies" are served at the beginning, followed by substantial dishes of meat and poultry, with special soups in the middle and a fish to end the dishes.

("To have fish" is pronounced exactly the same as "surplus", in Mandarin and Cantonese, so the Chinese frequently use this pun and choose fish to symbolically end the main dishes.) Then, one fried rice and often one noodle dish will be served. This is the host saying, with traditional polite modesty, "Excuse my humble fare which may not have been sufficient, so please fill up with some grain food!"

HOW TO EAT RICE

The proper way is to raise the bowl with one hand and perch it on your lower lip and then, holding the chopsticks with the other hand, to shuffle the rice into your mouth without dropping the grains on to the table or floor. Rice symbolises blessings in life for the Chinese and it is therefore vital for you to grab your blessings rather than pick away at them.

In China it is considered good manners to hold the bowl on your lower lip and to shuffle in the rice.

EATING OTHER DISHES

When you pick up a piece of food from one of the central dishes, it is quite all right to do so at the same time as another person so long as your chopsticks do not end up fighting in the dish. Having picked up the pieces, remember to make a gesture of touching the rice in the bowl, however momentarily, before putting the food into your mouth.

When a piece is large in size, whether with or without bone, it is polite to eat it in bites rather than in one gulp. The bones can be sucked, quietly, before being gently spat out on to the side plate.

The main aim should be to enter into the spirit of the meal and to *enjoy* yourself. Don't forget, however, if you are host, to always put some choice pieces on to the bowl or saucer of your guests.

WHAT TO DRINK WITH CHINESE FOOD

Like table manners, the Chinese are casual about what they drink with their meals. Traditionally, they drank warmed up rice wine with their food and tea after the meal, but some Chinese have now adopted a habit of drinking beer or cognac or whisky, sometimes straight and sometimes diluted, with the meal. In Chinese restaurants abroad a custom has developed of serving tea throughout the meal. Many Westernized Chinese have also found that some Western table wines, especially white or rosé, go well with Chinese food. Many Chinese never drink anything with their food; they are, on the other hand, more particular about the tea they drink after the meal. There is a wide choice of tea to serve after the meal – jasmin, keemun, Oolong, iron goddess of mercy or Tit-koon-yum, Pu-erh from Yunnan and chrysanthemum, to name but a few. Jasmin is a green tea scented with jasmin petals, originally beloved of the Shanghaiese but now popular throughout China and abroad. Tit-koon-yum from Fukien, gleaming with a dark lustre, releases its subtle fragrance slowly after it has been infused in the pot for some minutes. Pu-erh tea is believed to have a slight medicinal property, and is excellent after a meal of rice dishes.

USING CHOPSTICKS

Perch the chopsticks on the first knuckles of the third and middle fingers so that they lie parallel to each other, resting in the crook of the thumb. Lay the thumb on top of the chopsticks to secure them – the lower chopstick should remain more or less stationary while the upper one is manoeuvred by the first and middle fingers in a pincer movement.

INGREDIENTS

Beans and Bean Products

Beans and bean products play a prominent rôle in Chinese cooking where they are used in much the same way as dairy products in the West. The soy bean, one of the most ancient staples grown in China, is richer in protein than any other food of equivalent weight. However, because they are hard to digest as beans, they are usually processed into sauces or, more importantly, bean curd. Many imitation meat dishes, the backbone of Buddhist vegetarian food, are based on the numerous forms of bean curd. Fermented bean products are very important seasonings in savoury cooking, while the red azuki bean, whole or in paste form, is used in many sweet dishes.

豆腐 **Bean curd, fresh**
Made from a mixture of finely ground soy beans and water, bean curd is used extensively in Chinese cookery.

豆腐泡 **Bean curd, puffed**
Deep-fried pieces of fresh bean curd, used to absorb tastes and juices.

三邊腐竹 **Bean curd sheet**
Thin, dried sheet of bean curd, has to be moistened before use.

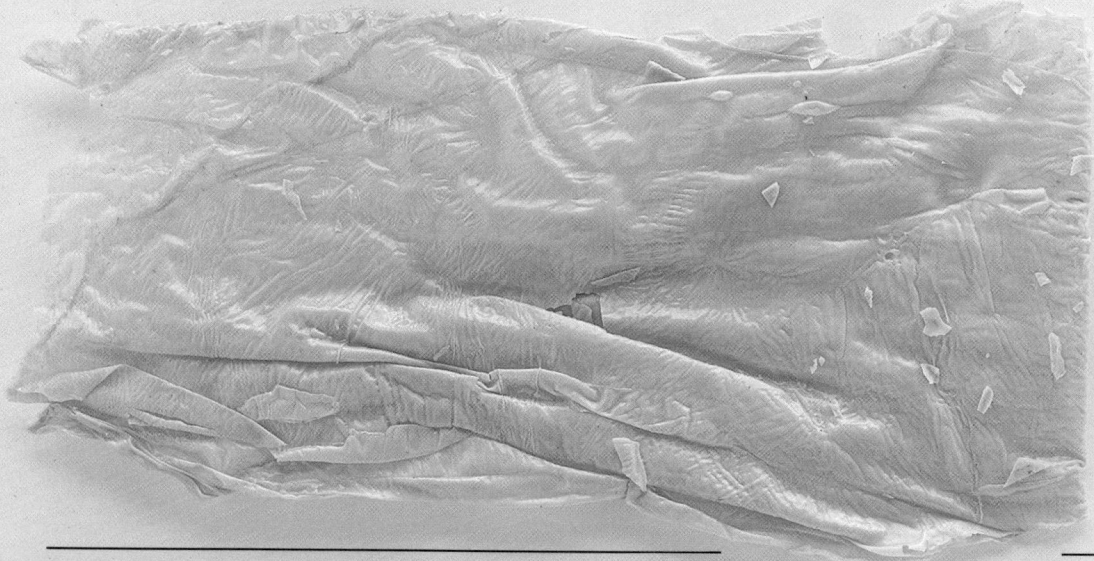

Black beans, fermented
Whole soy beans preserved in salt and ginger.

紅豆 **Red beans**
Highly proteinous azuki bean, most commonly used for puddings in Chinese cookery.

紅豆沙 **Red bean paste**
Thick paste made from puréed, sweetened red beans, frequently used as a sweet filling.

 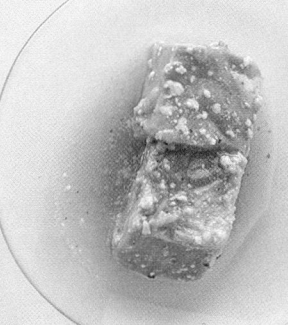 

Bean curd "cheese", red fermented
Fresh bean curd, fermented with salt, and rice wine.

辣椒腐乳 **Bean curd "cheese", white fermented**
Fresh bean curd, fermented with or without chilli.

磨豉醬 **Crushed yellow bean sauce**
Purée of fermented yellow soy beans, wheat flour, salt and water.

Szechwan chilli paste
Spicy hot paste of dried chilli and crushed yellow bean sauce.

豆瓣醬 **Soy bean paste**
Paste of crushed soy beans combined with chilli, sugar and salt.

麵豉 **Yellow beans in salted sauce**
Whole yellow soy beans fermented with salt, wheat flour and sugar.

13

Cereals, Grains and Noodles

Long-grain white rice is the most important staple for the Chinese and it is usually eaten with every meal. Noodles are generally of secondary importance, apart from in the North where wheat is the main crop and they are eaten just as much as rice. Symbolically rice is blessing in life and noodles are longevity. Not surprisingly, therefore, noodles are always served for a birthday celebration.

春卷皮 **Spring roll wrapper**
Paper-thin wrapper made from wheat flour and water.

雲吞皮 **Wonton wrappers**
Made from wheat flour, egg and water and used specifically for wontons.

糯米 **White glutinous rice**
Sticky when cooked, this rice is used for both savoury and sweet dishes.

占米 **Long-grain rice**
The hulled, polished grains of this variety remain the ideal staple for the Chinese.

沙河粉 **Sarhor noodles**
Made from rice ground with water, which is then steamed into thin sheets before being cut.

米粉 **Dried rice noodles**
White, wiry noodles made from rice flour.

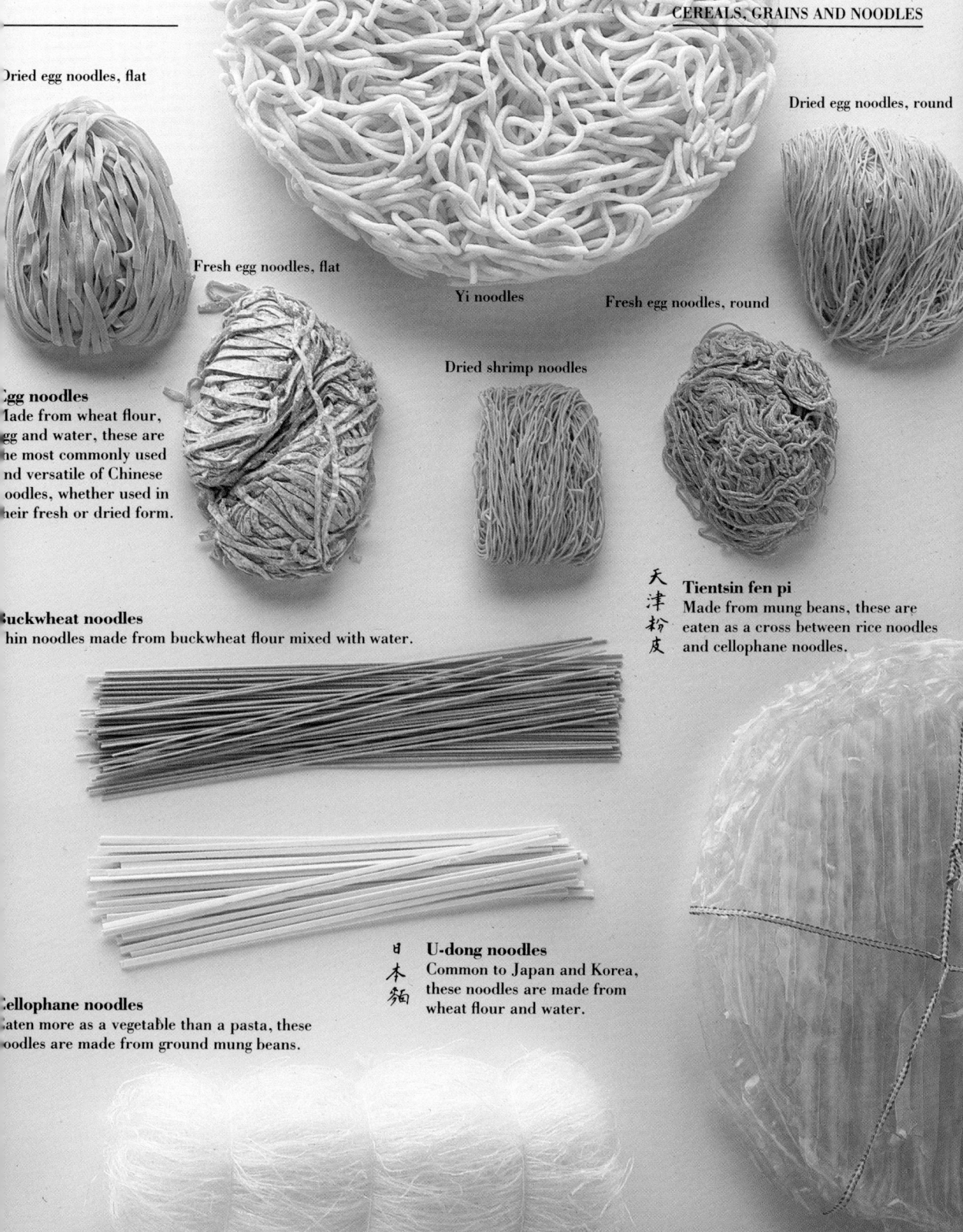

Dried egg noodles, flat

Dried egg noodles, round

Fresh egg noodles, flat

Yi noodles

Fresh egg noodles, round

Dried shrimp noodles

Egg noodles
Made from wheat flour, egg and water, these are the most commonly used and versatile of Chinese noodles, whether used in their fresh or dried form.

Buckwheat noodles
Thin noodles made from buckwheat flour mixed with water.

天津粉皮 **Tientsin fen pi**
Made from mung beans, these are eaten as a cross between rice noodles and cellophane noodles.

日本麵 **U-dong noodles**
Common to Japan and Korea, these noodles are made from wheat flour and water.

Cellophane noodles
Eaten more as a vegetable than a pasta, these noodles are made from ground mung beans.

Dried Products

One cannot get very far with Chinese cooking without using dried fungi. They are used, according to variety, to provide texture or taste, and very often hold the balance of quality in a dish, making a simple dish taste outstanding. Black mushrooms, used whole or sliced into small pieces, provide their own taste but also absorb that of others. Both cloud ears and golden needles absorb tastes and are often used to give texture to stir-fried pork or beef dishes; wood ears, which need to be cooked longer, are best in soups.

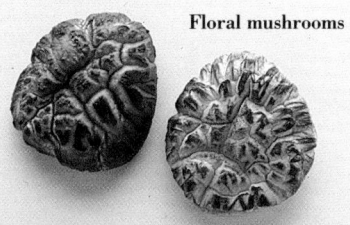

Floral mushrooms

Chinese mushrooms, dried and reconstituted
These edible tree fungi vary in both quality and price, the most expensive being the floral mushroom (top right). The medium-sized mushrooms are most frequently used in this book.

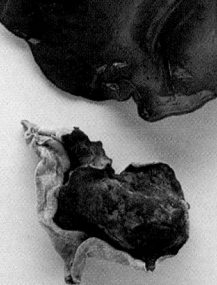

Straw mushrooms, canned

Wood ears
Large, edible mushrooms cultivated in large quantities in Western China.

Straw mushrooms
Cultivated on rice straws in paddy fields, they are used more for their texture than their taste.

Straw mushrooms, dried

Cloud ears
Like wood ears, these mushrooms are grown in Western China but they are more delicate in taste.

金針 Golden needles
The dried buds of the tiger lily flower, generally used for their texture.

陳皮 Tangerine peel
Dried peel which is often used with star anise and Szechwan peppercorns.

紅棗 Dried red dates
Sweet, prune-like fruit of the jujube tree.

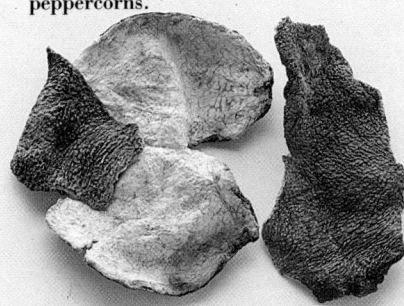

椰油 Creamed coconut
Concentrated coconut milk in a solid form.

栗米粉 Cornflour
Fine white starch extracted from maize, used as a thickener.

生粉淀粉 Potato flour
Made from cooked potatoes, this flour produces a more gelatinous sauce than cornflour.

馬蹄粉 Water chestnut flour
Made from ground water chestnuts, this is used when a lighter sauce is required.

氷糖 Rock sugar
Crystallized cane sugar.

大菜 Agar-agar
Gelatinous thickener derived from seaweed.

Dried Products

Chinese dried products, used as either the main ingredient or as a seasoning for more bland ingredients, are regarded as second to none. Abalone, scallops, oysters and shrimps, although delicious fresh, are much richer in taste and more interesting in texture when dried. Bird's nest, shark's fin and edible jellyfish actually have no fresh counterpart in Chinese cooking and always have to be reconstituted before cooking.

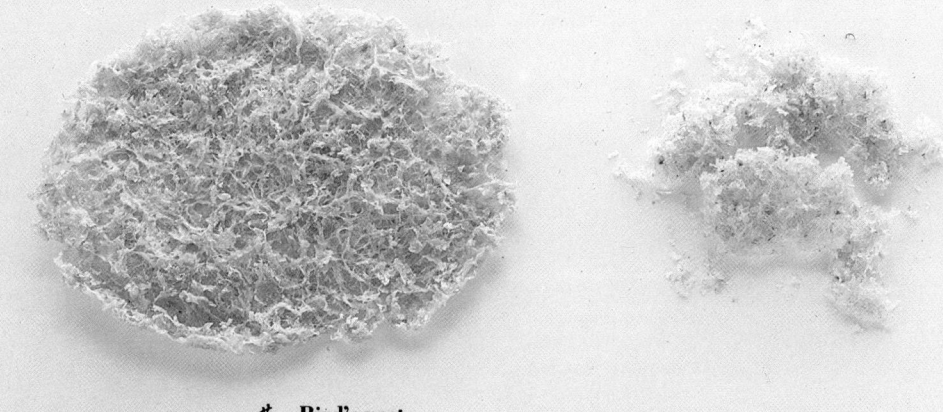

燕窩 **Bird's nest**
Nests of the swallows of the Collocalia genus who line their nests with a thick mixture of predigested seaweed which then dries to a hard, transparent layer.

Pork liver

Pork and duck liver

臘腸 **Chinese sausages**
Wind-dried sausages made of pork or pork and duck liver. Both should be cooked before use.

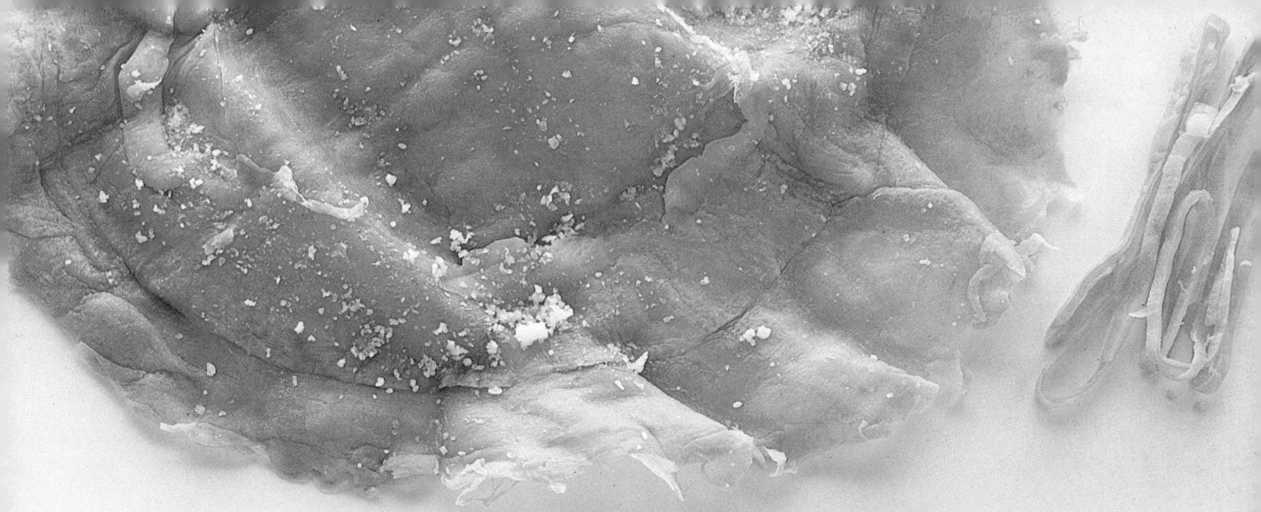

海哲皮 **Edible jellyfish**
Preserved and dried in salt, the layers must
be soaked in frequent changes of water
before use.

魚翅 **Shark's fin**
The cured fins from more than one species of shark.
The processed fins (right), are more economical to
use.

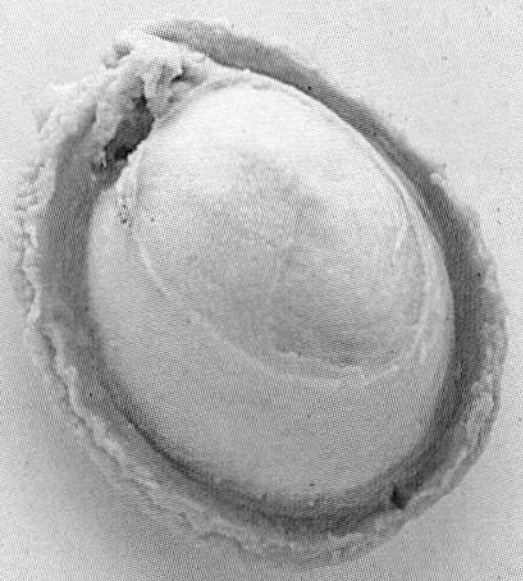

罐頭鮑魚 **Abalone**
Firmly fleshed mollusc which is usually only available
canned. The juice is useful for soups and sauces.

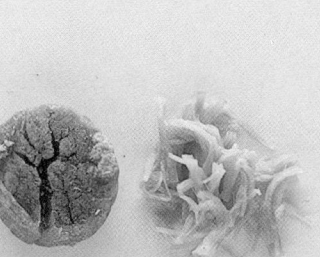

干貝 **Dried scallop**
Deriving their name from the
shell's shape, these molluscs have
a deliciously sweet taste.

蠔豉 **Dried oyster**
Dried and salted, these molluscs
add a smoky taste to other
ingredients.

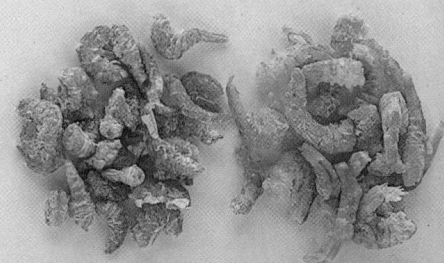

蝦米 **Dried shrimps**
Dried shelled shrimps of various
sizes, frequently used as a
seasoning and in stuffing.

Herbs and spices

Relatively few herbs and spices are used to produce the sophisticated simplicity of Chinese cuisine. The three indispensable ones are ginger, spring onions and garlic, especially for stir-fried dishes. Next in line are star anise, Szechwan peppercorns and cinnamon, all of which enrich the taste of soy sauce-based, slow-cooked dishes. Chillies, especially the dried red ones, are part and parcel of Western regional cuisine whereas coriander is beloved of the Northern people.

葱 Spring onions
An essential ingredient in Chinese cuisine. Both green and white parts are used.

蒜 Garlic
One of the three indispensable ingredients of Chinese cooking, along with ginger and spring onions.

乾葱頭 Shallots
Similar to, but less pungent than onions, they can, however, be used in the same way.

香菜 Coriander
Also known as Chinese parsley, it is used as both a garnish and a seasoning.

卤
水
料 **Mixed spices**
Used in flavour-potting, the ready made-up packets usually contain star anise, Szechwan peppercorns, cinnamon, ginger, fennel, cloves, liquorice and cardamom.

五香粉 **Five-spice powder**
Liquorice-tasting powder used, sparingly, in marinades.

花椒粉 **Ground roasted Szechwan peppercorns**
Dry-roasted then ground up, used to add aroma to other ingredients.

花椒 **Szechwan peppercorns**
Not spicy hot like peppercorns, the roasted variety produce a slightly numbing effect.

辣椒乾辣椒 **Chilli**
Indispensable hot ingredient of Szechwan cooking.

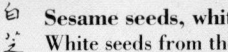

白芝麻 **Sesame seeds, white**
White seeds from the sesame plant.

八角 **Star anise**
Pungent liquorice-tasting spice used to add flavour to meat and poultry.

Fresh ginger

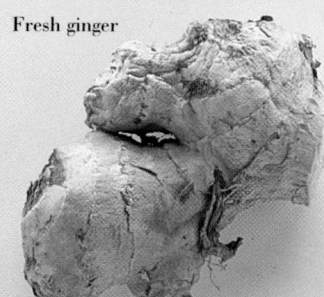

Dried ginger

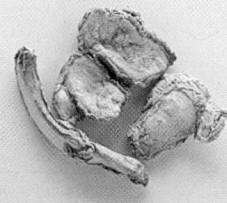

Ground ginger

生薑 **Ginger**
The third essential ingredient in Chinese cooking, used to provide flavour and to counteract any rank odour of other ingredients.

桂皮 **Cassia bark**
Dried bark of an evergreen tree, often confused with cinnamon (left), which can be used as an alternative.

Cinnamon stick

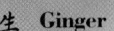

Vegetables

The Chinese love to eat vegetables, and the leafy green vegetables of the brassica family are their special favourites. They boil or stir-fry them, but only for a short time so that the vegetables retain both their crispness and their vitamins. They frequently use a little meat to enhance the taste of vegetable dishes, and conversely use some vegetables in meat dishes to provide an interesting texture.

菜心 **Chinese flowering cabbage**
This vegetable is usually served stir-fried or simply blanched.

芥菜 **Mustard green**
This more pungent variety of mustard green is served pickled, braised or in soup.

芽菜 **Bean sprouts**
Tender sprouts of
mung beans, used to
provide a crunchy
texture.

雪豆 **Mange tout**
Tender, flat green peapods
with barely-formed peas.
Usually served lightly blanched or stir-fried.

紹菜 **Chinese celery cabbage**
Sweet, mild-flavoured
cabbage, usually stir-fried
or braised.

白菜 **Chinese white cabbage**
Although similar in taste to Swiss
chard, it is nevertheless sweeter and
juicier.

芥菜 **Mustard green**
This variety of mustard
green is less bitter than
many others, and it is
usually served
blanched or stir-fried,
or in soup.

韭菜 **Chinese chives**
Used to provide
flavour, they are
stronger than chives,
although more fibrous
in texture.

Vegetables

As with many Chinese ingredients, texture is important in a vegetable: the spongy hair seaweed is both an absorber of sauce and a provider of texture; water chestnuts and bamboo shoots are pure texture foods. The flesh of winter melon is succulent and subtle while the slimy taro goes especially well with duck. Ginkgo nuts and baby corn on the cob, often used in vegetarian dishes, add colour and variety to a dish. The three preserved vegetables are popular seasonings for meat, soups and other vegetables.

冬瓜 **Winter melon**
Green gourd, the flesh of which becomes almost transparent when cooked. It is often used in soup with pork, chicken or duck.

馬蹄 **Chinese water chestnuts**
Crisp, sweet-tasting sedge bulb, used to provide a crunchy texture. They are also ground into flour.

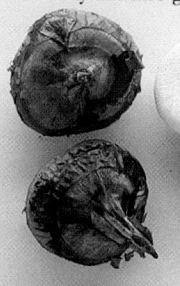

芋頭 **Taro**
Root vegetable, freqently cooked with duck or fatty pork.

髮菜 **Hair algae**
Product of the Kansu and Sinkiang provinces, this rather tasteless ingredient is used to absorb flavour and provide a slippery texture.

竹筍 **Bamboo shoots**
Young shoots of bamboo plants, used for their texture in many Chinese dishes.

白果 **Ginkgo nuts**
Tender, mild-tasting nuts from the Ginkgo tree.

咸酸菜 **Pickled mustard green**
Mustard green preserved in brine.

珍珠筍 **Young corn**
Miniature corn on the cob, used in both vegetable and meat dishes.

雪菜 **Red-in-snow**
Red-rooted variety of mustard plant which sprouts up through the spring snows.

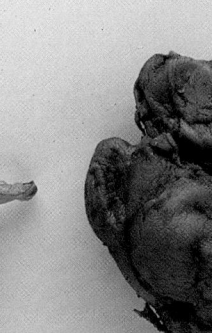

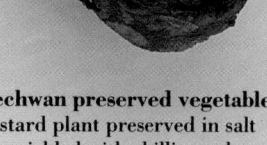

榨菜 **Szechwan preserved vegetable**
Mustard plant preserved in salt then pickled with chilli powder.

Sauces, Oils, Wines and Vinegars

Because so many Chinese dishes are stir-fried or deep-fried oil is obviously an important ingredient, but it is also important for the flavour it gives to marinades. Sauces of various types are used in marinades and to add flavour to cooked ingredients. Soy sauce is the most basic but also the most important seasoning. Used with salt, it helps to turn simple ingredients into Chinese cuisine.

SAUCES

Thick soy sauce

Thin soy sauce

醬油 **Soy sauce**
Made from fermented soy beans with wheat or barley, salt, sugar and yeast.

蠔油 **Oyster sauce**
Made from oyster juice, wheat flour, cornflour and glutinous rice, salt and sugar.

辣椒醬 **Chilli sauce**
Made from crushed chillies, vinegar, salt and plums.

海鮮醬 **Hoisin sauce**
Soy beans, wheat flour, salt, sugar, vinegar, garlic, chilli and sesame oil combined.

甜麵醬 **Sweet bean sauce**
Made from crushed yellow bean sauce combined with sugar.

蝦醬 **Shrimp paste**
Ground shrimps fermented in brine; available in two strengths.

魚露 **Fish sauce**
A combination of fish, salt and water.

芝麻醬 **Sesame paste**
Pulverised sesame seeds. Tahini paste should not be used instead.

OILS

栗米油 **Corn oil**
A polyunsaturated oil from the sweetcorn plant.

芝蔴油 **Sesame oil**
Dark, aromatic oil from roasted white seeds.

花生油 **Groundnut oil**
Rich, monounsaturated oil with a nutty flavour.

FATS

辣油 **Hot chilli oil**
Oil in which red chilli flakes have been steeped.

雞油 **Chicken fat**
Chicken fat rendered down by slow frying.

猪油 **Lard**
Rendered pork fat.

WINES AND VINEGARS

高梁酒 **Kao-liang liqueur**
Very strong spirit made from sorghum.

茅台酒 **Moutai wine**
Distinctive spirit made from wheat and sorgham.

紹興酒 **Shaohsing wine**
Popular wine made from fermented glutinous rice and yeast.

玫瑰露酒 **Mei-kuei-lu wine**
Made from Kao-liang spirit and rose petals.

鎮江香醋 **Chinkiang vinegar**
Thick fragrant liquid with low vinegar content.

江浙醋 **Red vinegar**
Low vinegar content; frequently used as a dip.

米醋 **Rice vinegar**
Used for cooking and pickling vegetables.

EQUIPMENT

The wok

A wok fitted with a lid is an essential cooking utensil as it is suitable for all methods of Chinese cooking, especially stir-frying. It varies in size but for family use a 35cm (14 inch) one made of carbon iron is ideal.

竹擦 Wok brush
Stiff wooden brush used for cleaning the wok after use.

鑊 The wok
Generally made of iron, these round-bottomed pans allow the heat to spread rapidly and evenly, which is essential in Chinese cooking. They are available with both wooden and iron handles – both styles should be used with a glove. Woks can be used for stir-frying, deep-frying, boiling and steaming.

蒸籠 Bamboo steamer
Small steamer placed on wooden trivet; used with wok lid or own bamboo one.

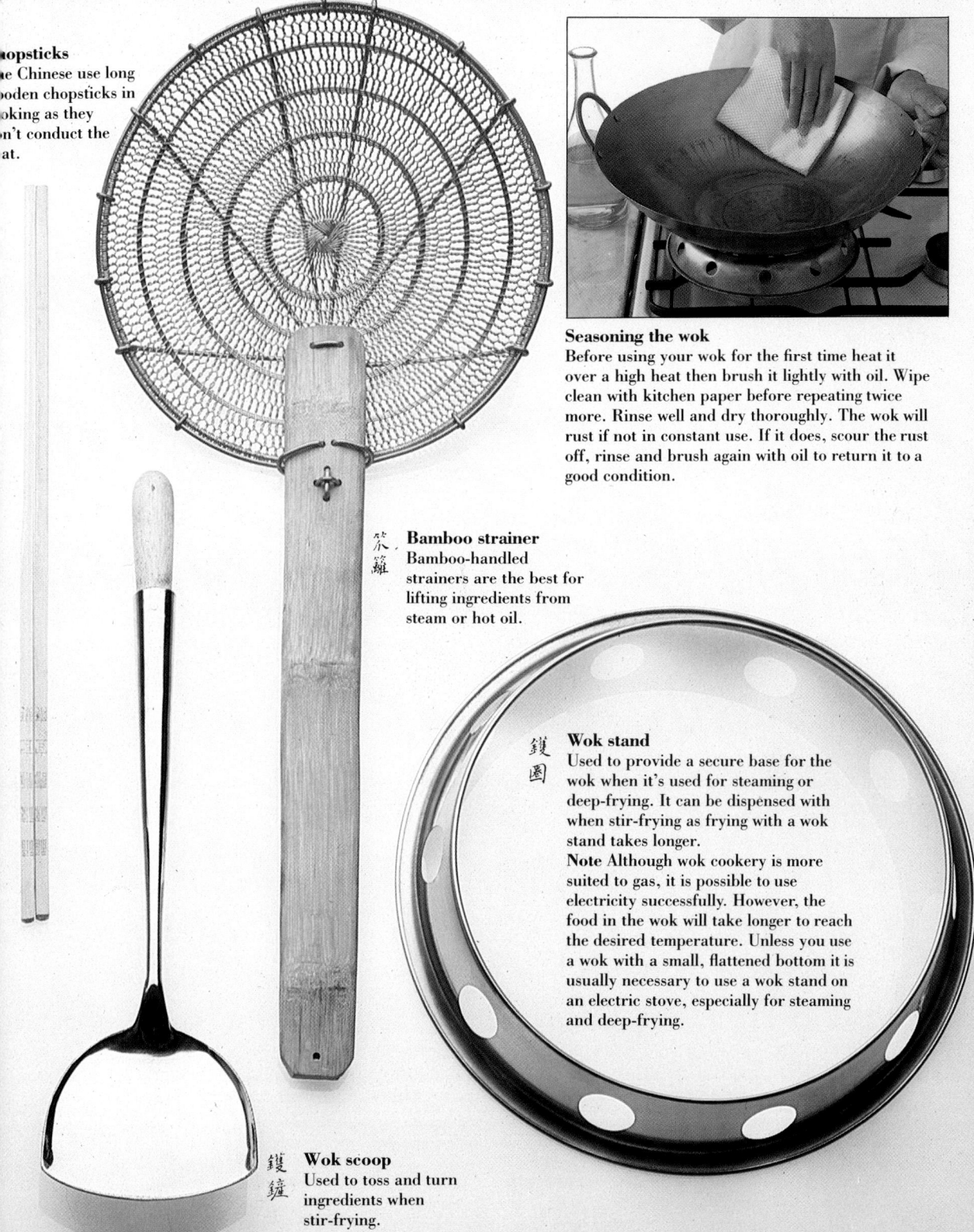

opsticks
e Chinese use long
oden chopsticks in
oking as they
n't conduct the
at.

Seasoning the wok
Before using your wok for the first time heat it over a high heat then brush it lightly with oil. Wipe clean with kitchen paper before repeating twice more. Rinse well and dry thoroughly. The wok will rust if not in constant use. If it does, scour the rust off, rinse and brush again with oil to return it to a good condition.

笊籬 **Bamboo strainer**
Bamboo-handled strainers are the best for lifting ingredients from steam or hot oil.

鑊圈 **Wok stand**
Used to provide a secure base for the wok when it's used for steaming or deep-frying. It can be dispensed with when stir-frying as frying with a wok stand takes longer.
Note Although wok cookery is more suited to gas, it is possible to use electricity successfully. However, the food in the wok will take longer to reach the desired temperature. Unless you use a wok with a small, flattened bottom it is usually necessary to use a wok stand on an electric stove, especially for steaming and deep-frying.

鑊鏟 **Wok scoop**
Used to toss and turn ingredients when stir-frying.

Steamers and cleavers

There are two basic types of steamer: specially designed metal ones which act as both water boilers and food containers, and traditional-style bamboo steamers which fit on top of a wok in which the water is boiled. These come in various sizes, from small (see page 28) for dimsum to those large enough to hold a whole fish (see below).

The other method of steaming doesn't require a steamer but is just as effective, especially for everyday use (see page 45). Instead, the food (on a heatproof plate) is held above the water in the wok by a metal or bamboo trivet, and the steam is retained by a tightly fitting wok lid. For any cutting, fine or rough, all you need is a medium-weight cleaver and a solid wooden board.

蒸籠 **Steamer**
Made of stainless steel or aluminium, this specially designed steamer has a lower container for the water, on which sit one or two perforated containers for the food. The food is placed on a heatproof dish or muslin, and then covered with a tightly fitting lid.

Assembled metal steamer
Slotting snugly together so that all the steam is directed up through the holes to the food, this steamer can sit directly on the source of the heat.

Bamboo steamer in wok
This traditional-style steamer can be used with one or more baskets to hold the food. The wok must rest on a wok rim for stability.

Cleaver

One of medium weight, about 9 x 20cm (3½ x 8 inches), made of carbon or stainless steel is ideal for general use.

If you find this too big, try one of the more slender, lighter cleavers, below. In China, this type is frequently used to carve Peking duck.

竹
墊

Bamboo mat
To prevent meat from sticking during slow cooking it should be placed on this latticed mat, placed inside the cooking pot.

砧
板

Chinese chopping board
A solid, wooded base is essential for chopping, and one 5cm (2 inches) thick and 27.5-30cm (11-12 inches) in diameter is ideal. When new they should be soaked in water and oiled frequently to prevent splitting.

TECHNIQUES

Cutting vegetables

In Chinese cooking, all vegetables are cut up into uniformly small pieces because this allows them to cook quickly without losing their crunchiness; it also means that they can absorb the taste of the oil and seasonings, despite the short cooking time. Some vegetables are cut according to their natural shape (for example, broccoli and cauliflower are cut into florets); others are sliced, shredded, diced or roll cut depending on the dish. For stir-frying, Chinese celery cabbage is shredded, but for braising it is cut into larger pieces. Bamboo shoots, if braised, are cut into wedges but if put into a stir-fried dish they are thinly sliced. Chinese mushrooms can be sliced thinly or more thickly, quartered or cut into small cubes. Root vegetables such as carrots and white radishes are roll cut to expose as many surfaces to the heat as possible; celery is traditionally cut diagonally to make it look more attractive.

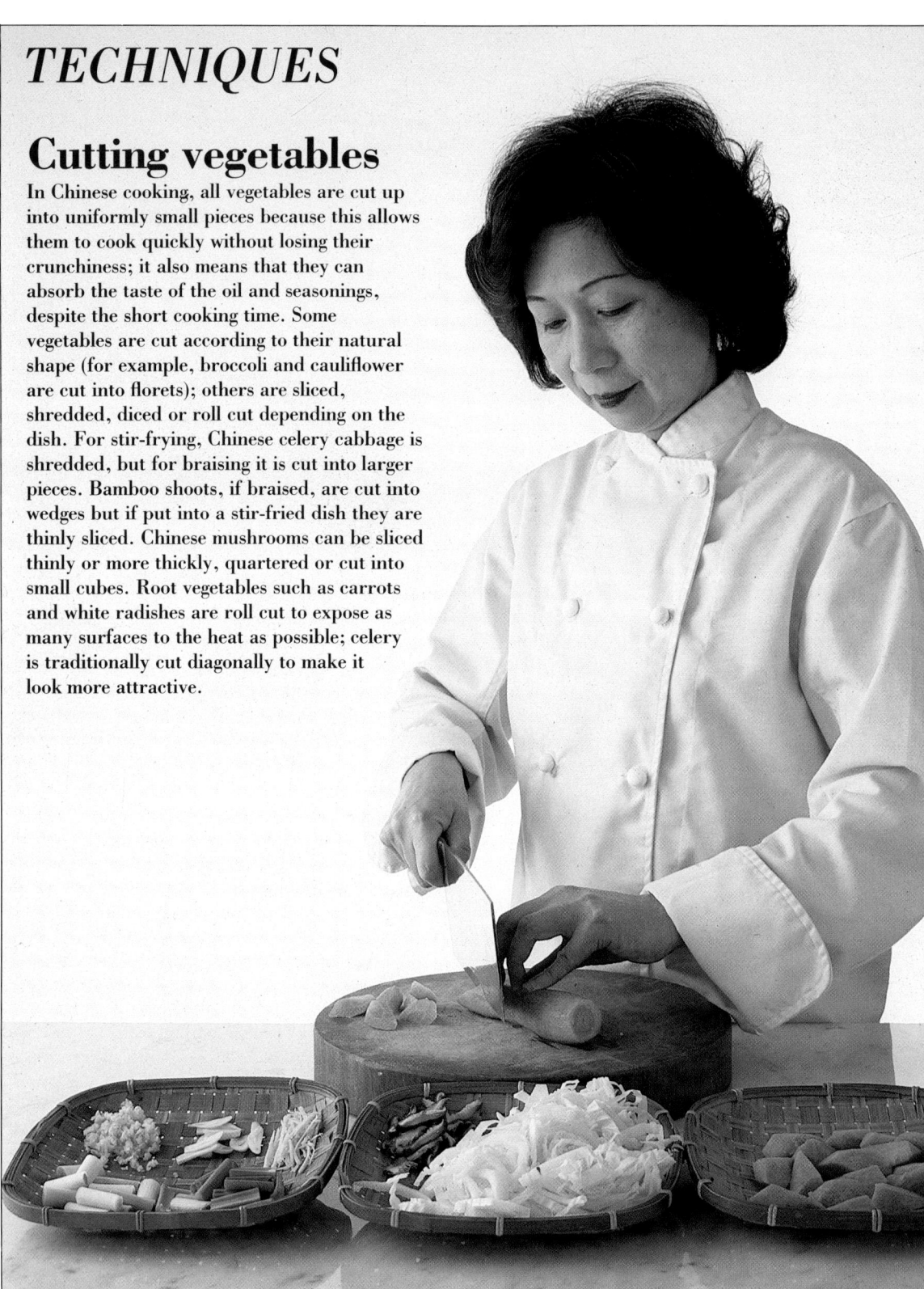

HOLDING THE CLEAVER

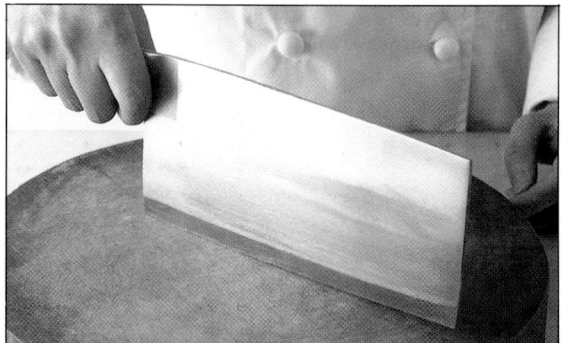

Method 1 *Curl your fingers tightly around the handle which should rest in the palm of your hand. This way, the cleaver will cut downwards with its own weight.*

Method 2 *Hold the handle in your palm as before, but slide your index finger down the side of the blade. This allows you more control using your thumb and forefinger.*

GUARDING

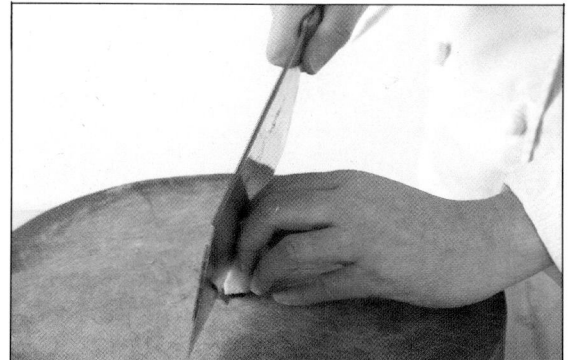

Hold the food with your fingertips turned under, knuckles forward so that they act as a guide for the cutting blade. Never lift cleaver higher than knuckles.

SLICING

Put the blade about 3mm (⅛ inch) from one edge and slice downwards. Regulate thickness by moving fingers further away from, or nearer to, edge being cut.

SHREDDING

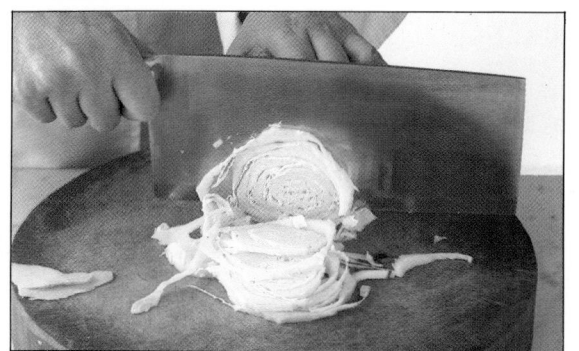

Cut the food into uniform slices about 3-6mm (⅛-¼ inch) wide, depending on preference. Cut across these slices to form shreds. With vegetables other than cabbage, stack the slices before slicing them into strips.

DIAGONAL CUTTING

Hold the top of the food firmly, with your fingers at a slant of 60°. Cut down at this angle and continue down to the end of the vegetable.

ROLL CUTTING

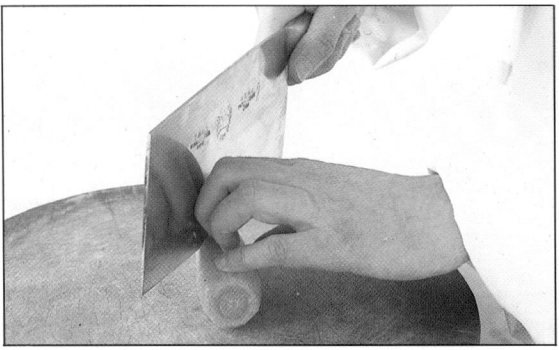 

1 *Hold one end of the vegetable firmly, then make a diagonal cut.*

2 *Roll the vegetable a quarter turn towards you and make another diagonal cut. Continue rolling and cutting.*

CUTTING SPRING ONIONS

BRUSHES

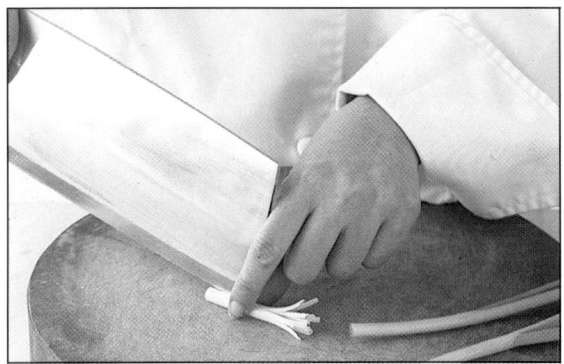 

1 *Trim the white ends of the spring onions into 6.5cm (2½ inch) lengths. Make repeated cuts through both ends, leaving the central section intact.*

2 *Place the onions in iced water and refrigerate for several hours. This will make the ends curl up, forming the brushes.*

SILKEN THREADS

Cut off the roots and any withered tops. Chop into 5-7.5cm (2-3 inch) lengths. Slice along the length of the spring onions and then cut the two halves into strands.

FIVE-WAY SPRING ONIONS

Top: *trimmed;* **middle left:** *sliced;* **middle centre:** *silken threads;* **middle right:** *brushes;* **bottom left:** *small rounds;* **bottom right:** *diagonal cut*

CUTTING GARLIC AND GINGER

SILKEN THREADS

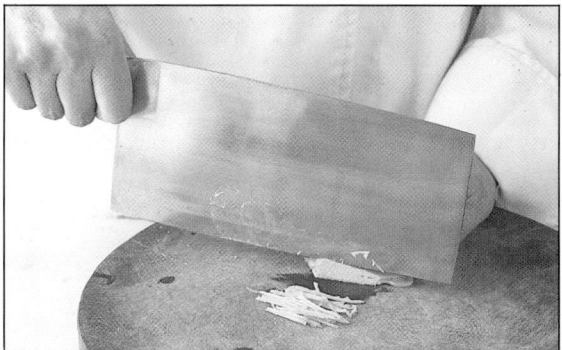

1 *Slice thinly. Arrange the slices on top of each other.*

2 *Place the cleaver carefully, and then cut slices into narrow strips.*

CRUSHING GARLIC

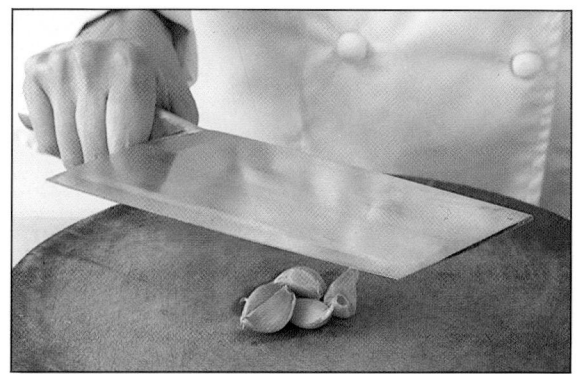

1 *Lay the unpeeled cloves on a wooden board. Using the side of the cleaver, bang down on the garlic firmly.*

2 *Separate the flesh from the skin by peeling one from the other.*

FINELY CHOPPED

Place the garlic on a wooden board. Crush with the cleaver, remove the skin, then chop repeatedly until finely minced.

THREE-WAY GARLIC AND GINGER

Top: *ginger root; sliced; silken threads; finely chopped*
Bottom: *garlic cloves; sliced; silken threads; finely chopped*

Cutting Meat

Because Chinese cooking methods rely on the rapid cooking of ingredients, any meat used has to be cut up into small, uniformly sized pieces. Invariably for stir-frying, and sometimes for steaming, the meat should be cut up into thin slices, matchstick strips or cubes. This way it can be quickly stir-fried or steamed without losing any of its tenderness.

Beef should always be cut across the grain otherwise it will be tough; pork or chicken can be cut either along or across the grain. Although the cutting up of meat into small pieces is time-consuming, it is an integral part of Chinese cooking and it is essential if you want the meat to taste good.

MATCHSTICK CUT

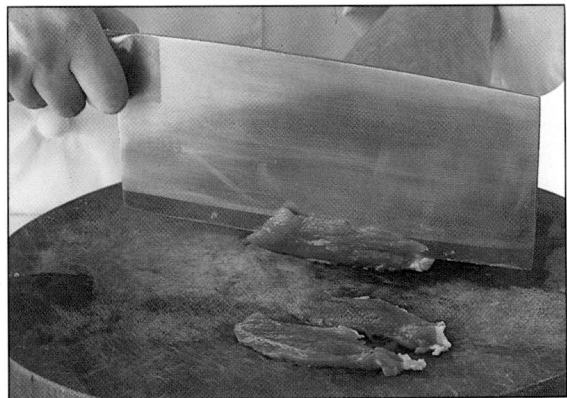

1 *Cut the meat into thin slices about 3mm (⅛ inch)*
thick.

2 *Lay the slices on top of each other and cut them into*
narrow slivers like matchsticks.

RECTANGULAR CUT

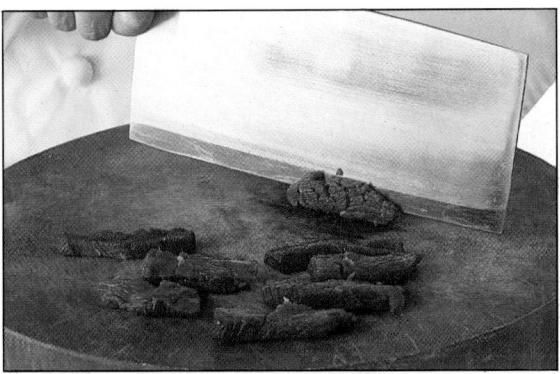

1 *Cut the meat into manageable pieces about 4cm (1½*
inches) wide.

2 *Turn the chunks on their sides and then cut* across the
grain *into rectangular slices about 6mm (¼ inch) thick.*

SLIVERED CUT

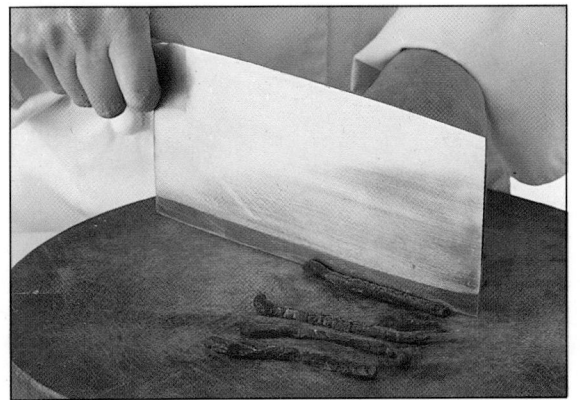

PAPER THIN CUT

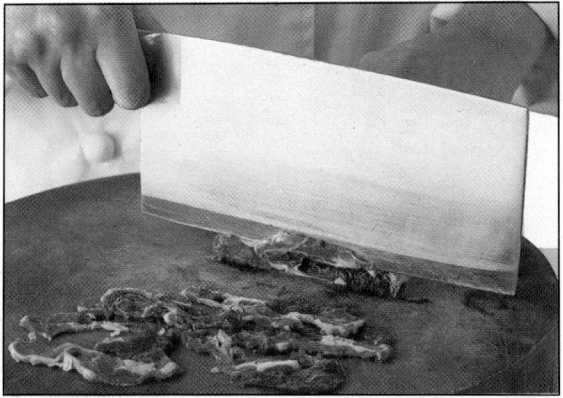

Cut 5mm (⅕ inch) slices of beef. Lay them flat and cut
into long slivers. Use especially for Dry-fried beef.

Slice the meat as thinly as possible. Freezing the meat for
a couple of hours beforehand makes this easier.

MATCHSTICK HEADS

1 *Slice the ham into uniformly-sized strips. Gather the strips together so that they're lying alongside each other.*

2 *Holding them firmly with your free hand, cut across them to form small dice.*

CUBED CHICKEN

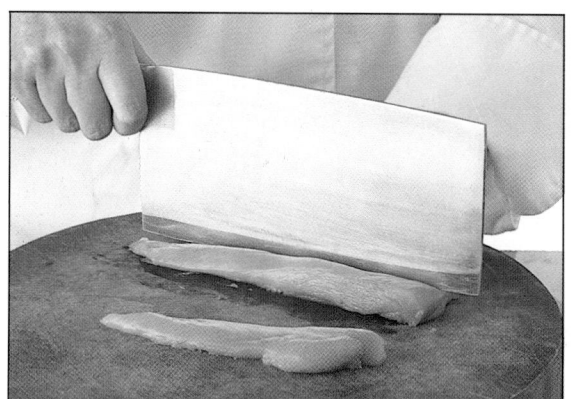 

1 *Cut the breast lengthwise into about three long strips.*

2 *Gather the strips together then cut across them to form cubes of a uniform size.*

MARCH CHOPPING

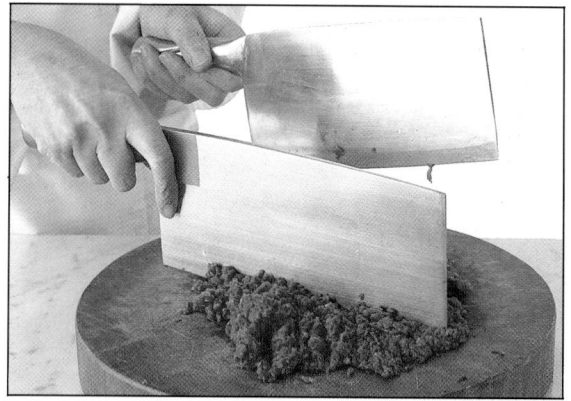 

1 *Cut the meat into small pieces. Using one or two cleavers, rhythmically chop the meat, moving from side to side.*

2 *As the meat spreads slip one cleaver under one side and use it to flip the meat into the centre then repeat the chopping.*

SPECIAL TECHNIQUES

RECONSTITUTING MUSHROOMS

1 *Rinse ingredients. Put in a bowl and pour on enough warm water to cover by about 4cm (1½ inches).*

2 *Leave for about 20-30 minutes or until they have become swollen and soft.*

DEVEINING PRAWNS

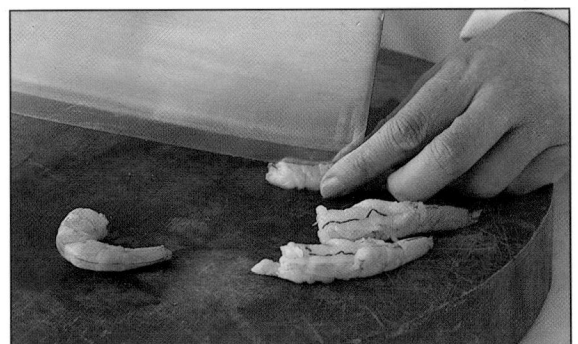 

1 *Shell the prawns. Hold the tail end firmly then make a small cut along the centre of the back.*

2 *Pull out the black vein and throw it away.*

MINCING PRAWNS

1 *Shell and devein the prawns and cut up roughly. Using the broad side of the cleaver press down on the prawns to flatten them.*

2 *Repeatedly chop the prawns until they are finely minced.*

Stir-frying

Stir-frying is the unique contribution of the Chinese to world cooking. When cooked with this method, meat is tender, vegetables are crisp, and they both have a unique fragrance. Because speed and instant control are essential, gas is preferable to electricity (cooking also takes longer on an electric burner).

In Chinese cooking there are two types of deep-frying. In one, the ingredients are deep-fried until crisp and cooked through; in the other they are deep-fried just long enough to seal in their juices. This is known as "going through the oil", and is a preparatory step to the sophisticated stir-frying invariably used in Chinese restaurants. Although it produces a more refined result in certain dishes it is not essential for everyday cooking.

STIR-FRYING

1 *Stir-frying is a very quick cooking technique so prepare all the ingredients before you start. Add the marinade to the main ingredient and stir well. If oil is to be added, blend it in last.*

2 *Heat the empty wok over a high heat until smoke rises (you may also notice a slight blue/rainbow effect at the bottom). Heating the wok before adding the oil prevents the meat or fish from sticking.*

3 *Gently add the oil (usually about 45-60ml [3-4tbsp]), and swirl it around to coat half way up the side of the wok.*

4 *If you're using garlic, add this to the oil. Steady the wok with a gloved hand as you do so.*

5 *As soon as the garlic has started to sizzle and take on colour, add the ginger. Stir.*

6 *As soon as the ginger starts to sizzle add the white part only of the spring onion (the green part needs less cooking and is added later). Stir well.*

7 *Add the main ingredient (meat, fish or shellfish). Slide the scoop under the food to the bottom of the wok; turn and toss until the food is partially cooked.*

8 *Splash in the wine or sherry around the side of the wok and continue to stir until the sizzling subsides.*

9 *Add any other ingredients which need heating or reheating and stir and toss.*

10 *Make a well in the centre of the wok and pour in the well-mixed sauce. Stir until the sauce has thickened and turned glossy.*

11 *Add the green parts of the spring onion which need the least cooking. Stir and toss briefly.*

12 *Scoop out the stir-fried ingredients on to a warm serving plate. Serve immediately.*

DEEP-FRYING

1 Put the wok on a stand. Pour in enough oil to half fill the wok. Turn the heat on high.

2 If you're using a thermometer, put it in after you've poured in the oil. Heat until the thermometer registers the required temperature.

3 When you notice the oil "moving" put in a piece of stale bread. The oil will be at 180°C (350°F) when the bread browns in about 60 seconds.

4 Using long wooden chopsticks, carefully add the food to the oil. If you don't feel confident about this, use tongs.

5 Using long wooden chopsticks, move the food around. This prevents any pieces from sticking together.

6 Using a large hand strainer (or a perforated spoon or disc), carefully remove the food from the oil. Drain on kitchen paper before serving.

Steaming

Steaming is the technique that evolved when a moist dish was required as an alternative to a roasted one. Compared with dishes cooked by other methods, steamed dishes are more subtle in taste and seem to bring out the freshness of the ingredients more. Thus, the fresher the ingredients, the better they are for steaming. In fact, steamed dishes cover the whole spectrum of ingredients: meat, poultry, vegetables (not leaf vegetables), breads, buns, hot hors d'oeuvres (dimsum), seafood and especially fish. Preparation for steaming often entails cutting up ingredients, marinating them and then putting them on to a heatproof plate so that the juices from the food and the seasonings can be served with the dish itself.

USING AN ALUMINIUM STEAMER

1 *Put the boiling water into the lower container so that it fills about half of the container.*

2 *Place whatever is to be steamed on a heatproof plate and put it into the steamer container. Place the lid securely on top.*

USING A WOK

1 *Put the base of a small bamboo steamer or metal trivet into the wok. Fill with boiling water to within 2.5cm (1 inch) of the container supporting the food.*

2 *Place whatever is to be steamed on a heatproof plate, and put it carefully on the stand. Place the wok lid on securely.*

ADDING THE CONDIMENTS TO STEAMED FISH

1 *When the fish is cooked, turn off the heat. Put in the spring onion and ginger then pour over the prepared heated oil.*

2 *If you're going to add ham, sprinkle it on top. Pour over the soy sauce and serve immediately.*

HORS D'OEUVRES

Pickled Vegetables Cantonese Style

廣東泡菜

INGREDIENTS

1 long cucumber, about 450g (1lb), halved
350g (12oz) young carrots, peeled
4-5 sticks celery, about 225g (8oz), trimmed
10ml (2tsp) salt
60ml (4tbsp) sugar
60ml (4tbsp) rice or white wine vinegar

Serves 10

Illustrated opposite

True to form, Cantonese pickled vegetables are sweet and sour rather than spicy, and their unique taste is achieved by a harmonious and subtle blending of salt, sugar and vinegar.

1 Discard the seedy pulp from the cucumber. Slice diagonally into thickish pieces at about 7mm ($\frac{1}{3}$ inch) intervals.

2 Roll-cut the carrots (see page 34).

3 Diagonally slice the celery into pieces about the same size as the cucumber.

4 Put the vegetables into a large clean bowl. Sprinkle over the salt, mix together and leave to stand at room temperature for 2½-3 hours during which time excess water will be drawn out. Drain thoroughly or squeeze out excess water but leave damp.

5 Return to a clean bowl. Add the sugar and vinegar, mix thoroughly and leave for about 3 hours at room temperature or overnight in the refrigerator. Serve chilled.

Facing page, clockwise from the top: Crisp stir-fried shrimps (see page 48); Pickled vegetables Cantonese-style (see above); Edible jellyfish with cucumber (see page 49)

Crisp Stir-fried Shrimps

INGREDIENTS
500g (1lb 2oz) fresh or frozen
raw peeled shrimps or prawns,
cut into 2-cm (¾-inch) pieces
groundnut or corn oil for
deep-frying
15ml (1tbsp) Shaohsing wine or
medium dry sherry

FOR THE MARINADE
5ml (1tsp) salt
15ml (1tbsp) cornflour
1 egg white

FOR THE SAUCE
5ml (1 tsp) cornflour
60ml (4 tbsp) clear stock
1.25ml (¼tsp) sugar
salt to taste

Serves 6

Illustrated on page 47

Texture is the essence of this dish. The quickly cooked shrimps should be crisp yet tender, and the longer they are marinated in the refrigerator – up to 3 days – the better their texture becomes. The delicate colour of the shrimps needs no garnish.

1 If frozen shrimps are used, defrost thoroughly. Wash the shrimps under cold running water. Pat dry with kitchen paper but leave damp. Put into a bowl (a).

2 *Prepare the marinade:* sprinkle the salt over the shrimps and mix well. Stir in the cornflour, then add the egg white and stir again to coat the shrimps evenly and thoroughly (b). Cover and leave to marinate for at least 5 hours.

a   b

3 *For the sauce:* mix together the cornflour, stock and sugar in a small bowl. Put aside.

4 Half fill a wok or deep-fryer with oil. Heat until just hot (150°C/300°F). Carefully add all the shrimps and fry for 30-45 seconds, separating them with a pair of long chopsticks or a long-handled wooden spoon. Remove the shrimps before they are quite cooked with a hand strainer or perforated disc and drain on kitchen paper.

5 Pour most of the oil into a container, leaving only about 30ml (2tbsp) in the wok. Reheat until smoke rises. Quickly add the shrimps to the wok and stir a few times with a wok scoop or metal spatula. Splash in the wine or sherry around the side of the wok. When the sizzling dies down, pour in the well-stirred sauce. Continue to flip and toss for a few more seconds. Add salt to taste, if necessary. Remove the mixture to a warm serving plate. Serve immediately.

Edible Jellyfish with Cucumber

Do not be put off by the initial rubbery appearance of the jellyfish which is sold in sheets, folded and packed into plastic bags with large grains of salt in-between the folds. When properly prepared, edible jellyfish gives great pleasure to those who enjoy food as much for texture as for taste. This is certainly why the Chinese seek it.

1 Shake off all the sandy salt from the jellyfish. Wash in 3 changes of water, squeezing to get rid of some of the excess saltiness.

2 Put into a large, deep bowl and fill up with cold water. Leave to soak, changing the water at 60-minute intervals and squeezing the jellyfish each time. Test by tasting: if the jellyfish is totally bland, it is ready.

3 *Prepare the dressing:* mix together the vinegar, soy sauce, sugar, oil and mustard.

4 Squeeze out excess water. Put on a board and cut into thin strips about 3mm (⅛ inch) wide. Pour hot water over the strips to make them curl up. Drain well and pat dry.

5 Cut the cucumber diagonally into slices about 3mm (⅛ inch) thick. Stack a few pieces together at a time (a) and cut into sticks about 5mm (⅕ inch) wide (b).

INGREDIENTS
450g (1lb) preserved edible jellyfish
½ long cucumber

FOR THE DRESSING
5ml (1tsp) rice or cider vinegar
30ml (2tbsp) thin soy sauce
2.5ml (½ tsp) sugar
15ml (1tbsp) sesame oil
2.5ml (½ tsp) made-up mustard

Serves 4

Illustrated on page 47

a   b

6 Arrange the cucumber on the serving plate and place the jellyfish in the centre.

7 Just before serving, add the well-stirred dressing to the jellyfish, then mix in the cucumber.

Shredded Chicken with Tientsin Fen-Pi

This pleasant Northern dish is served cold with a slightly tangy sauce, and because it can be prepared completely in advance it is very handy for entertaining. The fen-pi, literally meaning the skin of flour, must not be soggy if the dish is to be successful.

INGREDIENTS

2 small chicken breasts, skinned and boned, or 225g (8oz) chicken breast fillet
600ml (1 pint) clear stock or water
4 pieces Tientsin fen-pi, each about 22.5cm (9 inches) in diameter
½ long cucumber, about 225g (8oz)

FOR THE SAUCE

15ml (1tbsp) rice or white wine vinegar
10ml (2 tsp) hot made-up mustard
2.5ml (½tsp) salt
2.5ml (½tsp) sugar
60ml (4tbsp) thin soy sauce
8 turns white pepper mill
15ml (1tbsp) sesame oil
45ml (3 tbsp) groundnut or corn oil

Serves 6

Illustrated opposite

1 Put the stock or water in a saucepan and bring to the boil. Add the chicken flesh and simmer, covered, for about 5 minutes. Remove from the heat and leave to steep in the liquid for 15 minutes without disturbing. Remove and leave to cool.

2 *Prepare the sauce:* mix together the vinegar, mustard, salt, sugar, soy sauce, pepper and oils.

3 Bring a large pan of water, about 1.75 litres (3 pints), to a fast boil. Put in the fen-pi, one by one, so that they will not stick to each other. Cover, then remove from the heat for 5 minutes. Drain, then put the fen-pi into a pan of cold water, handling with care.

4 Fold each fen-pi into 3, then cut crosswise at 1cm (½ inch) intervals. Transfer to a serving plate.

5 Cut the cucumber diagonally into thin slices, leaving them in an ordered pile. Then cut the pile into thin strips. Place on top of the fen-pi.

6 Going with the grain, tear the chicken by hand into thin strips and put on top of the cucumber.

7 Just before serving, pour the sauce over, mix well and serve.

Note: if the dish is not to be served straight away, the ingredients can be individually refrigerated, covered, and assembled just prior to serving.

Facing page, clockwise from the top: Shredded chicken with Tientsin fen-pi (see above); Steamed scallops in the shell (see page 53); Spiced salt spareribs (see page 52)

Spiced Salt Spareribs

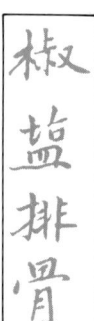

INGREDIENTS
700g-1.1kg (1½-2½lb) meaty
  pork spareribs
22.5-37.5ml (1½-2½tbsp)
  cornflour
groundnut or corn oil for
  deep-frying
5-7.5ml (1-1½tsp) spiced salt

FOR THE MARINADE
4-6.25ml (¾-1¼tsp) spiced salt
22.5-37.5ml (1½-2½tbsp) thin
  soy sauce
5-7.5ml (1-1½tsp) sugar
8-10 turns black pepper mill
10-15ml (2-3tsp) Shaohsing wine
  or medium dry sherry

FOR THE SPICED SALT
30ml (2 tbsp) salt
4ml (¾tsp) ground roasted
  Szechwan peppercorns
2.5ml (½tsp) five-spice powder

Serves 6-8

Illustrated on page 51

If you have trouble finding spareribs, use boneless shoulder or pork chump chops to make this dish. You will find the result just as deliciously satisfying.

1 Ask the butcher to cut up the spareribs one by one, and then chop them into pieces about 5cm (2 inches) long. This, of course, can also be done at home if you possess a heavy kitchen cleaver, a thick chopping board and a strong arm. Put the meat into a dish.

2 *Prepare the spiced salt:* add the salt to a dry wok and stir-fry over a moderate heat for about 4 minutes or until it takes on colour slightly. Remove from the heat and add the Szechwan peppercorns and five-spice powder. Mix well and leave to cool. (Spiced salt can be kept in a covered jar for a long time.)

3 *Prepare the marinade:* add the spiced salt, soy sauce, sugar and wine or sherry to the spareribs. Blend well. Leave to marinate for about 2 hours, turning the pieces over 2-3 times for better absorption.

4 Pour off any liquid marinade that has not been absorbed. Sprinkle over the cornflour and mix well to coat.

5 Half fill a wok or deep-fryer with oil. Heat to a temperature of 180°C (350°C) or until a cube of stale bread browns in 60 seconds. Place the spareribs on a large hand strainer or in a deep-frying basket. Dip into the oil 2-3 times while you separate the pieces with a pair of long chopsticks. Slide the pieces into the oil if you are using a hand strainer and a wok, or leave the deep-frying basket in the deep-fryer. Deep-fry for about 3 minutes or until the pieces begin to surface. Remove and keep nearby.

6 Reheat the oil to the same temperature. Return the spareribs to the oil and deep-fry a second time for about 1 minute or until crisp and thoroughly cooked. Remove and drain on kitchen paper before removing to a warm serving plate.

7 Sprinkle over the spiced salt. Mix thoroughly, then serve.

Note: left-over spareribs can be reheated – wrap in foil and place in a preheated oven at 190°C (375°F) mark 5 for 20 minutes.

Steamed Scallops in the Shell

A Cantonese dish at its simplest and best. The fresh scallops are steamed with just a touch of garlic, then served with a sauce to add zest to their natural sweetness. The details of preparation, seemingly elaborate, are nevertheless worth observing if you wish to make this simple yet sophisticated dish.

1 Ask the fishmonger to open the scallops on the cup side of the shells rather than on the flat side. If they have already been opened on the flat side, ask for the cup shells so that you can transfer the scallop meat to them. Remove the frills or rims, sandy and black impurities and the muscles, leaving only the white meat and the corals or roes. Separate the corals from the meat; save the corals for another recipe or freeze them. Rinse the scallop meat and pat dry, leaving them on the shells.

2 *Prepare the sauce:* divide the spring onions into 2 portions and put into 2 serving bowls. Heat a wok until smoke rises. Add the oil and swirl it around, lower the heat, then add the ginger and chilli. Remove from the heat. After a few seconds, add the soy sauces and water and bring to simmering point. Pour this mixture over the spring onion in the bowls.

3 Half fill a wok or deep-fryer with oil. Heat to a temperature of 180°C (350°F) or until a cube of stale bread browns in 60 seconds. Put the garlic into a small wire sieve. Dip the sieve into the oil momentarily 3-4 times or until the garlic has taken on colour. Save the oil for other deep-frying purposes.

4 Place 4-5 pieces of garlic and the same amount of green spring onion on each scallop. Place the scallops in a wok or steamer; some shells can perch on top of other shells as long as they are not pressing down on the meat.

5 Steam over a high heat for about 7-10 minutes. The scallops will have turned opaque and be just cooked. There will be juice in the shell.

6 Remove each shell carefully, taking care not to spill the juice, and put on a large serving platter or on individual plates. Serve hot.

7 To eat, put a small amount of sauce on the meat, then break up to absorb the sauce. As host or hostess, do encourage your guests to pick up the shell and drink the tasty juice as well.

INGREDIENTS

20 large scallops

groundnut or corn oil for deep-frying

6-8 cloves garlic, peeled and diced

4-6 large spring onions, green parts only, cut into rounds

FOR THE SAUCE

4-6 large spring onions, white parts only, cut into silken threads (see page 34)

45-60ml (3-4tbsp) groundnut or corn oil

2cm (¾ inch) fresh ginger root, peeled and cut into silken threads (see page 35)

3-4 fresh green chillies, seeded and cut into rounds

30ml (2tbsp) thick soy sauce

30ml (2tbsp) thin soy sauce

30ml (2tbsp) water

Serves 6-8

Illustrated on page 51

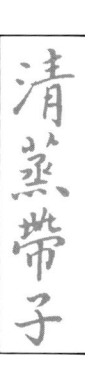

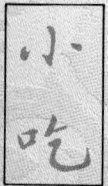

Deep-fried Appetizers

This is not literally a menu, so never try to make all seven at once. Rather, attempt one or two at a time and you will have fun both making them and eating the delicious results with your guests.

炸
五
香
卷 **Deep-fried five-spice rolls**
Aromatic pork-filled rolls, served with tomato, chilli and soy sauces (see page 195).

百
花
釀
蟹
鉗 **Stuffed crab claws**
An elegant combination of prawn and crabmeat, cri on the outside, tender ar juicy on the inside (see page 197).

鳳尾蝦

Phoenix-tail prawns
Deep-fried prawns served
with deep-fried pepper (see
page 198).

錦鹵雲吞

Deep-fried wontons
Crisp parcels of prawns,
served with a sweet and
sour sauce (see page 194).

紙包蝦

Prawns wrapped in rice paper
Deep-fried rolls of prawns, ham
and bamboo shoots, served with
a chilli sauce (page 199).

特式春卷

Special spring rolls
Delicious, deep-fried
packets filled with a
seafood, meat and
vegetable mixture
(see page 196).

炸牛奶

Deep-fried milk
Smooth, creamy filling of
coconut cream and
crabmeat, with a crisp
outside (see page 198).

Ginger Soup with Pork and Wood Ears

老薑肉片湯

INGREDIENTS

15g (½oz) wood ears,
    reconstituted (see page 39)
175g (6oz) lean pork
30-45ml (2-3 tbsp) groundnut or
    corn oil
25-50g (1-2oz) fresh ginger root,
    peeled and sliced into slivers
15ml (1tbsp) Shaohsing wine or
    medium dry sherry
2.5ml (½ tsp) salt
10ml (2tsp) thin soy sauce
1.1 litres (2 pints) clear stock
3 spring onions, cut into 1-cm
    (½-inch) sections

Serves 6

Illustrated opposite

This is a favourite summer soup of the Hunanese, who appreciate the cooling effect that the ginger brings on a humid day.

1 Drain excess water from the wood ears but leave damp. Break up the larger pieces.

2 Slice the pork into strips, about 4 x 1cm (1½ x ½ inch) and 3mm (⅛ inch) thick.

3 Heat a wok over a high heat until smoke rises. Add the oil and swirl it around. Add the ginger and stir a few times. Put in the pork and, sliding the wok scoop or metal spatula to the bottom of the wok, turn and toss for about 30 seconds. Add the wood ears, lowering the heat so that they do not make explosive sounds or fly out of the wok. Stir and turn for another 30 seconds.

4 Add the wine or sherry, salt, soy sauce and stock. Bring to the boil. Spoon off the foam that surfaces. Lower the heat, cover and simmer for 10-15 minutes. Taste for seasoning, then add the spring onion and immediately remove from the heat.

5 Transfer to a large warm soup tureen or individual soup bowls and serve hot.

Facing page, clockwise from the top: Dried scallop soup (see page 59); Egg drop soup (see page 58); Ginger soup with pork and wood ears (see above); Bean curd soup (see page 58)

Egg Drop Soup

INGREDIENTS

1 egg
900ml (1½ pints) clear stock
2.5ml (½tsp) salt
2.5ml (½tsp) sugar
5ml (1tsp) thin soy sauce
2 long spring onions, green parts
   only, cut into tiny rounds

Serves 4

Illustrated on page 57

This is the most basic Chinese soup and can be made in an instant with some clear stock and an egg. The soup's success, however, depends on the technique of adding the egg to the soup.

1 Beat the egg lightly.

2 Put the stock into a saucepan or wok and bring to the boil. Reduce the heat to a minimum. Stream in the beaten egg either through the gap of 2 chopsticks or along the back of a fork held about 20-25cm (8-10 inches) above the saucepan, moving the chopsticks or fork in a circular motion so that the egg covers the whole surface of the stock.

3 Remove from the heat and cover for 45 seconds to allow the egg to set into tender flakes. Add the salt, sugar and soy sauce, and sprinkle on the spring onion. Give the soup 2-3 generous stirs.

4 Transfer to a large warm soup tureen or individual soup bowls and serve.

Bean Curd Soup

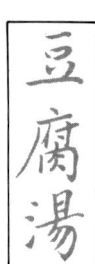

INGREDIENTS

2 cakes bean curn
100g (4oz) frozen petits pois
salt
900ml (1½ pints) clear stock
thin soy sauce to taste
15-30ml (1-2tbsp) groundnut or
   corn oil

Serves 4

Illustrated on page 57

A simple but refreshing soup which is also very healthy – a vegetarian's delight.

1 Cut each cake of bean curd into 32 cubes: cut lengthwise into 4 pieces, then crosswise into another 4 pieces and then halve each piece. Steep in hot water for 10-15 minutes. Drain, handling with care so as not to break them.

2 Place the peas in a saucepan of boiling salted water and simmer for about 3 minutes. Drain.

3 Put the stock, bean curd and peas in a saucepan and bring to the boil. Season with salt and a little soy sauce. Add the oil. Remove to a large warm soup tureen or individual soup bowls and serve.

Dried Scallop Soup

Dried scallops used to be relatively cheap in China and Dried scallop soup was the poor man's Shark's fin soup. However, times have changed and this soup, with its contrast in texture between the tender scallops and the crisp bamboo shoots, is now one of the most sought-after first courses, second only to the Shark's fin and Bird's nest soups.

1 Rinse the dried scallops, rubbing with your fingers to get rid of the white filmy substance which is sometimes found on their surface.

2 Put into a large saucepan and add about 1.4 litres (2½ pints) water. Bring to the boil and skim off the white foam that surfaces. Reduce the heat and simmer fast for 1¾-2 hours until the scallops are tender and the liquid has reduced to about 1 litre (1¾ pints). Check the water level from time to time and add more water if necessary.

3 Using a perforated spoon, transfer the scallop pieces to a dish. Shred using a knife and fork or with the fingers. Be sure to pick out and discard the hard muscles which are whole and easily recognizable. Return the shredded scallops to the saucepan.

4 Stack the bamboo slices, a few at a time, and cut into very thin strips similar to the length of the scallops. Add to the saucepan. (The procedure up to this point can be done several hours in advance.)

5 Just before serving bring the soup to a gentle simmer. Add the salt and well-stirred dissolved potato flour, stirring as it thickens.

6 Stream in the beaten egg, either between the gap of 2 chopsticks or along the back of a fork, moving the chopsticks or fork in a circular motion at the same time. Remove from the heat and cover for 45 seconds to allow the egg to set in tender flakes.

7 Transfer to a warm soup tureen or individual soup bowls and serve.

Note: the soup can be reheated slowly over a moderate heat.

INGREDIENTS

10 dried scallops, about 100g (4oz)
100g (4oz) canned bamboo shoots, thinly sliced
2.5ml (½tsp) salt
30ml (2tbsp) potato flour, dissolved in 60ml (4tbsp) water
1 large egg, lightly beaten with 1.25ml (¼tsp) salt

Serves 4-6

Illustrated on page 57

Bird's Nest Soup

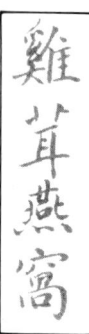

INGREDIENTS
100g (4oz) loose bird's nest
4 thickish slices fresh ginger root, peeled
2 large spring onions
1.1-1.4 litres (2-2½ pints) prime stock (see page 225)
30ml (2tbsp) cornflour, dissolved in 30ml (2tbsp) water
salt to taste
½-1 quantity Chicken velvet (see page 63)
25g (1oz) best ham, ideally Chinhua, York or Virginia, finely chopped

Serves 10

Illustrated opposite

Like Shark's fin soup, Bird's nest soup reaches the heights of Chinese cuisine, though Westerners are often put off by the name and the fact that it is produced by swallow's saliva. On its own, bird's nest is bland, and its function is to provide texture, rather than taste, to the soup. A very rich, prime stock is therefore essential as a base, as is the Chicken velvet. And yet, without the bird's nest, no amount of prime stock or chicken velvet could produce the unique quality of this soup.

1 Soak the bird's nest in about 1.4 litres (2½ pints) tepid water for several hours or overnight. Drain through a fine sieve. It will have increased about 4 times in weight.

2 With a pair of tweezers, remove any feathers or other impurities. Depending on the quality of the bird's nest, this could be a time-consuming task. Rinse in cold water 2-3 times and drain.

3 Put into a saucepan, add the ginger, spring onions and about 1.4 litres (2½ pints) boiling water. Return to the boil, then simmer for 10 minutes. Remove and discard the ginger and spring onions. Drain but leave damp. (The bird's nest can now be left in the refrigerator, covered, for 2-3 days before making the soup.)

4 Put the bird's nest and prime stock into a large saucepan and bring to a gentle simmer. Stir in the dissolved cornflour and let the soup thicken. Add salt to taste, if necessary.

5 Stir about 2 ladles of hot soup into the chicken velvet to make the purée thinner. Stream into the simmering soup, stirring to make a smooth consistency. Continue to simmer until the chicken is cooked.

6 Transfer to a warm soup tureen. Sprinkle the chopped ham on top in the centre. Serve hot.

Note: any leftover soup can be frozen.

Facing page, clockwise from the top: Bird's nest soup (see above); Shredded ham and beansprouts, mustard and vinegar for Shark's fin soup; Shark's fin soup (see page 62)

Shark's Fin Soup

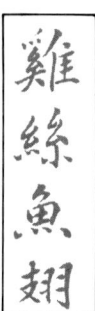

INGREDIENTS
300-350g (11-12oz) loose shark's
  fin
150g (5oz) chicken breast meat
4 slices fresh ginger root, each
  about 6mm (¼ inch) thick
3 large spring onions, halved
  crosswise
25g (1oz) lard
45ml (3tbsp) Shaohsing wine or
  medium dry sherry
15ml (1tbsp) groundnut or corn
  oil
1.2-1.4 litres (2¼-2½ pints)
  prime stock (see page 225)
salt to taste
thin soy sauce to taste

FOR THE MARINADE
2.5ml (½tsp) salt
1.25ml (¼tsp) sugar
3-4 turns white pepper mill
5ml (1tsp) Shaohsing wine or
  medium dry sherry
5ml (1tsp) cornflour
22.5ml (1½tbsp) egg white, lightly
  beaten
15ml (1tbsp) groundnut or corn
  oil

FOR THE SAUCE
45-60ml (3-4tbsp) water chestnut
  flour or potato flour
75ml (5tbsp) water
10ml (2tsp) thick soy sauce

TO SERVE
50g (2oz) lean ham, York,
  Virginia or Chinhua
225g (8oz) bean sprouts
Chinese red vinegar
hot made-up mustard

Serves 6

Illustrated on page 61

The Chinese are unanimous in their appreciation of shark's fin soup, and this very nutritious soup is rightly considered to be one of the most exotic examples of Chinese cuisine. A fin of the best quality is, however, extremely expensive and takes four days to prepare. The fin used in this recipe is sold in packages consisting of the cartilage with some fin needles and is already processed and then dried again. On its own, shark's fin has little taste but when combined with other ingredients in a prime stock, makes the perfect soup.

1 Put the shark's fin in a large container and pour over about 1.4 litres (2½ pints) hot water. Soak overnight or for a minimum of 6 hours.

2 Rub with fingers. Drain through a fine sieve so as not to lose any of the precious shark's fin needles while getting rid of fine sand. Repeat as many times as necessary. Put into a large saucepan.

3 Add about 1.7 litres (3 pints) water. Bring to the boil and simmer gently for about 2 hours, replenishing the water if it evaporates too quickly.

4 Test if the fin needles are ready: they should be tender yet still firm. Another way of testing is to press one between the thumb and the index finger: if it breaks easily, it is ready. Drain. If the fin is still hard, let the water cool, then drain. Return to the saucepan, add the same amount of water and boil gently for another hour or longer. Drain, taking care not to lose the needles.

5 Meanwhile, cut the chicken flesh into matchstick-sized pieces. Put into a small bowl.

6 *Prepare the marinade:* add the salt, sugar, pepper, wine or sherry and cornflour to the chicken. Stir in the egg white in the same direction and leave to marinate for 20-30 minutes. Blend in the oil.

7 Place about 1 litre (1¾ pints) water in a saucepan with the ginger, spring onions, half the lard and 30ml (2tbsp) of the wine or sherry. Bring to the boil. Add the shark's fin and boil gently for about 15 minutes. This curing process rids the fin of any remaining rank odour. Drain, discarding the ginger and spring onion.

8 Cut the ham into matchstick-sized pieces.

9 Pluck and discard the bean heads off the bean sprouts. Blanch in boiling water until the water returns to the boil. Drain, then refresh under cold running water. Drain thoroughly.

10 Arrange the ham and bean sprouts in bunches on 1 or 2 small serving dishes. Put the vinegar and mustard into separate saucers on the dining table.

11 *Prepare the sauce:* mix the flour, water and soy sauce thoroughly.

12 Heat a wok or saucepan over a high heat until hot. Splash in the remaining wine or sherry. As it sizzles, add the remaining lard and the oil. Pour in the prime stick, add the shark's fin and stir to mix. Slowly bring to the boil, then add the chicken, stirring to separate the pieces. Reduce the heat. Gradually add the well-stirred sauce to the soup, stirring as the soup thickens. Remove from the heat. Taste for seasoning, add salt and thin soy sauce, if necessary.

13 Transfer to a warm soup tureen and serve. To eat, each person puts some bean sprouts and ham into the bowl before adding the shark's fin soup. Some may also like to add a little vinegar or mustard to the soup.

Chicken Velvet

A preparation of finely minced chicken breast, which is made light and fluffy by the addition of egg white. It is used to add taste, texture and substance to soups, such as Winter melon soup (see page 65) and Bird's nest soup (see page 60).

1 Turn the chicken breast inside out and pull off the 2 fillets.

2 Hold the end of the white tendon of each fillet with the fingers of one hand and scrape the flesh away from it with a Chinese cleaver or knife. Discard the tendons.

3 Holding the large end of one chicken breast, scrape the flesh going with the grain from the small end all the way to the large end, discarding membranes and fat as you go. Repeat with the other breast and then with the 2 fillets.

4 Gather together the chicken flesh, sprinkle with the salt and start chopping, adding drops of the iced water and folding the flesh back to the centre from time to time. Chop for about 3 minutes or until the meat is very finely minced.

5 Scrape up the meat and transfer it to a bowl. Blend in the cornflour and egg and stir in the same direction until a light purée – the velvet – is achieved. This can be refrigerated, covered, for a few hours before it is used.

Note: steps 3 and 4 can be done in a food processor or blender, adding all the iced water and salt to the roughly cut up chicken breast before mincing.

INGREDIENTS
2 chicken breasts, about 450g (1lb), skinned and boned
2.5ml (½tsp) salt
10ml (2tsp) iced water
10ml (2tsp) cornflour
1 egg white, lightly beaten

Used in recipes on pages 61 and 67

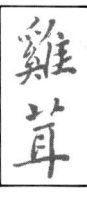

Sweetcorn Soup

INGREDIENTS

1 chicken breast, 175g (6oz)
  skinned and boned, or 100g
  (4oz) chicken fillet
225-285g (8-10oz) can sweetcorn
  kernels, drained
225-285g (8-10oz) can cream-style
  sweetcorn
1-2 eggs
1.25ml (¼tsp) salt
10ml (2tsp) groundnut or corn oil
298g (10½oz) can condensed
  cream of chicken soup
3 soup cans cold water

FOR THE MARINADE

1.25ml (¼tsp) salt
10ml (2tsp) thin soy sauce
6 turns white pepper mill
15ml (1tbsp) Shaohsing wine or
  medium dry sherry
5ml (1tsp) cornflour
60ml (4tbsp) water
5ml (1tsp) sesame oil
5ml (1tsp) groundnut or corn oil

Serves 6-8

Illustrated on page 67

This Cantonese soup, like Sweet and sour pork, is tremendously popular with non-Chinese, especially Westerners. Canned products are used here for labour-saving purposes. The soup will still be delicious if you want to make it very simple and omit the chicken.

1 Mince the chicken flesh finely in a food processor or mincer. Put into a bowl.

2 *Prepare the marinade:* add the salt, soy sauce, pepper and wine or sherry to the chicken. Sprinkle with the cornflour and stir in the water, 15ml (1tbsp) at a time, until the chicken becomes a smooth paste. Leave to stand for 15 minutes. Blend in the oils.

3 Roughly chop the sweetcorn kernels in a food processor, liquidizer or by hand. (They can be left whole.)

4 In a small bowl, beat the eggs lightly with the salt and oil. Put aside.

5 Pour the soup into a large saucepan and add the cold water gradually, stirring with a wooden spoon until smooth.

6 Stir in the sweetcorn kernels and cream-style sweetcorn.

7 Bring the soup mixture to just below boiling point over a moderate heat, stirring occasionally.

8 Combine about 90ml (6tbsp) of the hot soup liquid with the chicken paste, breaking up any lumps. Add to the rest of the soup, stirring in well, and gradually bring to the boil. Simmer for 1 minute to make sure that the chicken is cooked.

9 Stream in the beaten egg through the gap of a pair of chopsticks or along the back of a fork, moving the chopsticks or fork in a circular motion at the same time. Remove from the heat and cover for 45 seconds to allow the egg to set in tender flakes. Give the soup a final stir and then serve hot.

Note: left-over soup can be reheated, it can also be frozen. Instead of condensed soup, 1 litre (1¾ pints) clear stock (see page 225) can be used. In this case, use 2 cans cream-style sweetcorn and only 2 cans of water.

Winter Melon and Chicken Velvet Soup

In Hong Kong and China, some restaurants specialize in a very sophisticated dish, Winter Melon Pond. A whole winter melon of the perfect size is partially hollowed, filled with such delicacies as crabmeat, diced duck, pork, Chinese mushrooms and bamboo shoots and then steamed for hours to produce the most delectable soup. But it is not a practical dish to make at home. This recipe, however, is, and the melon is succulent in the soup.

1 Cut the winter melon into pieces that are easy to work with. Deseed only, leaving the pulpy flesh alone. Cut off the hard skin and discard. Dice all the pieces including the pulpy parts.

2 Put the winter melon and stock in a large saucepan and bring to the boil. Lower the heat and simmer, covered, for about 25-30 minutes or until the melon is tender and looks transparent.

3 Put the chicken velvet into a bowl and add several spoonfuls of boiling broth. Stir to blend, then pour into the boiling soup. Stir the soup to break up any lumps of the chicken velvet as it cooks and turns opaque. Taste and add salt, if necessary.

4 Pour the soup into a large warm soup tureen, sprinkle with the ham and serve.

Note: if desired, about 225g (8oz) cooked white crab meat can be added to the soup at the end of step 3. Fuzzy melon, though not the traditional ingredient for this soup, can be used as a satisfactory substitute.

INGREDIENTS

1 small winter melon or part of a large one, about 1.3-1.4kg (2¾-3lb)

1.1 litres (2 pints) prime stock (see page 225)

1 quantity Chicken velvet (see page 63)

salt to taste

50g (2oz) best ham, ideally Chinhua, York or Virginia, finely chopped

Serves 8

Illustrated on page 67

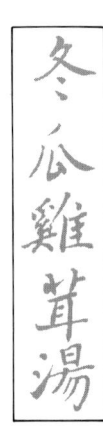

Wonton Wrapper Crisps Soup

片兒麵湯

INGREDIENTS
groundnut or corn oil for
   deep-frying
60 wonton wrappers, halved and
   folded in 2
225g (8oz) Cantonese roast duck
   with some skin, diced (see page
   209)
275g (10oz) cooked crabmeat,
   broken into chunks
100g (4oz) canned bamboo
   shoots, thinly sliced or diced
225g (8oz) canned straw
   mushrooms, drained and
   halved or quartered
2.5 litres (4½ pints) prime or
   clear stock (see page 225)
5-10ml (1-2tsp) salt
pepper to taste
15-30ml (1-2tbsp) thin soy sauce
12 spring onions, cut diagonally
   into 1-cm (½-inch) sections,
   white and green parts
   separated

Serves 10-12

Illustrated opposite

The tender wonton wrappers, deep-fried to a crisp before being dunked in the soup, lend special character to this dish. The colour of the ingredients, suspended in the clear soup, is especially attractive.

1 Half fill a wok or a deep-fryer with oil. Heat to a temperature of about 180°C (350°F) or until a cube of stale bread browns in 60 seconds. Add a batch of wonton wrappers, about 20 at a time; they will sizzle and expand at once. Remove to kitchen paper before they turn brown, using a hand strainer or perforated disc. Repeat until all are done.

2 Put the duck, crabmeat, bamboo shoots and straw mushrooms into the stock and bring to the boil. Add the salt, pepper and soy sauce. Add the white spring onion and, finally, the wonton wrappers. (It is always better to add the wonton wrappers at the last moment so that they retain their crispness.) Dunk them with a wooden spoon. Remove from the heat and add the green spring onion.

3 Serve immediately, either from a communal bowl or in individual bowls.

Note: wonton wrappers can be deep-fried ahead of time and, if kept in an airtight container, will remain crisp for more than a week. With some salt sprinkled on them, they are quite a novelty to serve with drinks. Cantonese roast duck, see page 209, is also available in some Cantonese restaurants, whole or in portions.

Facing page, clockwise from the top: Wonton wrapper crisps soup (see above); Cantonese wonton soup (see page 68); Sweetcorn soup (see page 64); Winter melon and chicken velvet soup (page 65)

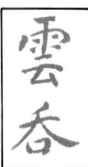

Cantonese Wonton Soup

Wontons, or small dumplings, served in broth, are a national Chinese snack. The main ingredient for wonton filling is pork, but in Kwangtung shrimps and prawns are also used, because they are so easily available. This addition gives the wontons a much more interesting taste and texture.

INGREDIENTS

350g (12oz) pork, with about 50g (2oz) fat
100g (4oz) raw shelled shrimps
6 spring onions, cut into tiny rounds
50-75g (2-3oz) canned bamboo shoots, finely chopped
1 egg yolk
90 wonton wrappers, each about 7.5cm (3 inches) square
1 egg white, lightly beaten
salt
6-8 leaves Cos lettuce or Chinese celery cabbage, shredded crosswise into 2.5-cm (1-inch) pieces
1.4 litres (2½ pints) prime and clear stocks, mixed together (see page 225)
80ml (16tsp) groundnut or corn oil

FOR THE MARINADE

5ml (1tsp) salt
2.5ml (½tsp) sugar
15ml (1tbsp) thin soy sauce
5ml (1tsp) thick soy sauce
10 turns black pepper mill
7.5ml (1½tsp) Shaohsing wine or medium dry sherry
5ml (1tsp) potato flour
45-60ml (3-4tbsp) water
10ml (2tsp) sesame oil

TO SERVE

ground pepper
sesame oil
thin soy sauce

Makes 80-90 wontons; serves 8 as lunch

Illustrated on page 67

1 Chop the pork by hand or mince it. Put into a large bowl.

2 Pat dry the shrimps. Cut into the size of petits pois and add to the pork.

3 *Prepare the marinade:* add the salt, sugar, soy sauces, pepper, wine or sherry and potato flour to the pork. Stir in the water in the same direction, 15ml (1tbsp) at a time.

4 Pick up the pork mixture with one or both hands and throw it back into the bowl or on to a flat surface. Repeat this action about 100 times to achieve the desired light and yet firm texture.

5 Add half the spring onion and all the bamboo shoots to the pork mixture, mix well and leave to marinate for 20-30 minutes. Then blend in the sesame oil.

6 Just before ready to wrap the wontons, stir in the egg yolk which will bind the filling to the wrappers.

7 Wrap the wontons. There are 2 ways to do this:

The quick way. Put about 5ml (1tsp) filling in the centre of 1 wrapper placed on the palm of the hand. Gather together the corners of the wrapper with the other hand (a) and give it a twist in the middle to secure the wrapping (b). Repeat until all the filling is used up.

a   b

The classic way. Put about 5ml (1tsp) filling in the centre of 1 wrapper placed at an angle, like a diamond, on the palm of the hand or on a flat surface. Fold the bottom half upwards (c) to make a triangle, then turn the triangle to point towards you. Fold the 2 side corners backwards (d) and, using one finger, smear a little egg white on one corner (e) and put the other corner on top, pressing to secure them (f). Turn up the front flaps (g), to make the wonton look like a hat (h).

c   d   e

f   g   h

8 Bring a large saucepan of salted water to the boil. Blanch the lettuce or cabbage for about 1 minute, remove with a hand strainer or perforated spoon and transfer to a bowl.

9 Put the stock in another saucepan and bring to simmering point.

10 Bring the water in the large saucepan to the boil again. Plunge in the wontons, no more than 20 at a time, and return to the boil, stirring gently to separate them. Continue to boil, uncovered, for about 3 minutes until the wontons are cooked and float to the surface.

11 Remove with a hand strainer to individual serving bowls, allowing about 10 wontons per bowl. To each bowl, add a pinch of the remaining spring onion, a few pieces of lettuce or cabbage and 10ml (2tsp) oil, and then pour over a ladleful of stock (about 175ml [6fl oz]). Everyone can help themselves to ground pepper, sesame oil and soy sauce placed on the table.

Note: wontons freeze well and can therefore be made in advance up to step 7 and frozen. Make sure, however, to cook the defrosted wontons a little longer in boiling water. Wonton soup can also be served with cooked egg noodles in the stock. Allow fewer wontons per bowl when served in this way.

Cantonese Fire Pot

INGREDIENTS
350-450g (12oz-1lb) fresh or
    frozen medium raw prawns in
    the shell, without heads
1 Dover sole, or sea bass, about
    450g (1lb), skinned and boned
10 large scallops, white meat only
2 chicken breasts, skinned and
    boned
350-450g (12oz-1lb) beef, rump,
    skirt or fillet
450g (1lb) Chinese celery cabbage
1 large Cos or Webbs lettuce
450g (1lb) spinach, washed and
    trimmed
1 bunch watercress, washed and
    trimmed
4 cakes bean curd
450g (1lb) dried egg noodles or
    700g (1½lb) fresh noodles
about 2.3-2.8 litres (4-5 pints)
    clear stock
groundnut or corn oil

FOR THE DIPS
8 eggs
thick or thin soy sauce
groundnut, corn or sesame oil
salt
freshly ground black pepper
hot made-up mustard
chilli sauce

Serves 8 as dinner

Illustrated opposite

A Cantonese fire pot reflects what's easily available in the region, and it therefore consists of seafood as well as meat and vegetables. If you do not want to use the traditional charcoal-burning fire pot for cooking at the table, use a heatproof bowl and burner or an electric pot.

1 Shell and devein the prawns (see page 39). Halve lengthwise.

2 Cut the fish fillets across into 2.5cm (1 inch) pieces.

3 Wash and pat dry the scallops. Remove and discard the hard muscles. Place each one on its side and cut into 3-4 pieces.

4 Cut the chicken flesh into thin slices, about 3mm (⅛ inch) thick.

5 Cut the beef across the grain into slices about 5 x 4cm (2 x 1½ inches) and 6mm (¼ inch) thick.

6 Cut each Chinese celery cabbage stalk across at about 2.5cm (1 inch) intervals.

7 Break up the lettuce leaves into large pieces.

8 Steep the bean curd in hot water for 15 minutes. Drain, handling with care. Cut each into 8 pieces.

9 Bring a large pan of water to the boil. Add the noodles, return to the boil and continue to cook for a few minutes or until *al dente*. Pour into a colander and refresh under cold running water. Drain.

10 Arrange all the ingredients either on individual plates or together on several plates. The meat and seafood slices can be laid overlapping each other. Put on the dining table.

11 Arrange all the dips in small dishes and put on the dining table.

12 To serve, provide each person with one bowl and a side plate, one pair of bamboo chopsticks and one small wire strainer.

13 Crack 1 egg into each bowl and beat lightly. Pour 10ml (2tsp) soy sauce on to each saucer and add 2.5ml (½tsp) oil. This can be replenished by individuals later.

14 Have the stock simmering in a saucepan.

15 Pour sufficient stock into the heated pot to come about half way up the sides, and bring back to the boil. Add about 45ml (3tbsp) oil.

Facing page, top left to right: Lamb for Mongolian fire pot (see page 72); buckwheat and cellophane noodles; Chinese celery cabbage; coriander leaves; spring onions; sesame paste dip. *Bottom left to right:* prawns, white fish and scallops for Cantonese fire pot (see above); bean curd and fresh noodles; lettuce and Chinese celery cabbage; egg, mustard, chilli sauce, pepper, salt, sesame oil; soy sauce; beef and chicken. *Centre:* traditional fire pot with stock and strainers

16 To eat, everyone picks up one or two morsels of either meat or seafood, places them into the strainer and then lowers it into the fire pot to cook. If you have no strainers, simply use chopsticks to hold and dip the food into the boiling stock to cook. Remove after some seconds or as soon as the food is cooked. Dip into the egg and season with the other condiments before eating. (If you dislike the raw egg idea, dispense with it.)

17 When a fair amount of meat and seafood has been eaten put the vegetables and the bean curd in stages into the pot. Let everyone help themselves from the pot.

18 Whenever necessary, replenish the stock level with more stock or water. Add more oil and bring to the boil again before cooking more food in the pot.

19 When most of the dishes, vegetables and bean curd have been eaten and the broth is getting richer and richer, add the noodles. The broth and noodles can then be enjoyed by everyone.

Mongolian Lamb Fire Pot

This Mongolian dish, which has long since become part and parcel of Peking food, ranks second in fame only to the Peking duck (see page 209).

1 Ask the butcher to bone the lamb for you. If possible, freeze for about 3-4 hours so that the meat becomes firm and easy to cut into paper-thin slices.

2 Meanwhile, soak the cellophane noodles in plenty of boiling water in a bowl. Leave for a minimum of 20-30 minutes to expand. Drain. Make 2-3 cuts with scissors to shorten them. Transfer to a serving bowl.

3 Slice the celery cabbage at 2.5cm (1 inch) intervals. Put on to a plate.

4 Plunge the noodles into plenty of boiling water, return to the boil, then continue to cook for several minutes until they are soft yet *al dente*. Drain and rinse under cold running water. Put on to a plate or into a bowl.

5 *Prepare the dip:* put the sesame paste into a fairly large serving bowl and gradually add about 120ml (4fl oz) of water to dilute, stirring until smoothly blended. Add about 45-60ml (3-4tbsp) water to the red bean curd and blend to a creamy consistency. Pour into the serving bowl, then add the wine or sherry, sugar, soy sauce, the oils and fish sauce and stir until well mixed.

6 Take the lamb out of the freezer. Trim excess fat and cut into as paper-thin slices as you can possibly manage. Ideally, each slice

INGREDIENTS

½ leg of lamb, ideally spring lamb, about 1.2kg (2½lb)
100g (4oz) cellophane noodles
1 Chinese celery cabbage, about 800g (1¾lb), trimmed
225g (8oz) dried egg or buckwheat noodles

FOR THE DIP

120ml (8tbsp) sesame paste, well stirred in the jar
2 cakes fermented red bean curd or about 60ml (4tbsp) and 30ml (2tbsp) own juice
90ml (6tbsp) Shaohsing wine or medium dry sherry
45ml (3tbsp) sugar
120ml (8tbsp) thin soy sauce
45-60ml (3-4tbsp) hot chilli oil (see page 225)
45-60 (3-4tbsp) sesame oil
60ml (4tbsp) fish sauce
100g (4oz) coriander leaves, chopped into small pieces
10-12 large spring onions, cut into small rounds

Serves 6 as dinner

Illustrated on page 71

should be about 10 x 4cm (4 x 1½ inches). Arrange them on several serving plates in single layers but overlapping each other. Refrigerate, covered, until ready to eat.

7 Put all the ingredients on the dining table.

8 Pour boiling water into the pot to come about half way up the sides, and bring back to the boil. The feast is now ready to commence.

9 To serve, provide each person with a pair of bamboo chopsticks (not plastic or lacquered ones), a small wire strainer made specially for fire pot feasts (optional), a bowl and a small plate.

10 To eat, everyone spoons some sauce into their bowl and adds some coriander leaves and spring onions. Everyone picks up 1-2 slices of lamb at a time, puts them into the strainer (or uses chopsticks) and immerses them in the water in the pot. Remove after a few seconds (or longer if very well done meat is preferred). The meat is then dipped into the sauce before eating.

11 After about half of the lamb has been consumed and the water in the pot has become a tasty broth, put in the cabbage and cellophane noodles in stages for everyone to share. Dip them into the sauce before eating. Whenever necessary, replenish the water level in the pot.

12 After about three-quarters of the lamb has been consumed, put in half or all of the remaining noodles. Dip into the sauce then eat them.

13 At the end of the feast, the broth in the pot is shared. Each person spoons some into their bowl, mixes it with the remaining sauce and then drinks it.

A Western or Szechwan Menu

四川菜

To a dish, this menu for eight, with its delicious tastes and aftertastes, offers the full spectrum of Szechwan flavours from *spicy and numbing to salty, sweet and vinegary. The dishes can be prepared and enjoyed individually, or two or three at a sitting.*

银絲卷 **Silver-thread buns** Steamed bun, always served with Fragrant and crispy duck (see page 201).

荷葉夾 **Lotus leaf buns** Steamed bun for Fragrant duck (see page 200).

香酥鴨 **Fragrant and crispy duck** Marinated and steamed before being deep-fried, the meat in this dish simply melts off the bone (see page 200).

Hot and sour soup
Spicy hot soup with pork, mushrooms and bean curd (see page 202).

Fish fragrant shredded pork
Finely sliced pork combined with chilli paste, garlic, ginger and spring onion (see page 203).

Dry-fried four seasonal beans
Delicious hot or cold, this dish combines deep-fried beans with a tangy flavouring (see page 203).

Pang pang chicken
Peppery hot dish served cold with cucumber and spring onion (see page 204).

Sautéed Mackerel

INGREDIENTS

1 large mackerel, about 700-800g (1½-1¾lb), cleaned with head left on
2.5ml (½tsp) salt
250ml (8 fl oz) groundnut or corn oil
6 thin slices fresh ginger root, peeled
1cm (½ inch) fresh ginger root, peeled and cut into silken threads (see page 35)
4-6 spring onions, cut into small rounds

FOR THE SAUCE

15ml (1tbsp) thin soy sauce
15ml (1tbsp) thick soy sauce
2.5ml (½tsp) sugar
10ml (2tsp) Shaohsing wine or medium dry sherry

Serves 2 as a main course; 4 with 2 other dishes

Illustrated opposite

To sauté or shallow-fry is another basic Chinese method of cooking fish; the technique is explained in this recipe for mackerel. Another fish which lends itself to sautéing is pomfret, which abounds in South China, India and South East Asia but is only available frozen in Europe. Red snapper, red mullet and whiting, among others, are also delicious sautéed.

1 As the mackerel at this weight is probably long, halve it crosswise. Rub the salt all over the skin, crevices and cavity. Leave to stand for about 15 minutes.

2 *Prepare the sauce:* mix together the soy sauces, sugar and wine or sherry.

3 Heat a wok or a heavy frying pan over a high heat until smoke rises. Pour in the oil, tip the wok carefully to swirl it around the sloping edges, then pour all but about 45ml (3tbsp) into a container. Reheat the oil, add the ginger slices and fry until brown, then discard. Lower the heat, wait until the oil is less hot and then add both pieces of mackerel. Fry for about 5 minutes to brown the skin, then turn over and brown the other side for about 5 minutes. Turn over again and continue to shallow-fry for about another 3 minutes, adding about 15ml (1tbsp) oil around the edges of the fish. Repeat with the other side.

4 Pour the sauce all over the fish and sprinkle on the shredded ginger. Cover and continue to cook for about 3 minutes. Sprinkle on the spring onion and cook, covered, for a few more seconds. Remove to a warm serving plate and pour the sauce from the wok or frying pan over the fish.

5 Either put the 2 pieces of mackerel side by side or join to form a "whole" mackerel. Arrange the spring onion on top and serve.

Facing page, from the top: Abalone with Chinese mushrooms (page 79); Steamed prawns in mixed bean sauce (page 78); Sautéed mackerel (see above)

Steamed Prawns in Mixed Bean Sauce

雙又鼓蒸蝦

INGREDIENTS

350g (12oz) medium or large prawns in the shell, without heads
few coriander leaves, torn into pieces

FOR THE SAUCE

15ml (1tbsp) fermented black beans
15ml (1tbsp) salted yellow beans
2.5ml (½tsp) sugar
5ml (1tsp) sesame oil
60-75ml (4-5tbsp) groundnut or corn oil
4-6 cloves garlic, peeled and finely chopped
1-2cm (½-¾ inch) fresh ginger root, peeled and finely chopped
½-1 fresh green or red chilli, seeded and sliced into tiny rounds
15-22.5ml (1-1½tbsp) Shaohsing wine or medium dry sherry

Serves 4-6 with 2-3 other dishes

Illustrated on page 77

I first tasted this dish in 1980 in one of the famous restaurants of my home town, Hong Kong, and thought it tasted heavenly. There was no question of their letting me into their cookery secret, so I experimented on my own and came up with this concoction. I think you will enjoy it, too!

1 Mash the black beans and salted yellow beans together with the sugar and sesame oil into a paste.

2 Heat a wok over a high heat until smoke rises. Add the oil and swirl it around. Add the garlic, and as soon as it takes on colour, put in the ginger. Stir. Quickly add the mashed bean paste, stir well, and then add the chilli. Splash in the wine or sherry around the side of the wok. As soon as the sizzling dies down, lower the heat, stir well and then remove the sauce to a container and allow to cool.

3 Remove and discard the prawn legs. Pat dry. Split lengthwise into 2, except for the tails (a), discarding their veins (b). Arrange around a heatproof serving dish with a slightly raised edge.

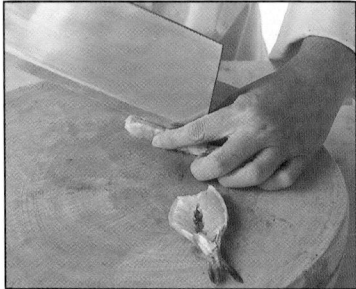 

a b

4 Spoon the sauce on to the prawns, scraping up every bit of oil as well.

5 Steam in a wok or steamer, over a moderately high heat for 3-4 minutes (see page 44). Check to see if the prawns are cooked. Scatter the coriander leaves over the prawns. Replace the lid and steam for a brief moment to partially cook the coriander leaves.

6 Remove from the heat and spoon the sauce on to the prawns and coriander leaves. Serve immediately from the dish in which they were cooked.

Abalone with Chinese Mushrooms

Dried abalone, which ranks with shark's fin and bird's nest in gastronomic prestige, is sadly out of the question for most people's pockets; these days canned abalone graces even the best tables. Although it lacks the depth of taste found in dried abalone, its subtle taste and slightly chewy texture still satisfy the palate of many a gourmet.

1 Put the mushrooms in a saucepan and pour over 900ml (1½ pints) boiling water. Return to the boil, then lower the heat and simmer for 1 hour until tender. When cool, clip off the stems and discard. Squeeze out excess water but leave damp. (They can be prepared hours ahead of time.)

2 Tear the lettuce leaves into large pieces.

3 Drain the abalone, reserving the juice. Slice the abalone into pieces about 3mm (⅛ inch) thick.

4 Pour the can juice into a saucepan, add 15ml (1tbsp) of the oil and bring to the boil. Immerse the lettuce in it, return to the boil and cook for 1 minute; the lettuce will be cooked yet still crisp. Transfer with a slotted spoon to a sieve placed over a bowl so that it will continue to drain. Pour the drained stock back into the saucepan.

5 Heat a wok over a high heat until smoke rises. Add the remaining oil and swirl it around. Add the white spring onion and stir a couple of times. Splash in the Shaohsing wine or sherry around the side of the wok, then add the stock saved from the lettuce, the oyster sauce, thick soy sauce to enhance the colouring, and sugar. Bring to the boil.

6 Now add the mushrooms and abalone and slowly return to the boil. Cover, lower the heat and simmer for about 2 minutes to let the abalone and mushrooms absorb the flavour.

7 Spread the lettuce on a warm serving plate.

8 Trickle the well-stirred dissolved potato flour into the sauce, stirring as it thickens. Tip in the green spring onion.

9 Remove the ingredients to the serving plate, arranging the mushrooms on the lettuce, cap side up, then the abalone. Pour the sauce all over. Serve hot.

INGREDIENTS

16 dried Chinese mushrooms (the thick and floral ones are best), washed
1 medium lettuce, Webbs or Iceberg, washed and trimmed
1 can best abalone, 425-450g (15-16oz)
drained can juice from abalone
75ml (5tbsp) groundnut or corn oil
3 spring onions, cut into 2.5-cm (1-inch) sections, white and green parts separated
15ml (1tbsp) Shaohsing wine or medium dry sherry
45ml (3tbsp) oyster sauce
7.5ml (1½tsp) thick soy sauce
2.5ml (½tsp) sugar
15ml (1tbsp) potato flour, dissolved in 30ml (2tbsp) water

Serves 4 with 2 other dishes

Illustrated on page 77

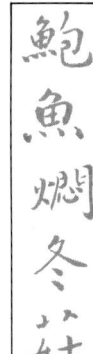

One Fish for Two Dishes:

Stir-fried Fish Fillet

炒魚球

INGREDIENTS

500-550g (1lb 2oz-1¼lb) fillet
   from 1 small halibut weighing
   1.2-1.4kg (2¾-3lb)
groundnut or corn oil for
   deep-frying
6 thin slivers fresh ginger root,
   peeled
225g (8oz) mange tout, trimmed
salt
2 cloves garlic, peeled and cut
   diagonally into slivers
1-2 shallots, skinned and
   chopped
15ml (1tbsp) Shaohsing wine or
   medium dry sherry

FOR THE MARINADE

2.5cm (1 inch) fresh ginger root,
   peeled and finely chopped
1.25ml (¼tsp) salt
1.25ml (¼tsp) sugar
6 turns white pepper mill
5ml (1tsp) Shaohsing wine or
   medium dry sherry
7.5ml (1½ tsp) cornflour
15ml (1tbsp) egg white, lightly
   beaten

FOR THE SAUCE

2.5ml (½tsp) potato flour
45ml (3tbsp) clear stock
30ml (2tbsp) oyster sauce
5ml (1tsp) thin soy sauce

*Serves 4-5 with the soup and 2
   other dishes*

Illustrated on page 83

*When a firmly textured fish is large enough, the Chinese often make
two dishes out of it: stir-frying the fillet and making a soup with the
head and carcass. This practice is especially common in the South
of China, where the yield from the sea enriches the table with such
delicious fish as grouper and perch. Small turbot, rascasse and brill
are also suitable for this purpose.*

1 Ask the fishmonger to fillet the halibut for you, removing the skin
as well. Take the head and carcass home to make soup (see right).

2 Pat the fillet dry. Halve (a), then cut the fillet lengthwise into
similarly sized strips. Cut strips across (b), into pieces about 2.5 x
3.5cm (1 x 1½ inches). Put into a dish.

a   b

3 *Prepare the marinade:* put the chopped ginger in a garlic press in
2 batches with 2 drops of water each time and squeeze the juice over
the fish. Discard the pulp. Add the salt, sugar, pepper, wine or
sherry, cornflour and egg white to the fish. Mix well to coat. Leave
to marinate for 15 minutes.

4 *Prepare the sauce:* mix together the potato flour, stock, oyster
sauce and soy sauce.

5 Bring a large pan of water to the boil. Add 5ml (1tsp) salt and
15ml (1tbsp) oil. Plunge in the mange tout and, once the water has
returned to the boil, pour into a colander and refresh under cold
running water. Drain thoroughly.

6 Half fill a wok or deep-fryer with oil. Heat to a temperature of
180°C (350°F) or until a cube of stale bread browns in 60 seconds.
Let the fish "go through the oil" carefully for about 10 seconds,
using a pair of long chopsticks to separate the pieces. Quickly
transfer to a dish using a large hand strainer. The fish is now half
cooked.

7 Pour the oil into a container to be used again, leaving only about 45ml (3tbsp) in the wok.

8 Reheat the oil over a high heat. Add the garlic and, as it sizzles, add the ginger slices and shallots and stir for a few seconds to release their aroma. Return the fish to the wok and toss and turn for about 30 seconds or until very hot. Splash in the wine or sherry around the side of the wok, continuing to turn and stir as it sizzles. Pour in the well-mixed sauce, stirring as it thickens. Return the mange tout to the wok; turn and toss to mix. Remove the fish mixture to a warm serving plate. Serve immediately.

Note: other vegetables, like broccoli, Chinese broccoli or fresh mushrooms, can also be used as complementary ingredients to the fish.

Bean Curd Soup with Fish Stock

1 Wash the fish carcass thoroughly. Put into a large saucepan.

2 Add the water, ginger and spring onion, and bring to the boil. Skim off the scum that surfaces. Reduce the heat to maintain a fast simmer for 30 minutes. Drain and discard all the solids. Season with salt.

3 Meanwhile, slice the pork into thin slivers. Put into a bowl.

4 *Prepare the marinade:* add the salt, sugar, soy sauce, pepper, wine or sherry, potato flour and water to the pork. Stir to coat. Leave to marinate for 15 minutes. Blend in the oil.

5 Slice the bean curd into thin strips or pieces of the same size.

6 Return the fish stock to the boil. Add the oil. Add the bean curd and mange tout and bring to the boil again. Add the pork, using a pair of chopsticks or a fork to separate the pieces. Reduce the heat and simmer for 1-2 minutes, depending on the thickness of the pork.

7 Remove from the heat. Add the spring onion.

8 Remove to a warm soup tureen or individual bowls and serve piping hot.

INGREDIENTS
750-800g (1lb 10oz-1¾lb) head
    and carcass of 1 small halibut
1.1 litres (2 pints) water
2.5cm (1 inch) fresh ginger root,
    peeled and bruised
2 large spring onions, quartered
2.5ml (½tsp) salt
100g (4oz) lean pork
2 cakes bean curd, drained
30ml (2tbsp) groundnut or corn
    oil
25g (1oz) mange tout, trimmed
    (or blanched petits pois)
2-3 spring onions, green parts
    only, cut into small rounds

FOR THE MARINADE
2.5ml (½tsp) salt
1.25ml (¼tsp) sugar
10ml (2tsp) thin soy sauce
3-4 turns white pepper mill
5ml (1tsp) Shaohsing wine or
    medium dry sherry
2.5ml (½tsp) potato flour
15ml (1tbsp) water
15ml (1tbsp) groundnut or corn
    oil

*Serves 4-5 with the stir-fried fillet
    and 2 other dishes*

Illustrated on page 83

Braised Fish Hunan-Szechwan Style

The essence of this dish is the gradual absorption of the Szechwan chilli paste, a favourite seasoning in Hunan-Szechwan cuisine. The dish is made all the more aromatic by the addition of garlic and ginger.

INGREDIENTS
1 sea bass, grey mullet or trout, about 625-700g (1lb 6oz-1lb 8oz), cleaned with head left on
2.5ml (½tsp) salt
250ml (8fl oz) groundnut or corn oil
3-4 cloves garlic, peeled and finely chopped
2.5cm (1 inch) fresh ginger root, peeled and finely chopped
30-60ml (2-4tbsp) Szechwan chilli paste (see page 226) or hot soy bean paste
15ml (1tbsp) Shaohsing wine or medium dry sherry
2.5ml (½tsp) sugar
120ml (4fl oz) clear stock or water
15ml (1tbsp) hot chilli oil (see page 225)
6-8 spring onions, green parts only, cut into small rounds

Serves 4 with 2 other dishes

Illustrated opposite

1 Blot the fish dry. Rub salt all over the fish including the cavity. Leave to stand for about 15 minutes.

2 Heat a wok over a high heat until smoke rises. Pour in the oil. Tip the wok carefully to swirl it all around the sloping edges. Pour all but 30ml (2tbsp) oil back into a container.

3 Lower the heat. Add the fish at once and brown for about 2 minutes. Slip 2 metal spatulas underneath the fish and turn over carefully. Brown the other side for about 2 minutes. Remove to a plate and keep nearby.

4 Turn up the heat. Add another 30ml (2tbsp) oil to the wok and heat until smoke rises. Now add the garlic and ginger and, as they sizzle, add the Szechwan chilli or hot soy bean paste, wine or sherry and sugar. Pour in the stock or water and bring to the boil, stirring to mix. Return the fish to the wok, lower the heat, cover and simmer in the sauce for about 12-15 minutes. Turn the fish over carefully and simmer, covered, for about 12-15 minutes until the fish is cooked and some of the sauce has been absorbed.

5 Remove the cover. Turn up the heat to reduce the sauce, spooning it on to the fish continually. Remove only the fish to a warm serving plate.

6 Add the hot chilli oil to the sauce, then the spring onion. Stir and cook for a few seconds, then scoop the sauce on to the fish. Serve immediately.

Facing page, clockwise from the top: Bean curd soup with fish stock (page 81); Braised fish Hunan-Szechwan-style (see above); Stir-fried scallops in oyster sauce (page 84); Stir-fried fish fillet (page 80)

Stir-fried Scallops in Oyster Sauce

INGREDIENTS

4 large dried Chinese mushrooms, reconstituted (see page 39)
10-12 large scallops, fresh or frozen
75ml (5tbsp) groundnut or corn oil
4 cloves garlic, peeled and finely chopped
6 thin slices fresh ginger root, peeled
4 spring onions, cut into 2.5-cm (1-inch) sections, white and green parts separated
15ml (1tbsp) Shaohsing wine or medium dry sherry
4-6 sticks celery, cut diagonally into thin slices
sesame oil to taste

FOR THE MARINADE

white pepper to taste
5ml (1tsp) cornflour
½ egg white, lightly beaten

FOR THE SAUCE

2.5ml (½tsp) potato flour
5ml (1tsp) water
1.25ml (¼tsp) salt
30ml (2tbsp) oyster sauce
45ml (3tbsp) juice from cooked scallops

Serves 4-6 with 2-3 other dishes

Illustrated on page 83

Another classic Cantonese dish. You may think it gilding the lily to add the savoury/sweet-tasting oyster sauce to the inherently sweet scallops, but your palate will be delighted with the result.

1 Drain and squeeze out excess water from the mushrooms but leave damp. Quarter them.

2 Wash the scallops, remove and discard the hard muscle. Pat dry and separate the corals from the scallops. Place each scallop on its side and slice into 2-3 pieces. Pat dry again and put into a dish. Halve the corals horizontally and put into another dish.

3 *Prepare the marinade:* add white pepper to taste, a good 2.5ml (½tsp) cornflour and a little over half of the egg white to the scallops and stir to coat. Add the remaining cornflour and egg white to the corals. Leave to marinate for 10 minutes.

4 *Prepare the sauce:* dissolve the potato flour in the water. Stir in the salt and oyster sauce and put aside.

5 Heat a wok over a high heat until smoke rises. Add 37.5ml (2½tbsp) of the oil and swirl it around. Add half the garlic and as soon as it sizzles and takes on colour, add half the ginger, then half the white spring onion. Stir and tip in the scallops immediately. Sliding the wok scoop or metal spatula to the bottom of the wok, turn and toss for 30-60 seconds or until the scallops are barely cooked, and have become whitish. Splash half the wine or sherry around the side of the wok and continue to stir. As soon as the sizzling dies down, drain in a sieve placed over a bowl to catch the juice that will continue to drip from the scallops.

6 Add 22.5ml (1½tbsp) oil to the wok and swirl it around. Stir in the rest of the garlic, ginger and white spring onion. Add the coral and stir and toss as before for about 1 minute. Splash the remaining wine or sherry around the side of the wok, stir, cover, lower the heat and cook for about 2 more minutes or until the corals become firm to the touch. Remove to the sieve over the bowl. While the corals are being cooked, add 45ml (3tbsp) scallop juice to the potato flour and oyster sauce mixture. Blend thoroughly and keep nearby.

7 Turn up the heat again, add the remaining 15ml (1tbsp) oil to the wok and swirl it around. Tip in the celery, stir, and then add the mushrooms. Stir and toss for 30-60 seconds; the celery should remain crisp. Make a well; pour in the well-stirred sauce and when it bubbles add the scallops and corals. Add the green spring onion and then remove to a warm serving plate. Sprinkle on some sesame oil to enhance the flavour. Serve immediately.

Deep-fried Fish with Sweet and Sour sauce

A sweet and sour sauce goes especially well with deep-fried food, not just because it whets one's appetite but, more importantly, because it counteracts any trace of grease. Such is, indeed, the case with fish. There are regional variations and personal preferences, but in the main a sweet and sour sauce is a mixture of vinegar and sugar, balanced by salt, and made more interesting by the addition of other condiments. Try this one and then concoct your own.

1 If the wok in which the fish will be deep-fried is large enough (35cm [14 inches or over]) leave the fish whole; otherwise cut it in half. Make 2-3 diagonal slashes across the thickest part of both sides of the fish, taking care not to go right to the edges.

2 *Prepare the marinade:* squeeze the ginger in a garlic press with 2 drops of water and mix the juice with the wine or sherry and salt. Rub both sides of the fish, including the crevices and the cavity, with the mixture. Leave to marinate for about 15-30 minutes. Discard any excess liquid.

3 *Prepare the sweet and sour sauce:* drain and squeeze out excess water from the mushrooms but leave damp. Cut into small cubes. Cook the petits pois in boiling water for 2 minutes, drain. Mix together the dissolved potato flour, vinegar, sugar, ketchup, salt, soy sauce, wine or sherry and water. Heat a wok (if you have a second one), or a saucepan, over a high heat until smoke rises. Add 45ml (3tbsp) of the oil and swirl it around. Add the garlic, then the onion or shallot and fry for about 1 minute, stirring. Add the mushrooms, petits pois and bamboo shoots. Stir the liquid mixture once more to blend, then pour into the wok or saucepan. Bring to the boil, stirring continuously as it thickens. Keep aside.

4 Half fill a wok or deep-fryer with oil. Heat to a temperature of 190°C (375°F) or until a cube of stale bread browns in 50 seconds.

5 While the oil is heating, brush the egg yolk over both sides of the fish, then sift the cornflour over it, smoothing it for evenness.

6 Lower the fish into the oil and deep-fry for about 7-8 minutes or until the skin is crisp. Turn over carefully and deep-fry the other side for about the same time.

7 Remove with a hand strainer or perforated disc and drain on kitchen paper. Transfer to a warm serving dish. If the fish has been cut into 2 halves, put together to look whole again.

8 Reheat the sauce until simmering, stir in the remaining 15ml (1 tbsp) oil and pour all over the fish. Serve immediately.

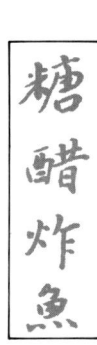

INGREDIENTS

1 red snapper or grey mullet, about 1-1.1kg (2¼-2½lb), cleaned with head left on
groundnut or corn oil for deep-frying
1 egg yolk
about 45ml (3tbsp) cornflour

FOR THE MARINADE

2.5cm (1 inch) fresh ginger root, peeled and finely chopped
5ml (1tsp) Shaohsing wine or medium dry sherry
5ml (1tsp) salt

FOR THE SWEET AND SOUR SAUCE

3 dried Chinese mushrooms, reconstituted (see page 39)
50g (2oz) petits pois
10ml (2tsp) potato flour, dissolved in 30ml (2tbsp) water
60ml (4tbsp) rice or wine vinegar
60ml (4tbsp) sugar
60ml (4tbsp) tomato ketchup
5ml (1tsp) salt
7.5ml (1½tsp) thick soy sauce
10ml (2tsp) Shaohsing wine or medium dry sherry
250ml (8fl oz) water
60ml (4tbsp) groundnut or corn oil
1 clove garlic, peeled and finely chopped
1 small onion or 3 shallots, skinned and diced
50g (2oz) canned bamboo shoots, diced

Serves 6 with 3 other dishes

Illustrated on page 87

Stir-fried Squid in Shrimp Paste

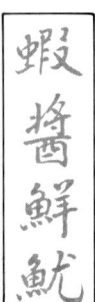

INGREDIENTS
1 large squid, about 700g (1½lb)
    or body pouch pieces only
10ml (2tsp) thin soy sauce
5ml (1tsp) potato flour
60ml (4tbsp) water
groundnut or corn oil for
    deep-frying
22.5ml (1½tbsp) shrimp paste
3-4 cloves garlic, peeled and
    finely chopped
25g (1oz) fresh ginger root,
    peeled and finely chopped
6 spring onions, cut into 1-cm
    (½-inch) diagonal slices, white
    and green parts separated
15ml (1tbsp) Shaohsing wine or
    medium dry sherry

Serves 4-5 with 3 other dishes

Illustrated opposite

On its own, shrimp paste has a strong, almost unpleasant, odour while squid is very bland. However, when stir-fried together with garlic, this peasant dish, although an acquired taste, can delight even the most sophisticated palate.

1 Cut off the head of the squid from the body pouch. Cut off the eyes and discard them. Rinse in cold water, then cut the tentacles into 4-cm (1½-inch) sections.

2 Slit the body pouch open lengthwise as far as the innards. Pull these out and discard. Remove the transparent bone and peel off the reddish skin; discard. Rinse in cold water.

3 Turn the body pouch inside out. Lay it flat on a board and, using the sharp edge of a knife, score in a criss-cross pattern. Cut into pieces about 5 x 2.5cm (2 x 1 inches).

4 Immerse the squid momentarily in plenty of boiling water and as soon as the pieces curl up, pour into a colander and rinse under cold running water. This makes the squid crisp and tender. Drain thoroughly and dry.

5 Mix together the soy sauce, potato flour and water. Put aside.

6 Half fill a wok or deep-fryer with oil. Heat until just hot, about 150°C (300°F). Add the squid and let it "go through the oil" for about 10 seconds. Remove with a hand strainer and keep close by. Pour all but about 45ml (3tbsp) of the oil into a container and save for other uses.

7 Dilute the shrimp paste with 15ml (1tbsp) water, stirring to blend.

8 Reheat the oil until it smokes. Add the garlic and, when it sizzles, add the ginger. Stir a couple of times and add the white spring onion. Stir a few more times, then pour in the shrimp sauce. Cook for a few seconds, stirring, then return the squid to the wok. Sliding the wok scoop or metal spatula to the bottom of the wok, turn and toss for about 10-20 seconds or until thoroughly hot. Splash in the wine or sherry around the side of the wok. When the sizzling dies down, add the well-stirred dissolved potato flour mixture. Continue to stir while this thickens. Tip in the green spring onion.

9 Remove to a warm serving plate. Serve immediately.

Note: steps 1-6 can be prepared several hours in advance. Instead of 1 large squid, small squids can be used.

Facing page, clockwise from the top: Stir-fried squid in shrimp paste (see above); Stir-fried clams in black bean sauce (see page 88); Deep-fried fish with sweet and sour sauce (see page 85)

Stir-fried Clams in Black Bean Sauce

INGREDIENTS

24 clams, about 1.4kg (3lb)
45ml (3tbsp) groundnut or corn oil
4-5 cloves garlic, peeled and finely chopped
1cm (½ inch) fresh ginger root, peeled and finely chopped
4-5 spring onions, cut into 2.5-cm (1-inch) sections, white and green parts separated
22.5ml (1½tbsp) fermented black beans, rinsed, mashed with 2.5ml (½tsp) sugar
30ml (2tbsp) Shaohsing wine or medium dry sherry
15ml (1tbsp) thick soy sauce
45ml (3tbsp) clear stock or water
5ml (1tsp) potato flour, dissolved in 15ml (1tbsp) water
sesame oil to taste (optional)

Serves 4-6 as a first course

Illustrated on page 87

Black bean sauce and clams go together for the Chinese as horseradish and roast beef do for the English.

1 Leave the clams in water with a little salt until ready to use. Scrub the shells very thoroughly.

2 Heat a wok over a high heat until smoke rises. Add the oil and swirl it around. Add the garlic, ginger and white spring onion. Stir and let them sizzle for a few moments to release their aroma. Add the mashed black beans and stir to mix. Tip in the clams. Sliding the wok scoop or metal spatula to the bottom of the wok, turn and toss for 30-45 seconds. Splash in the wine or sherry around the side of the wok, continuing to turn and stir. When the sizzling dies down, add the soy sauce and stock or water. Bring to the boil, cover, lower the heat to medium and cook for about 8 minutes.

3 Remove the opened clams with a pair of chopsticks or tongs to a warm serving platter and keep warm. Stir and turn the remainder a few times and cook, covered, for another 4-5 minutes so that they will open. Transfer the rest to the serving platter, leaving the sauce in the wok. Discard any clams that do not open.

4 Lower the heat, add the well-stirred potato flour to the sauce, stirring as it thickens. Tip in the green spring onion.

5 Scoop the sauce on to the clams and serve immediately. Sesame oil may be sprinkled on, if desired.

Lobster with Ginger and Spring Onion

The species of lobster found along the Chinese coast is the spiny lobster or crayfish and, significantly, the Chinese name for it is dragon prawn. The meat, compared to that of the true lobster, is slightly coarser, but cooking methods and recipes are the same for both. Only fresh lobsters are fit for consumption; they can be kept alive up to 3 days in the vegetable compartment of the refrigerator.

1 *Prepare the sauce:* mix together the flour, water, soy sauce and oyster sauce. Put the sauce aside.

2 Kill and chop up the lobsters. Before starting, make sure that strong rubber bands are around the pincers. Lay the lobsters flat, one at a time, on a chopping board, and steady them with one hand. Pierce the centre of the head where there is a cross, with the pointed end of a strong knife, pressing firmly all the way down in order to paralyze the nerve and hence kill the lobster instantly. Split it in half along the back, all the way to the tail, cutting through both the shell and the flesh. Remove and discard the pouch of grit from the head, as well as the dark gut running along the body. Remove the tiny eggs, if any, and the greenish creamy substance (tomalley) which can be cooked separately if wished. Twist the joints to dislodge the 2 claws from the body. Lay each half of the body flat and, using a kitchen cleaver, chop each into 3 pieces. Remove the gill from the head, close to the shell. Lay the claws on the board and bang them, one by one, with either the broad side of the cleaver or a hammer until the shell is cracked at various points so that it will not be necessary to use crackers when eating them. Cut each claw into 2 at its obvious joint.

3 Put all the head and claw pieces into one large bowl and the body pieces into another. Pat dry with kitchen paper.

4 Half fill a wok or deep-fryer with oil. Heat to a temperature of 180°C (350°F) or until a cube of stale bread browns in 60 seconds. Carefully lower all the head and claw pieces into the oil and let them "go through the oil" for about 20-30 seconds so that their juices are sealed in. Remove immediately with a large hand strainer and put on to a large platter.

5 Reheat the oil and let the body pieces "go through the oil" for about 10 seconds.

6 Empty the oil into a container and save it for other purposes. Wash and dry the wok.

7 Heat the wok over a high heat until smoke rises. Add 45ml (3tbsp) oil and swirl it around. Add the ginger, stir, and let it sizzle for about 1 minute to fully release its aroma. Add the white spring onion

INGREDIENTS

2 lobsters, each about 700g (1½lb)
groundnut or corn oil for deep-frying
45ml (3tbsp) groundnut or corn oil
75g (3oz) fresh ginger root, peeled and cut into thin slices
10-12 large spring onions, cut diagonally, white and green parts separated
22.5ml (1½tbsp) Shaohsing wine or brandy
150ml (¼ pint) prime stock (see page 225)

FOR THE SAUCE

5ml (1tsp) potato flour
60ml (4tbsp) water
7.5ml (½tbsp) thin soy sauce
22.5ml (1½tbsp) oyster sauce

Serves 6 as a first course

Illustrated on page 91

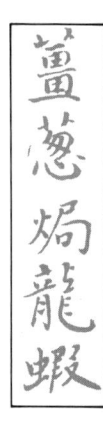

and stir a few times. Now return *all* the lobster and, sliding the wok scoop or metal spatula to the bottom of the wok, turn and toss the pieces until thoroughly hot. Splash in the wine or brandy around the side of the wok, continuing to stir as it sizzles.

8 Pour in the stock, cover and cook for about 2 minutes, at the end of which most of the liquid will have been absorbed. Add the well-stirred sauce, tip in the green spring onion and stir and toss until the sauce thickens.

9 Remove to a large, warm serving platter. Serve immediately.

Spiced-salt Prawns

INGREDIENTS
450g (1lb) fresh or frozen
    medium raw prawns in the
    shell, without heads
30ml (2tbsp) salt
5ml (1tsp) five-spice powder
5ml (1tsp) ground roasted
    Szechwan peppercorns
5ml (1tsp) ground black pepper
groundnut or corn oil for
    deep-frying

Serves 6 with 3 other dishes

Illustrated opposite

This dish, with its subtly spicy flavour, is very popular in Hong Kong, one of the leading capitals of Chinese food. The prawns used are left with their shells on because this protects the meat from the intense heat of deep-frying, keeping them succulent.

1 If frozen prawns are used, defrost thoroughly. Wash the shells well; remove and discard the legs.

2 Devein: using a satay stick or a strong needle, pierce the flesh at the joints of the shell sections and remove the black veins.

3 To make the spiced-salt, heat a wok over a medium heat until hot but not smoking. Add the salt and stir continuously for about 4 minutes or until very hot and slightly greyish in colour. Remove to a small bowl, add the five-spice powder, ground roasted Szechwan peppercorns and pepper. Mix well.

4 Half fill a wok or deep-fryer with oil. Heat to a temperature of 180°C (350°F) or until a cube of stale bread browns in 60 seconds. Add the prawns and deep-fry for 30-45 seconds or until they have curled up and turned red, indicating that they are cooked. Remove with a large hand strainer or perforated disc and drain.

5 Empty the oil into a container and save it for other cooking purposes. Wash and dry the wok.

6 Reheat the wok until hot. Add 15ml (1tbsp) of the spiced-salt and return the prawns to the wok. Over a medium heat flip and turn the prawns in the salt for about 30 seconds so that the salt permeates the prawns. Remove to a warm serving plate. Put the remaining salt on a small saucer for additional dipping at the table.

7 To eat, the Chinese pick up a prawn with a pair of chopsticks, take a bite and then shell it with their teeth whilst savouring the spicy taste. If this method seems impossible, shell with your fingers.

Facing page, from the top: Lobster with ginger and spring onion (page 89); Spiced salt prawns (see above)

Stir-fried Prawns in Tomato Sauce

INGREDIENTS

225g (8oz) fresh or frozen raw
   prawns, in the shell, without
   heads
1.25ml (¼tsp) salt
225g (8oz) tomatoes
75ml (5tbsp) groundnut or corn
   oil
4-5 cloves garlic, peeled and
   finely chopped
4 spring onions, cut into 2.5-cm
   (1-inch) sections, white and
   green parts separated
10ml (2tsp) thin soy sauce
2.5ml (½tsp) sugar
2.5ml (½tsp) potato flour,
   dissolved in 15ml (1tbsp) water

Serves 2 with 1 other dish

Ilustrated opposite

The Cantonese like to bite into prawns that are "crisply firm", and to achieve this texture Cantonese chefs leave out the ginger and wine when preparing them.

1 If frozen prawns are used, defrost thoroughly. Shell and devein the prawns (see page 39). Pat dry with kitchen paper and put into a bowl.

2 Sprinkle with half the salt, which will firm up the prawns. Leave for about 15 minutes.

3 Plunge the tomatoes into a bowl of very hot water and leave for 5-10 minutes. Peel off the skins. Cut the flesh into slices.

4 Heat a wok over a high heat until smoke rises. Add the oil, swirl it around and heat until very hot. Add the garlic and half the white spring onion. Stir a few times to release their aroma and add the prawns. Sliding the wok scoop or metal spatula to the bottom of the wok, flip and turn in rapid succession for about 1 minute or until the prawns have curled up and turned pink in colour. Scoop on to a warm plate, leaving behind as much oil as possible.

5 Add the remaining white spring onion to the wok. Tip in the tomatoes and stir well. Season with the remaining salt, the soy sauce and sugar. Cover and cook over a medium heat for 2-3 minutes.

6 Add the well-stirred dissolved potato flour.

7 Return the prawns to the wok and tip in the green spring onion. Turn up the heat, stir and turn until the prawns are very hot. Remove to a warm serving plate.

Facing page, clockwise from the top: Steamed trout with black beans and garlic (see page 95); Stir-fried prawns in tomato sauce (see above); Sizzling rice with shrimps and tomato sauce (see page 94)

Sizzling Rice with Shrimps and Tomato Sauce

INGREDIENTS
225g (8oz) raw peeled shrimps
groundnut or corn oil for
    deep-frying
350-400g (12-14oz) canned
    tomatoes, chopped
2.5ml (½tsp) salt
2.5-5ml (½-1tsp) sugar
10-15ml (2-3tsp) thin soy sauce
15ml (1tbsp) Shaohsing wine or
    medium dry sherry
450ml (16fl oz) clear stock
22.5-30ml (1½-2tbsp) cornflour,
    dissolved in 60ml (4tbsp) clear
    stock or water
12 pieces guoba

FOR THE GUOBA
375-400g (13-14oz) cooked rice
15-30ml (1-2tbsp) groundnut or
    corn oil

FOR THE MARINADE
2.5ml (½tsp) salt
10ml (2tsp) cornflour
½ egg white or 15ml (1 tbsp)

Serves 4 with 3 other dishes

Illustrated on page 93

In many Chinese households rice, the staple food, used to be cooked in a large, round copper pot. When there was a layer of cooked rice stuck to the bottom of the pot, it would be carefully removed, roasted over a slow fire and then used again. These roasted rice pieces, called guoba, led to the invention of sizzling rice dishes in Eastern regional cuisine. This dish is also called "Thunder bolt out of the blue" because of the sizzle caused by the boiling sauce when poured on to the crispy guoba.

1 *Prepare the gouba:* loosen the rice and leave to dry for 4-5 hours.

2 Lightly brush 2 baking trays with the oil. Form the rice into 14-16 thin cakes, squares or circles, about 6.5cm (2½ inches) across, and place on the baking trays (a).

3 Put them, one tray at a time if necessary, on the top shelf of a preheated oven at 220°C (425°F) gas mark 7 and roast for about 20 minutes or until the underneath of the cakes is brown. If the surface still looks pale, loosen the cakes with a palette knife or spatula, turn them over and roast for another 5 minutes.

4 Take the baking trays out of the oven and leave the guoba to cool. Store in an airtight container. (They can also be eaten on their own, if sprinkled with a little salt.)

5 If frozen shrimps are used, defrost thoroughly. Wash twice in cold water to make them as white as possible. Drain well or pat semi-dry with kitchen paper. Put into a bowl.

6 *Prepare the marinade:* add the salt, cornflour and egg white to the shrimps. Stir in the same direction to coat evenly. Leave to marinate in the refrigerator for a minimum of 3 hours or overnight.

7 Half fill a wok or deep-fryer with oil. Heat until just hot, about 150°C (300°F). Add the shrimps and let them "go through the oil" for about 30 seconds, separating them with a pair of long chopsticks or a wooden spoon. The shrimps, having turned pinkish, will be almost cooked. Remove with a large hand strainer and keep nearby.

8 Heat 2 casseroles or ovenproof soufflé dishes in a preheated oven at about 140°C (275°F) gas mark 1. One is for serving the sizzling rice at the table, the other is for the boiling sauce.

9 Put the chopped tomato, salt, sugar, soy sauce, wine or sherry and stock in a saucepan and slowly bring it almost to the boil. Reduce the heat and stir in the dissolved cornflour. Leave over a low flame or on a hot plate.

10 Reheat the oil until it reaches 190°C (375°F) or until a cube of

stale bread browns in 50 seconds. Carefully add the pieces of guoba and deep-fry for about 2 minutes or until they are golden (b). Remove and transfer to the serving dish. Keep warm in the oven.

a   b

11 Add the shrimps to the tomato sauce and bring to a fast boil.

12 Take the serving dish containing the guoba to the table. Take the other dish out of the oven and pour the boiling sauce into it. Pour the sauce over the guoba at the table – there will be a great deal of sizzling. Serve as soon as the sizzling subsides.

Steamed Trout with Black Beans and Garlic

When more condiments are needed to enhance the flavour of a fish, it is often steamed with fermented black beans and garlic and then garnished with spring onion. Rainbow trout and grey mullet, among others, are delicious steamed this way.

1 Pat the fish dry. Lay them on a heatproof serving dish with slightly raised sides. Place 2 slices of ginger into the cavity of each fish.

2 Mix together the black beans and garlic, and then spread on the fish.

3 Steam in a wok or steamer over a high heat for 6-8 minutes until the fish is cooked and the flesh flakes easily (see page 45).

4 Remove from the heat and sprinkle the spring onion on the fish.

5 Heat the oil in a small saucepan over a high heat until smoke rises. Pour it over the spring onion. The sizzling oil partially cooks it, enhancing the flavour.

6 Remove the fish from the wok or steamer. Add the soy sauce.

7 To serve, scrape the condiments on the fish to the side. Peel and discard the uppermost skin. Spoon some of the condiments and sauce back on to the fish and serve.

INGREDIENTS

2 trout, about 350g (12oz) each, cleaned with heads left on
4 thin slices fresh ginger root, peeled
30ml (2tbsp) fermented black beans, rinsed and partially mashed with 2.5ml (½tsp) sugar and 5ml (1tsp) Shaohsing wine; leave some beans whole
4-6 cloves garlic, peeled and finely chopped
2-3 spring onions, cut into small rounds
60ml (4tbsp) groundnut or corn oil
30ml (2tbsp) thick soy sauce

Serves 4 with 2 other dishes

Illustrated on page 93

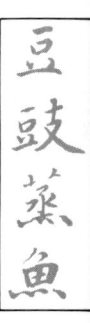

A Southern or Cantonese Menu

廣東菜

Cantonese and Fukienese cuisines, the two distinctive representatives of the Southern region, specialize in seafood. Hence this predominantly seafood menu for eight. However for those less fond of seafood there are more than enough classic meat and poultry dishes from the south from which to choose.

蟹扒蘆笋 **Asparagus with crabmeat**
Sweet-tasting combination of firm asparagus and tender crabmeat (see page 205).

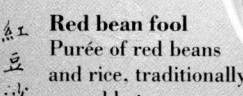

紅豆沙 **Red bean fool**
Purée of red beans and rice, traditionally served hot (see page 208).

香芒牛肉 **Stir-fried fillet of beef with mango**
Colourful dish combining sweet and savoury tastes (see page 207).

干燒明蝦 **Dry-fried prawns**
Prawns lightly fried in a tangy sauce of ginger, garlic, chilli and soy sauc (see page 206).

雪山蝦球 **Golden prawn balls**
Deep-fried balls of prawn meat and water chestnuts with a crunchy bread coating (see page 206).

清蒸鱸魚 **Clear-steamed sea bass**
Simply steamed then served with spring onion, ginger, garlic and oil poured on top (see page 205).

POULTRY AND EGGS

Stir-fried Chicken with Mange Tout

雪豆雞丁

INGREDIENTS
2 chicken breasts, about 450g
   (1lb), when skinned and boned
225g (8oz) mange tout, trimmed
salt
groundnut or corn oil for
   deep-frying
3-4 thin slices fresh ginger root,
   peeled
3-4 cloves garlic, peeled and
   finely chopped
4 spring onions, cut into 2.5-cm
   (1-inch) sections, white and
   green parts separated
15ml (1tbsp) Shaohsing wine or
   medium dry sherry

FOR THE MARINADE
1.25ml (¼tsp) salt
10ml (2tsp) thin soy sauce
4 turns white pepper mill
10ml (2tsp) Shaohsing wine or
   medium dry sherry
5ml (1tsp) cornflour
22.5ml (1½tbsp) egg white, lightly
   beaten
15ml (1tbsp) groundnut or corn
   oil

FOR THE SAUCE
5ml (1tsp) potato flour
90ml (6tbsp) clear stock or water
30ml (2tbsp) oyster sauce
7.5ml (½tbsp) thick soy sauce

Serves 4-6 with 2-3 other dishes

Illustrated opposite

A pleasant Southern stir-fried dish of tender and tasty chicken with crunchy mange tout. The oyster sauce, a special produce of the South, adds a pleasing taste to the dish.

1 Cut the chicken flesh into large cubes. Put into a bowl.

2 *Prepare the marinade:* add the salt, soy sauce, pepper, wine or sherry, cornflour and egg white to the chicken and stir in the same direction to coat. Leave to marinate for 15-30 minutes. Blend in the oil so that the lumps of chicken will not stick to each other.

3 Bring a pan of water (about 1.7 litres [3 pints]) to the boil. Add 5ml (1tsp) salt and 15ml (1tbsp) oil. Plunge in the mange tout and, as soon as the water returns to the boil, pour into a colander and refresh under cold running water. Drain. They will remain crisp and vivid for 2-3 hours.

4 *Prepare the sauce:* mix together the potato flour, stock or water, oyster sauce and soy sauce.

5 Half fill a wok or deep-fryer with oil. Heat to a temperature of 180°C (350°F) or until a cube of stale bread browns in 60 seconds. Let the chicken "go through the oil" for about 30 seconds, separating the pieces with a pair of long chopsticks (see page 45). Remove with a large hand strainer and keep nearby.

6 Transfer all but about 15ml (1tbsp) oil to a container and save for later use. Reheat the oil and add the ginger. When it sizzles, add the mange tout. Reduce the heat to medium and stir and turn until the mange tout are very hot. Season with salt to taste, then remove to a warm serving plate and keep warm.

7 Wipe the wok clean. Turn the heat to high, add 30ml (2tbsp) oil and swirl it around. Add the garlic, let it sizzle, then add the white spring onion and stir to release the aroma. Return the chicken to the wok and turn and toss with the wok scoop or metal spatula for about 30-45 seconds. Splash in the wine or sherry around the side of the wok, stirring continuously as it sizzles. Pour the well-stirred sauce over the chicken. Lower the heat and continue to stir while the sauce thickens. Add the green spring onion, stir, then scoop the chicken mixture on top of the mange tout. Serve immediately.

Facing page, clockwise from the top: Duck stuffed with myriad condiments (see page 100); Sauce for duck; Stir-fried chicken with mange tout (see above)

Duck Stuffed with Myriad Condiments

INGREDIENTS

12-15 spring onions, white parts only, made into brushes (see page 34)

450g (1lb) taro, peeled

1 oven-ready duck, 1.8-2kg (4-4½lb)

15ml (1tbsp) thick soy sauce

FOR THE SAUCE STUFFING

¼ of whole dried tangerine peel, soaked in cold water, then cut into small pieces

4 cloves garlic, peeled and finely chopped

5cm (2 inches) fresh ginger root, peeled and finely chopped

3 shallots, skinned and finely chopped

2 whole star anise (16 segments)

90ml (6tbsp) crushed yellow bean sauce

75ml (5tbsp) hoisin sauce

15ml (1tbsp) sesame paste

5ml (1tsp) five-spice powder

10ml (2tsp) ginger powder

10ml (2tsp) salt

30ml (2tbsp) sugar

15ml (1tbsp) mei-kuei-lu wine or gin

Serves 6 with 3-4 other dishes

Illustrated on page 99

The best time to serve this famous Cantonese dish is in the autumn and winter. The sauce resulting from this subtly balanced blend of seasonings is delicious.

1 *Prepare the sauce stuffing:* mix together the tangerine peel, garlic, ginger, shallots, star anise, sauces, sesame paste, five-spice powder, ginger powder, salt, sugar and wine or gin. (This can be done hours in advance.)

2 Make the spring onion brushes and leave them in a bowl of water in the refrigerator. (This can also be done hours in advance.)

3 Slice the taro into pieces, about 1cm (½ inch) thick. Lay them on a large heatproof dish with raised edges.

4 The duck must be at room temperature, otherwise the steaming will take much longer. Dry both skin and cavity with kitchen paper. Chop off the pinions of the wings, save them for the stockpot.

5 Spoon the sauce stuffing into the cavity. To seal the tail end, fold the parson's nose inwards. If necessary, however, use either a thin poultry skewer or bamboo satay stick to thread through the skin. To seal the neck end, fold the flap of neck skin over the neck cavity.

6 Lay the duck on top of the taro in the heatproof dish, breast side up. Put the dish into a wok or steamer and steam (see page 45), tightly covered, for 1¼-1½ hours or until the duck is tender yet firm.

7 Drain the spring onion brushes and pat dry.

8 Remove the dish from the steamer and carefully transfer the duck to another dish. Brush some thick soy sauce over the skin to give it colour.

9 Turn the parson's nose outwards or remove the skewer. Spoon the sauce stuffing into a saucepan.

10 Transfer the taro to a warm serving platter and keep warm. Degrease the liquid remaining in the heatproof dish, then pour it into the saucepan.

11 Stir to blend the liquid and the sauce stuffing in the saucepan and simmer over a low heat for 5-10 minutes. Strain through a sieve and discard the solids. Return this sauce to the saucepan and bring to a simmer again.

12 Chop the duck either in the Chinese way (see right) or by your usual method. Arrange the pieces on top of the taro.

13 Pour some of the sauce over the meat. Garnish with spring onion brushes. Pour the remaining sauce into a sauce bowl and serve.

CHOPPING POULTRY CHINESE-STYLE

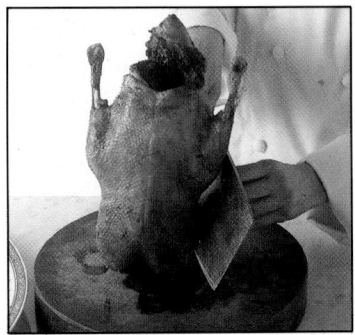

1 Slice off the wing on each side, cutting through the joint close to the body.

2 Slice off the leg on each side, cutting down through the joint close to the body.

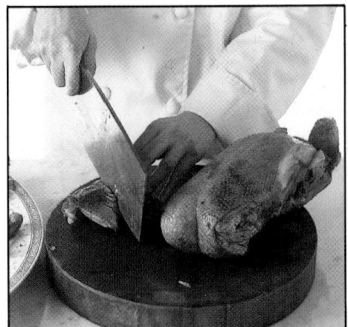

3 On each leg cut the drumstick and thigh apart. Cut both the thigh and drumstick in two.

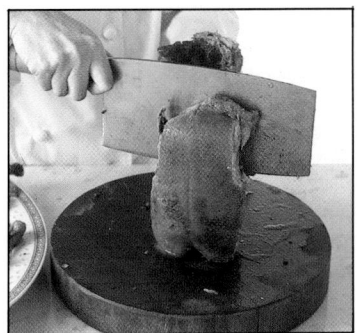

4 Split the carcass in half lengthwise so that the back and breast form two separate pieces.

5 Remove the breastbone with a knife, sliding it between the bone and the meat.

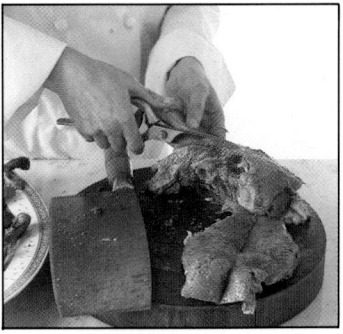

6 Using a pair of kitchen scissors cut the backbone out of the back piece, and discard.

7 Cut the back pieces crosswise into 1 inch (2.5cm) pieces.

8 Halve the breast meat lengthwise then cut crosswise into 1 inch (2.5cm) pieces.

9 Reassemble the bird with the breast meat on top of the back pieces.

Smoked Duck, Szechwan Style

INGREDIENTS

1 oven-ready duck, about 2.3kg (5lb)
26ml (1¾tbsp) salt
5ml (1 scant tsp) saltpetre powder
175g (6oz) plain flour
100g (4oz) brown sugar
60ml (4tbsp) black tea leaves
2 pieces fresh ginger root, each 1cm (½ inch), peeled and bruised
2 large spring onions
1 whole star anise (8 segments)
7.5ml (1½tsp) Szechwan peppercorns
30ml (2tbsp) Shaohsing wine or medium dry sherry
groundnut or corn oil for deep-frying
15ml (1tbsp) sesame oil

Serves 6 with 3 other dishes

Illustrated opposite

The various cooking processes used in this dish may seem overly time-consuming, but the duck is at once rendered crispy and moist, smoky and aromatic.

1 Rub the salt thoroughly over the skin and inside the cavity, then rub the cavity only with saltpetre. Leave the duck in a cool place for about 10 hours or overnight.

2 Rinse the duck, especially the cavity, in plenty of hot water. Wipe dry. The duck is now ready for smoking.

3 Line a large wok with heavy-duty foil and place the flour, sugar and tea in the bottom. Place a metal trivet or bamboo stand on top. Place the duck on top, breast side up, and make sure that there is a gap between it and the smoking ingredients so as to allow free circulation of smoke. Put the wok cover on tightly.

4 Turn the heat on high until you see smoke coming out, then adjust it, making sure that plenty of smoke continues to come out. Smoke for 15 minutes, turn the duck over and smoke, breast side down, for another 15 minutes. Remove from the heat.

5 When cool enough to handle, transfer to a large heatproof dish, breast side up. Put half of the ginger, spring onion, star anise, peppercorns and wine or sherry into the cavity; put the other half on the breast.

6 Steam in a steamer or another wok for 1-1¼ hours (see page 45).

7 When cool enough to handle, transfer the duck to a rack and leave to cool. Remove and discard all the condiments. Dry with kitchen paper.

8 Half fill a wok or deep-fryer with oil. Heat to a temperature of 190°C (375°F) or until a cube of stale bread browns in 50 seconds. Carefully lower the duck into the oil, breast side down, and deep-fry for 3-4 minutes or until brown. With a wooden spoon or spatula in one hand and another inside the cavity, turn the duck over and deep-fry the other side until brown. Hot oil can also be spooned over the skin. Remove to a chopping board. Brush the sesame oil over the breast. The duck can be carved either in the Chinese way (see page 101) or by your usual method. Serve warm.

Note: if the duck is prepared in advance, it can be reheated in a preheated oven at 150°C (300°F) mark 2 for 30-45 minutes or until it's hot and the skin is crisp.

Facing page, clockwise from the top: Lettuce-wrapped chicken (see page 104); Smoked duck Szechwan-style (see above)

INGREDIENTS

2 large lettuces, Webb, Iceberg
  or round
8 medium dried Chinese
  mushrooms, reconstituted (see
  page 39)
50-75g (2-3oz) Szechwan
  preserved vegetable, rinsed
  and dried
6-8 water chestnuts, fresh peeled
  or canned drained
4-6 chicken breasts, about 1kg
  (2-2½lb), skinned and boned
150ml (10tbsp) groundnut or
  corn oil
50g (2oz) walnuts or blanched
  almonds
4-5 cloves garlic, peeled and
  finely chopped
6 spring onions, cut into tiny
  rounds, white and green parts
  separated
22.5ml (1½tbsp) Shaohsing wine
  or medium dry sherry

FOR THE MARINADE

4-5ml (¾-1tsp) salt
4-5ml (¾-1tsp) sugar
15ml (1tbsp) thin soy sauce
8-10 turns white pepper mill
10ml (2tsp) Shaohsing wine or
  medium dry sherry
7.5ml (1½tsp) cornflour
1 egg white, lightly beaten
30-45ml (2-3 tbsp) water
30ml (2tbsp) groundnut or corn
  oil
10ml (2tsp) sesame oil

FOR THE SAUCE

7.5ml (1½tsp) potato flour
135ml (9tbsp) clear stock
5-10ml (1-2tsp) thick soy sauce
  (for colouring)
30ml (2tbsp) oyster sauce

Serves 6 with 2 other dishes

Illustrated on page 103

Lettuce-wrapped Chicken

Although the chicken used here is delicious, an arguably more elegant (although more expensive) version of this Southern dish uses quail's meat and dried oysters.

1 Wash and dry the lettuce. Refrigerate to maintain crispness until almost ready to cook the chicken, then arrange the leaves on 1 or 2 plates.

2 Drain and squeeze out excess water from the mushrooms but leave damp. Dice into the size of petits pois.

3 Finely chop the Szechwan preserved vegetable, removing stringy fibres at the same time.

4 Mince the water chestnuts in a food processor or blender.

5 Chop the chicken flesh by hand or mince coarsely. Put into a large bowl.

6 *Prepare the marinade:* add the salt, sugar, soy sauce, pepper, wine or sherry, cornflour and egg white to the chicken. Stir to coat until well blended. Add the water, 15ml (1tbsp) at a time, and stir vigorously in the same direction to make the chicken lighter in texture.

7 Stir in the mushroom, preserved vegetable and water chestnut. Leave to marinate for 30 minutes. Blend in the oil and sesame oil.

8 *Prepare the sauce:* dissolve the potato flour in a small bowl with 30ml (2tbsp) of the stock. Stir in the remaining stock and add the soy sauce and oyster sauce.

9 Heat a wok until hot. Add the walnuts or almonds and stir continuously over a low to medium heat for about 3 minutes until crisp and fragrant. Remove and chop. Wash and dry the wok. (This step can be prepared several hours ahead.)

10 Reheat the wok over a high heat until smoke rises. Add 150ml (10tbsp) of oil and swirl it around until very hot. Add the garlic which will sizzle and take on colour almost instantly. Add the white spring onion, stir a couple of times and add the chicken. Sliding the wok scoop or metal spatula to the bottom of the wok, flip and toss for 2-3 minutes or until the chicken turns white, breaking up lumps at the same time. Splash in the wine or sherry around the side of the wok, stirring as it sizzles.

11 As soon as the sizzling dies down, lower the heat, push the ingredients to the side of the wok and pour the well-stirred sauce into the middle. When it bubbles, stir in the surrounding chicken, add the green spring onion and walnut or almond, still stirring to blend well. Remove to a warm serving plate and put in the centre of the table with the prepared lettuce (a).

12 To eat, each person takes 1 piece of lettuce at a time (b), spoons some chicken on to the lettuce (c), folds it to encase the chicken (d) and then eats it with the fingers.

a

b

c

d

Willow Chicken in Black Bean Sauce

INGREDIENTS

about 800g (1¾lb), pieces chicken thigh, skinned and boned

2 small green peppers, seeded

1-2 fresh green chillies, seeded (optional)

90ml (6tbsp) groundnut or corn oil

5-6 cloves garlic, peeled and cut into silken threads (see page 35)

4 spring onions, cut into 2.5-cm (1-inch) sections, white and green parts separated

45ml (3tbsp) fermented black beans, rinsed and mashed

15ml (1tbsp) Shaohsing wine or medium dry sherry

little sesame oil (optional)

chilli sauce (optional)

FOR THE MARINADE

2.5ml (½tsp) salt

2.5ml (½tsp) sugar

15ml (1tbsp) thin soy sauce

8 turns black pepper mill

10ml (2tsp) Shaohsing wine or medium dry sherry

5ml (1tsp) cornflour

30ml (2tbsp) egg white, lightly beaten

22.5ml (1½tbsp) groundnut or corn oil

FOR THE SAUCE

5ml (1tsp) cornflour

60ml (4tbsp) clear stock or water

10ml (2tsp) oyster sauce or 5ml (1tsp) thick soy sauce

Serves 6 with 3 other dishes

Illustrated on page 109

This dish takes its name from the willowy strips of the sliced chicken and pepper.

1 Cut the chicken flesh into strips, about 5mm (⅕ inch) thick. Put into a bowl.

2 *Prepare the marinade:* add the salt, sugar, soy sauce, pepper and wine or sherry to the chicken. Sprinkle with the cornflour, add the egg white and stir in the same direction to coat. Leave to marinate for 15-30 minutes. Blend in the oil.

3 Slice the peppers into long and narrow strips.

4 Slice the chillies into strips.

5 *Prepare the sauce:* mix together the cornflour, stock or water, oyster or soy sauce.

6 Heat a wok until hot. Add 15ml (1tbsp) of the oil and swirl it around. Add the pepper and stir and toss with the wok scoop or metal spatula constantly for about 2 minutes. When tender yet crunchy, remove to a warm plate and keep warm.

7 Wash and dry the wok.

8 Heat the wok over a high heat until smoke rises. Add the remaining oil and swirl it around. Add the garlic and when it sizzles and takes on colour add the chilli, white spring onion and then the black bean paste. Stir to blend with the garlic. Put in the chicken and stir and toss the strips for 2 minutes or until they turn whitish, scraping the paste from the bottom of the pan to coat.

9 Splash in the wine or sherry around the side of the wok and let it sizzle, stirring continuously. When the sizzling dies down, lower the heat and add the well-stirred sauce to the chicken. Continue to stir as the sauce thickens. Add the pepper and green spring onion and mix well. Remove to a warm plate and serve immediately. A little sesame oil can be sprinkled on top. For those who like an extra hot flavour, chilli sauce can be served at the table.

Note: in pursuit of gastronomic excellence, you could let the chicken "go through the oil" (see page 40), before stir-frying it in step 8. In such cases, simply stir-fry for a shorter time.

Chicken in Yunnan Steam-pot

A Yunnan steam-pot is basically a pottery casserole dish about 20cm (8 inches) in diameter and 10cm (4 inches) high with a cone-shaped chimney in the centre of the bowl. The pot, with its tightly-fitting lid, is placed in boiling water so that steam rises through the chimney to circulate inside and cook the ingredients. Chicken cooked in this way is tender and succulent, and the accompanying soup is pure and flavourful. The pot is available in some Chinese shops, but at a pinch, a double boiler could be used.

1 Drain and squeeze out excess water from the mushrooms but leave damp. Reserve the soaking liquid.

2 Slice the ham into large pieces.

3 Chop the chicken through the bones into serving pieces, using a kitchen cleaver, a mallet and kitchen scissors if necessary. Joint at the wings, thighs and drumsticks and slit the whole breast off from the back. Cut and discard the pinions, then halve each wing at the joint. Halve each thigh and drumstick crosswise. Halve the breast lengthwise, then cut each half crosswise into 3-4 pieces. Do not use the back; save it for the stockpot.

4 Bring a large saucepan of water to the boil and add the chicken pieces. Return to the boil and continue to boil for about 2 minutes so that the scum rises. Pour into a colander and rinse the chicken to get rid of any remaining scum.

5 Line the steam-pot with the mushroom, ham and chicken. Add the salt, pepper, ginger, spring onion and wine or sherry. Add sufficient water (including the mushroom water) to come within 2.5cm (1 inch) of the top of the chimney of the pot. Put the lid on.

6 Over a moderate heat, place the steam-pot on the rim of a small saucepan with boiling water inside, leaving a gap between the water level and the bottom of the steam-pot. Cook for 1-1¼ hours without disturbing. Replenish the water in the saucepan from time to time, removing the steam-pot to do so if necessary.

7 Remove from the heat. Spoon off excess fat, if any, on the surface.

8 Take the steam-pot to the dining table and serve from it. Use the soy sauce as a dip if preferred.

INGREDIENTS

12 medium dried Chinese mushrooms, reconstituted (see page 39)
225g (8oz) best ham, trimmed of fat
1 oven-ready chicken, 1.4-1.5kg (3-3¼lb) (or 2 double poussins)
5-6.25ml (1-1¼tsp) salt
4-6 turns white pepper mill
2 thickish slices fresh ginger root, peeled
2 spring onions, quartered
15ml (1tbsp) Shaohsing wine or medium dry sherry
thin soy sauce (optional)

Serves 6 with 3 other dishes

Illustrated on page 109

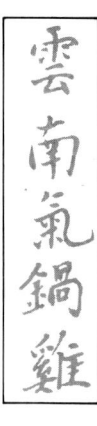

Red-braised Chicken with Chestnuts

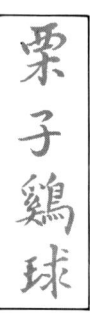

INGREDIENTS
20 medium dried Chinese
  mushrooms, reconstituted (see
  page 39)
450g (1lb) chestnuts
225g (8oz) canned bamboo shoots
45-60ml (3-4tbsp) groundnut or
  corn oil
1 oven-ready chicken, 1.8-2kg
  (4-4½lb)
45ml (3tbsp) Shaohsing wine or
  medium dry sherry
4 thickish slices fresh ginger root,
  peeled
2 whole star anise (16 segments)
2.5cm (1 inch) cinnamon stick
7.5ml (1½tsp) salt
5ml (1tsp) brown sugar
60-75ml (4-5tbsp) thick soy sauce
300ml (½ pint) clear stock

Serves 6-8 as a main course

Illustrated opposite

A popular national dish during autumn and winter when chestnuts are in season.

1 Drain and squeeze out excess water from the mushrooms but leave damp.

2 Make a cross in the shell of each chestnut and put into a saucepan of cold water. Bring to the boil and boil for 3-5 minutes, depending on the size of the chestnuts. Remove from the heat but leave the chestnuts in the water. Shell and peel the chestnuts as best you can.

3 Cube the bamboo shoots into the size of a small chestnut.

4 Chop the chicken through the bones into serving pieces, using a kitchen cleaver, a mallet and kitchen scissors, if necessary. Joint the wings, thighs and drumsticks and slit the whole breast off from the back. Cut and discard the pinions, then halve each wing at the joint; chop each piece crosswise into 2. Chop each thigh and drumstick crosswise into 2 or 3. Halve the breast lengthwise, then chop each half into 3-4 pieces. Do likewise with the back.

5 Heat a large, deep and heavy saucepan over a high heat until very hot. Add the oil and swirl it around. Add the dark meat of the chicken, turn and toss to brown for about 3 minutes. Add the white meat, mushroom and bamboo shoots and toss and turn for another 2-3 minutes.

6 Add the wine or sherry, ginger, star anise and cinnamon, continuing to stir until the sizzling dies down.

7 Add the salt, brown sugar and soy sauce. Adjust the heat, turning and stirring so that the chicken will be dyed by the soy sauce.

8 Pour in the stock and add the chestnuts. Bring to the boil and simmer fast for about 30 minutes until the ingredients are tender. (The cooking up to this point can be done up to a day in advance.)

9 Just before serving, bring slowly to the boil. Turn up the heat to the maximum and, as the sauce bubbles, spoon it over the ingredients. Repeat until the sauce has reduced and thickened, and the flavour has become richer. Remove to a warm serving dish and serve piping hot.

Facing page, clockwise from the top: Chicken in Yunnan steam-pot (see page 107; Willow chicken in black bean sauce (see page 106); Red-braised chicken with chestnuts (see above)

Chicken Glazed in Hoisin Sauce

INGREDIENTS
2-3 chicken breasts, about 450g (1lb), skinned and boned
90ml (6tbsp) groundnut or corn oil
5-6 cloves garlic, peeled and finely chopped
4-5 spring onions, cut into 2.5-cm (1-inch) sections, white and green parts separated
15-22.5ml (1-1½tbsp) Shaohsing wine or medium dry sherry
45ml (3tbsp) hoisin sauce
50g (2oz) roasted cashew nuts

FOR THE MARINADE
2.5ml (½tsp) salt
8 turns white pepper mill
10ml (2tsp) Shaohsing wine or medium dry sherry
5ml (1tsp) cornflour
½ egg white, lightly beaten
10ml (2tsp) sesame oil

Serves 4-6 with 2-3 other dishes

Illustrated opposite

The hoisin sauce adds colour and flavour to the chicken in this Northern dish, while the cashew nuts provide a pleasing contrast of texture.

1 Dice the chicken flesh into 2-cm (¾-inch) cubes. Put into a bowl.

2 *Prepare the marinade:* add the salt, pepper and wine or sherry to the chicken. Sprinkle with the cornflour and stir in the egg white to coat. Leave to marinate for 15-30 minutes. Blend in the sesame oil.

3 Heat a wok over a high heat until smoke rises. Pour in 75ml (5tbsp) of the oil and swirl it around. Add two-thirds of the garlic and the white spring onion. Stir with the wok scoop or metal spatula a few times, then add the chicken. Sliding the scoop or spatula to the bottom of the wok, turn and toss for about 2 minutes, lowering the heat so that the chicken does not become tough. Splash in the wine or sherry around the side of the wok. As soon as the sizzling dies down, remove the chicken, still a little undercooked, to a warm plate.

4 Increase the heat, add the remaining 15ml (1tbsp) oil and swirl it around. Add the remaining garlic and, as it sizzles, add the hoisin sauce and stir well. Return the chicken to the wok and toss in the sauce to glaze until just cooked. Mix in the cashew nuts and green spring onion. Remove to a warm serving plate. Serve immediately.

Facing page, from the top: Duck stuffed with glutinous rice (see page 112); Chicken glazed in hoisin sauce (see above)

Duck Stuffed with Glutinous Rice

Duck stuffed with glutinous rice is popular with most Chinese, irrespective of the region they come from. The stuffing can be made a day in advance and refrigerated but if it is, bring it out so that it will be at room temperature before being stuffed into the duck.

INGREDIENTS

1 oven-ready duck, 2-2.3kg (4½-5lb)
22.5ml (1½tbsp) thick soy sauce
75-90ml (5-6tbsp) groundnut or corn oil for deep-frying
5ml (1tsp) salt
22.5ml (1½tbsp) Shaohsing wine or medium dry sherry
1 whole star anise or 8 segments
5ml (1tsp) Szechwan peppercorns
¼ preserved tangerine peel, soaked in cold water for 20 minutes, drained
10-15ml (2-3tsp) potato flour, dissolved in 45ml (3tbsp) water
15-30ml (1-2tbsp) oyster sauce
350g (12oz) broccoli spears, trimmed

FOR THE STUFFING

15g (½oz) dried shrimps, rinsed
45ml (3tbsp) groundnut or corn oil
2 cloves garlic, peeled and finely chopped
3 spring onions, cut into small rounds
50g (2oz) pork, diced into size of matchstick heads
8 small dried Chinese mushrooms, reconstituted (see page 39) and chopped into size of matchstick heads
50g (2oz) canned bamboo shoots, chopped into size of matchstick heads
75g (3oz) glutinous rice, soaked in cold water for 2 hours, drained
2.5ml (½tsp) salt
22.5ml (1½tbsp) thin soy sauce
8 turns pepper mill

Serves 6 with 3 other dishes

Illustrated on page 111

1 Soak the shrimps in just enough boiling water to cover them, for 20 minutes. Drain, but save the liquid.

2 *Prepare the stuffing:* heat a wok over a high heat until smoke rises. Add the oil and swirl around. Add the garlic and spring onion and stir for a few seconds. Add the shrimps, stir, the pork, stir, and then the mushroom, bamboo shoots, glutinous rice and the shrimp liquid. Mix and stir for about 1 minute, partially cooking the mixture. Season with the salt, thin soy sauce and pepper. Remove to a bowl. Wash and dry the wok.

3 Boil a kettle of water. Pour over and scald the duck, turning it over several times to ensure even scalding. Wipe off excess water.

4 When the skin is still warm, brush all over with the thick soy sauce, not missing the wings and legs. Put on a wire rack.

5 Heat a wok over a high heat, add the oil, swirl it around and heat until smoke rises. Carefully lower the duck into the oil, breast side down, and fry for 1-2 minutes or until brownish in colour. With a wooden spoon or spatula held in one hand and another put inside the cavity, turn the duck over and fry the other side for another 1-2 minutes or until brownish. Turn off the heat. Remove to a larger plate. Discard the oil.

6 As soon as the duck has cooled a little, rub all over with the salt and wine or sherry. Pack the cavity loosely with the stuffing; there is no need to sew up either end.

7 Put into a large dish with about 2.5cm (1 inch) raised edges. Add the star anise, peppercorns and tangerine peel. Steam in a wok or steamer for 1¾-2 hours (see page 44). Remove carefully to a large heatproof serving platter. Keep warm in a low oven.

8 Spoon off most of the fat in the steaming dish. Strain the juices into a saucepan, discarding the spices: there should be about 300ml (½ pint). Slowly bring to a simmer. Trickle in the well-stirred dissolved potato flour, stirring as it thickens. Taste for flavour. Add the oyster sauce. Remove from the heat and keep hot.

9 Put the broccoli into a pan of boiling water with about 5ml (1tsp) salt and 15ml (1tbsp) oil. Return to the boil and cook for about 2-3 minutes until tender but still crisp. Drain thoroughly. Take the duck

out of the oven and arrange the broccoli around it. Pour the hot sauce over the duck and broccoli.

10 To serve the Chinese way, everybody can help themselves and pick from the duck. It is so tender that the meat will come away from the bones as the pressure of the chopsticks is applied. The stuffing can be spooned out of the cavity to be served with the meat.

Note: after the duck is steamed (step 7), if it is left in a pre-heated oven of 160°-180°C (300°-350°F) for 45-60 or 30-45 minutes, the skin will be crisp again. This time gap allows for drinks or other dishes to be served.

Scrambled Egg with Chinese Chives

1 Pick over the Chinese chives, snip off and discard both the hard top ends and the wilted tail ends. Wash and dry them well. Cut into 2.5-cm (1-inch) lengths.

2 Beat the eggs lightly in a large bowl with 15ml (1tbsp) of the oil until well blended and frothy. Add the salt and pepper and beat a few more times.

3 Heat a wok over a high heat until smoke rises. Add the remaining oil, swirl it around and heat until very hot. Add the Chinese chives, stir for about 20 seconds, then pour in the egg. Sliding the wok scoop or metal spatula to the bottom of the wok, keep turning and letting the egg go under to blend with the oil and chives. Continue in this way until all the egg has just set.

4 Remove from the heat while you scoop the egg and chives mixture on to a warm serving plate. Serve immediately.

Note: a small bunch of chives can be used as a substitute for Chinese chives.

INGREDIENTS
75-100g (3-4oz) Chinese chives
6 large eggs
120ml (8tbsp) groundnut or corn oil
2.5-4ml (½-¾tsp) salt
several turns pepper mill

Serves 6 with 2-3 other dishes

Illustrated on page 115

Whampoa Stir-fried Egg

INGREDIENTS
6 eggs
1.25-2.5ml (¼-½tsp) salt
250ml (8fl oz) groundnut or corn
oil (only about 105ml [7tbsp]
actually used)

Serves 4-6 with 2-3 other dishes

Illustrated opposite

Even if someone arrives unannounced, the Chinese will still extend an immediate invitation to stay for dinner with the stock phrase: "We'll just add another pair of chopsticks to the table." However, in the kitchen there will be a stir to whip up a quick and easy dish to add to those ready to be served; this egg dish foots the bill. It takes its name from Whampoa, a port near Canton, where the technique for stir-frying the eggs was originally invented. The tenderness of the egg has earned much fame for this Cantonese dish.

1 Beat the eggs lightly with the salt and 30ml (2tbsp) of the oil until well amalgamated.

2 Heat a wok over a medium heat until hot but not smoking. Add all the oil and swirl around 2-3 times to reach over half way up the sloping edges. Pour the oil back into a container and then return the wok to the burner. There will be some oil left in the wok.

3 Add 30ml (2tbsp) oil and heat until hot but not smoking. Pour in the egg slowly, stirring and folding with the wok scoop or metal spatula. As soon as all the egg has been poured in, start streaming in another 30-45ml (2-3tbsp) oil, little by little, around the side of the wok, while continuing to stir and fold. When the egg has set into tender flakes, remove from the heat and scoop at once on to a warm serving dish.

Facing page, clockwise from the top: Soy sauce chicken (see page 116); Scrambled eggs with Chinese chives (see page 113); Whampoa stir-fried egg (see above)

Soy Sauce Chicken

INGREDIENTS
2 whole star anise (16 segments)
5ml (1tsp) Szechwan peppercorns
15ml (1tbsp) groundnut or corn
oil
6 spring onions, halved crosswise
2-3 slices fresh ginger root, about
3mm (⅛ inch) thick, peeled
1 oven-ready chicken, 1.4kg
(3lb), at room temperature
250ml (8fl oz) thick soy sauce
30ml (2tbsp) Shaohsing wine or
medium dry sherry
60-75ml (4-5tbsp) brown sugar

*Serves 6 with 3 other dishes; or 4
as a main course*

Illustrated on page 115

*This is a whole chicken dish, beloved of the Southern Chinese. If the
chicken is hand-plucked in the old-fashioned way, it will be
coloured an even russet brown by the soy sauce and sugar mixture.
However, when a chicken is machine-plucked, as it usually is in the
West, the colouring will not be as successful. Fortunately, the
aromatic soy sauce taste is not affected in any way.*

1 To make the spiced liquid, put the star anise and peppercorns in
a saucepan with 350ml (12fl oz) water and bring to the boil. Reduce
the heat and simmer for about 15 minutes, reducing the liquid to
175ml (6fl oz). Drain and discard the spices.

2 Heat a wok over a high heat until smoke rises. Add the oil and
swirl it around. Add the spring onion and ginger, stir for about 10
seconds or until they have released their aroma. Remove from the
heat. Transfer the spring onion and ginger to the chicken cavity.

3 Wash the wok, then add the spiced liquid, soy sauce, wine or
sherry and sugar. Bring to the boil, stirring to make sure that the
sugar has dissolved.

4 Put the chicken in on its side. Using a large spoon, pour the
simmering sauce repeatedly over the chicken for 10 minutes.

5 With a spatula held in one hand and a wooden spoon put inside
the cavity, turn the chicken over to lie on the other side. Spoon the
simmering sauce over for another 10 minutes.

6 If too much sauce has evaporated, replenish with about 60ml (2fl
oz) water. Bring to simmering point again.

7 Cover and simmer for 20 minutes. Turn the chicken over again,
cover and continue to simmer for another 20 minutes until the
chicken is cooked. To test, pierce the thickest part of the thigh with
a chopstick. If no pink juices run out, the chicken is cooked.

8 Remove the chicken from the wok, tipping out the soy sauce from
the cavity. Put some of this sauce on the table to use as a dip. The
rest can be stored in the refrigerator and used to season other
ingredients.

9 To serve the chicken, carve either Chinese style (see page 101),
or in your usual way.

Variation: Soy sauce drumsticks or chicken wings
12 drumsticks or chicken wings or 6 of each. Pour the sauce
repeatedly over the drumsticks or wings for 10 minutes, then
simmer, covered, for about 20-30 minutes until cooked.

Kung Pao Chicken

A famous Szechwan dish which tempts the palate with a full range of tastes and aftertastes: peppery hot and spicy, savoury and slightly sweet and sour. It is said that this was a favourite dish of a Szechwan governor during the Ch'ing dynasty (1644-1911), after whose official title, "Kung Pao", the dish was named. The governor must have been fond of peanuts, for it is unthinkable not to add them.

1 Cut the chicken flesh into thin strips (a). Cut into cubes about 1cm (½ inch) square (b). Put into a bowl.

a   b

2 *Prepare the marinade:* add the salt, soy sauce, wine or sherry, cornflour and egg to the chicken. Mix well and leave to marinate for 15-30 minutes.

3 *Prepare the sauce:* mix together the soy sauce, chilli sauce, vinegar, sugar, cornflour, and water.

4 Heat a wok over a high heat until smoke rises. Add the oil and swirl it around. Add the dried chilli, stir, then add the garlic and ginger and stir to release their aroma. Add the chicken. Sliding the wok scoop or spatula to the bottom of the wok, turn and toss for about 60 seconds. Splash in the wine or sherry around the side of the wok, stirring and tossing continuously. Add the spring onion and continue to stir for another 30-45 seconds. The chicken should be almost cooked by now.

5 Add the well-stirred sauce to the wok. Continue to stir while it thickens.

6 Add the peanuts, stir to mix for a few times, then remove to a warm serving plate. Serve immediately.

INGREDIENTS

350g (12oz) chicken breast meat
60ml (4tbsp) groundnut or corn oil
2-3 long (about 7.5cm [3 inches] or more each) dried red chillies, or 4-5 smaller, seeded and cut into pieces
2 cloves garlic, peeled and diagonally sliced
4-6 thin slices fresh ginger root
15ml (1tbsp) Shaohsing wine or medium dry sherry
3 spring onions, cut into small rounds
50g (2oz) roasted peanuts

FOR THE MARINADE

2ml (⅓tsp) salt
10ml (2tsp) thin soy sauce
10ml (2tsp) Shaohsing wine or medium dry sherry
5ml (1tsp) cornflour
15ml (1tbsp) egg white, lightly beaten

FOR THE SAUCE

15ml (1tbsp) thick soy sauce
15-30ml (1-2tbsp) chilli sauce
10ml (2tsp) rice or white wine vinegar
10ml (2tsp) sugar
7.5ml (1½tsp) cornflour
90ml (6tbsp) clear stock or water

Serves 4 with 3 other dishes

Illustrated on page 119

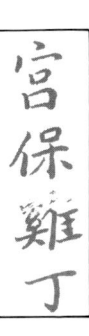

Sautéed Chicken Livers

In this simple dish, with its slightly piquant taste, the livers are partially browned so that they're crispy on the outside, but pink inside. As one of the dishes in a Chinese meal, rice would be served with it as usual, but as a main European course, noodles or spaghetti would do equally well. A green salad could be served afterwards.

INGREDIENTS
700g (1½lb) chicken livers, trimmed
7.5ml (1½tsp) cornflour
90-105ml (6-7tbsp) groundnut or corn oil
5-6cm (2-2½ inches) fresh ginger root, peeled and cut into slices
9-10 large spring onions, sliced diagonally into 1-cm (½-inch) sections, white and green parts separated
22.5ml (1½tbsp) Shaohsing wine or medium dry sherry

FOR THE MARINADE
4ml (¾tsp) salt
4ml (¾tsp) brown sugar
15ml (1tbsp) thick soy sauce
10 turns black pepper mill
10ml (2tsp) Worcestershire sauce
10ml (2tsp) Shaohsing wine or medium dry sherry

FOR THE SAUCE
7.5ml (1½tsp) cornflour
90ml (6tbsp) clear stock or water
10ml (2tsp) thick soy sauce
5ml (1tsp) Worcestershire sauce

Serves 4 as a main course; 8 with 3-4 other dishes

Illustrated opposite

1 Slice each liver into 2 or 3 pieces. Place in a colander to wash, and drain well. Put into a large bowl.

2 *Prepare the marinade:* add the salt, sugar, soy sauce, pepper, Worcestershire sauce and wine or sherry to the livers. Stir to mix well and leave to marinate for 1-2 hours, stirring occasionally.

3 *Prepare the sauce:* put the cornflour in a small bowl and stir in 30ml (2tbsp) of the stock or water to blend until smooth. Add the soy and Worcestershire sauces, and stir in the remaining stock or water.

4 Just before ready to cook, sprinkle the liver with the cornflour and stir to coat well.

5 Heat a wok over a high heat until smoke rises. Add the oil and swirl it around. Add the ginger and white spring onion and let them sizzle. As soon as the spring onion takes on colour, add the livers and brown for about 2 minutes, turning once or twice with a wok scoop or metal spatula to prevent sticking. Sprinkle with the wine or sherry and, when the sizzling has died down, lower the heat, cover and cook for about 2 minutes. Turn the livers over, add the green spring onion, cover and continue to cook for about 2 more minutes.

6 Pour the well-stirred sauce over the livers and stir until it thickens. Remove to a warm serving plate. Serve immediately.

Note: if pressed for time, instead of marinating the livers, pierce them with a fork to let the marinade permeate.

Facing page, clockwise from the top: Paper-wrapped chicken (see page 121); Dragon flying and phoenix dancing (see page 120); Sautéed chicken livers (see above); Kung Pao chicken (see page 117)

A Chicken For Two Dishes:

Dragon Flying and Phoenix Dancing

龍
飛
鳳
舞

INGREDIENTS

2 chicken breasts from a
  1.4-1.6kg (3-3½lb) chicken,
  skinned and boned
225g (8oz) medium raw prawns,
  without heads, shelled, halved
  and deveined
6.25ml (1¼tsp) salt
100g (4oz) mange tout, trimmed
groundnut or corn oil for
  deep-frying
50g (2oz) red-in-snow, rinsed
2-3 cloves garlic, peeled and
  finely chopped
3-4 spring onions, cut into 2.5-cm
  (1-inch) sections, white and
  green parts separated
15ml (1tbsp) Shaohsing wine or
  medium dry sherry

FOR THE MARINADE

2.5ml (½tsp) salt
2.5ml (½tsp) sugar
6 turns white pepper mill
5ml (1tsp) Shaohsing wine or
  medium dry sherry
5ml (1tsp) cornflour
15ml (1tbsp) egg white, lightly
  beaten

FOR THE SAUCE

4ml (¾tsp) potato flour
75ml (5tbsp) clear stock
15ml (1tbsp) oyster sauce

Serves 4-6 with 2-3 other dishes

Illustrated on page 119

The dragon and phoenix of the title are metaphors for the two main ingredients: chicken and prawns. As it is a very elegant dish, it is worth the trouble to use the "going through the oil" technique to seal in the juices of the ingredients before stir-frying them.

1 Cut the chicken flesh into large even-sized pieces. Put into a bowl.

2 *Prepare the marinade:* add the salt, sugar, pepper, wine or sherry, cornflour and egg white to the chicken. Stir in the same direction to mix well. Leave to marinate for 20-30 minutes.

3 Add 1.25ml (¼tsp) of the salt to the prawns.

4 Blanch the mange tout in plenty of boiling water with 5ml (1tsp) of the salt and 15ml (1tbsp) oil until the water returns to the boil. Pour into a colander and refresh under cold running water.

5 *Prepare the sauce:* mix together the potato flour, stock and oyster sauce.

6 Half fill a wok or deep-fryer with oil. Heat to a temperature of 180°C (350°F) or until a cube of stale bread browns in 60 seconds. Add the chicken and, using a long pair of chopsticks, separate the pieces and let them "go through the oil" for about 20 seconds (see page 40). Remove with a hand strainer and put on a plate nearby. Do not turn off the heat.

7 Add the prawns to the oil for about 20 seconds, separating the pieces with chopsticks. Remove to another plate nearby. Turn off the heat.

8 Pour the oil into a container for future use, leaving about 75ml (5tbsp) in the wok.

9 Reheat wok over a high heat until smoke rises. Add the garlic and, as it sizzles, add the white spring onion and stir. Add the red-in-snow and stir until hot. Return the chicken to the wok and, sliding the wok scoop or metal spatula to the bottom of the wok, turn and toss until almost cooked. Return the prawns to the wok, continuing to turn and stir. Splash in the wine around the side of the wok, stirring as it sizzles: both the chicken and prawns will be cooked by now. Add the mange tout. Sprinkle in the well-stirred sauce, stirring as it thickens. Add the green spring onion then remove to a warm serving dish. Serve immediately.

Paper-wrapped Chicken

The wind-dried sausage in this dish makes the chicken, already highly seasoned in the marinade, even spicier and richer in taste.

1 Skin and bone the drumsticks and thighs. Discard the pinions of the wings and chop each wing into 3 pieces. Scrape out the 2 oysters. Put into the bowl.

2 *Prepare the marinade:* add the soy sauce, sugar, wine or sherry, ginger, five-spice powder and oil to the chicken. Mix well. Leave to marinate for a minimum of 1 hour, turning the pieces occasionally.

3 Squeeze out excess water from the mushrooms but leave damp. Halve if small ones are used, quarter if large ones are used.

4 Slice the bamboo shoots into 24 pieces, each about 5mm (⅕ inch) thick.

5 Rinse the Chinese sausages and pat dry. Slice each diagonally into 8 pieces, making a total of 48.

6 About 10 minutes before the wrapping, add the mushroom and bamboo shoots to the chicken so that they can absorb some of the marinade.

7 Using a brush, thoroughly oil one side of 1 square of greaseproof paper. Put on a plate or work surface at an angle, like a diamond, and layer on it 1 piece of chicken between 2 strips of Chinese sausage, then 1 piece of bamboo shoot, and finally 1 piece of mushroom with a coriander leaf on top.

8 To wrap in the classic Chinese way, fold the bottom flap up towards the centre, then fold the 2 side flaps inwards on top of each other and finally fold the top flap down and tuck it squarely inside the opening. Repeat this process until all have been wrapped.

9 Half fill a wok or deep-fryer with oil. Heat to a temperature of 180°-190°C (350°-375°F) or until a cube of stale bread browns in 50-60 seconds. Slip 12 parcels into the oil, unsealed side down, and deep-fry for about 5 minutes if you like the chicken just done, or for about 8 minutes if you like it much more cooked and slightly charred. Turn them over for the last minute of cooking.

10 Remove with a large hand strainer and, holding it carefully above the oil, let excess oil from the parcels drain back into the wok or deep-fryer. Put the parcels on a warm serving plate. Reheat the oil and deep-fry the remainder as before.

11 Serve hot. As soon as the fingers can withstand the heat, open a parcel and savour its contents.

Note: any left-over parcels can be deep-fried again momentarily or put into a pre-heated oven of 180°C (350°F) gas 4 for 10 minutes.

INGREDIENTS

the rest of the chicken (or 6 drumsticks or thigh pieces), over 900g (2lb)

12 small or 6 large dried Chinese mushrooms, reconstituted (see page 39)

100-175g (4-6oz) canned bamboo shoots

6 wind-dried Chinese sausages, liver or pork or both

24 pieces greaseproof paper, each 20cm (8 inches) square

24 large pieces coriander leaves (optional)

groundnut or corn oil for deep-frying

FOR THE MARINADE

45ml (3tbsp) thin soy sauce

10ml (2tsp) sugar

10ml (2tsp) Shaohsing wine or medium dry sherry

5ml (1tsp) ginger powder

1.25ml (¼tsp) five-spice powder

15ml (1tbsp) sesame oil

Serves 8 as first course; 4 as a main course with a salad

Illustrated on page 119

A Northern or Peking Menu

北京菜

The main feature of this menu for six is, without doubt, the Peking duck with its pancake accompaniment. In fact, they alone, with any one of the other dishes, should make four people feel well fed and contented.

薄餅 **Mandarin pancakes**

北京填鴨 **Peking duck**
Tender duck served, traditionally, wrapped in a Mandarin pancake with hoisin sauce and spring onions (see page 209-210).

賽干貝松 **"Seaweed"**
Deep-fried spring greens garnished with sugar and almonds (see page 211).

酒溜魚片 **Fish in a wine sauce**
Delicate-tasting dish with firm white fish and cloud ears in a wine sauce (see page 211).

北京泡菜 **Pickled cabbage Peking-style**
Spicy dish served cold as an hors d'oeuvres or side dish (see page 212).

奶油津白 **Chinese celery cabbage in cream sauce**
An unusual dish, one of the few Chinese recipes using dairy produce (see page 212).

MEAT

Rustic Steamed Beef

A delicious family dish that is equally good to serve when entertaining.

1 Slice the beef into pieces, about 2.5 x 4cm (1 x 1½ inches) and 6mm (¼ inch) thick. Put into a bowl.

2 *Prepare the marinade:* add the ginger, salt, sugar, soy sauce, pepper, wine or sherry and potato flour to the beef. Add the water, 15ml (1tbsp) at a time, and stir in the same direction to coat the meat. Leave to marinate in the refrigerator for 20-30 minutes. Blend in the oil just before ready to steam.

3 Drain the cloud ears and golden needles and squeeze out excess water from the mushrooms but leave damp. Break up or cut the cloud ears into similarly sized pieces. Either split the golden needles in half lengthwise or halve crosswise. Slice the mushrooms into thin strips.

4 Put the cloud ears, golden needles and mushrooms together. Mix in the soy sauce and 15ml (1tbsp) of the oil.

5 Slice the preserved vegetable into very thin pieces.

6 Mix the cloud ears, golden needles, mushrooms and preserved vegetable into the beef. Spread out on a heatproof dish with sloping edges.

7 Steam the beef in a wok or steamer over a high heat for 10 minutes for medium-done beef or 13-15 minutes for well-done (see page 45). Remove from the heat. Add the spring onion and coriander leaves, if used, on top of the dish.

8 Heat the remaining 30ml (2tbsp) of oil in a small saucepan until just smoking. Pour over the spring onion to cook partially.

9 Remove the dish from the wok or steamer and serve immediately.

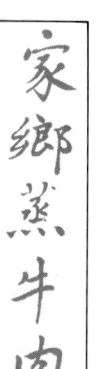

INGREDIENTS
350g (12oz) beef, fillet, rump or skirt, trimmed
30ml (2tbsp) cloud ears, reconstituted (see page 39)
1 small handful golden needles, about 5-6g (⅕oz), reconstituted (see page 39)
4 medium dried Chinese mushrooms, reconstituted (see page 39)
7.5ml (1½tsp) thick soy sauce
45ml (3tbsp) groundnut or corn oil
25g (1oz) Szechwan preserved vegetable, rinsed
3-4 spring onions, cut into 5cm (2-inch) sections, shredded lengthwise
2-3 coriander leaves, torn into pieces (optional)

FOR THE MARINADE
1cm (½ inch) fresh ginger root, peeled and finely grated
1.25ml (¼tsp) salt
1.25ml (¼tsp) sugar
15ml (1tbsp) thick soy sauce
6 turns black pepper mill
10ml (2tsp) Shaohsing wine or medium dry sherry
10ml (2tsp) potato flour
30ml (2tbsp) water
15ml (1tbsp) groundnut or corn oil

Serves 4 with 2 other dishes

Illustrated opposite

Facing page, clockwise from the top: Rustic steamed beef (see above); Twice-cooked pork (see page 126); Sweet and sour pork (see page 127)

Twice-cooked Pork

INGREDIENTS

450g (1lb) pork in one piece, 6-7.5cm (2½-3 inches) wide (middle section of belly with alternating lean and fat layers is ideal)

1 leek, trimmed

2-3 cloves garlic, peeled and thinly sliced

45ml (3tbsp) groundnut or corn oil

salt to taste

FOR THE SAUCE

22.5ml (1½tbsp) hot soy bean paste

15ml (1tbsp) thick soy sauce

1.25ml (¼tsp) salt

5ml (1tsp) sugar

15ml (1tbsp) Shaohsing wine or medium dry sherry

Serves 4-6 with 2-3 other dishes

Illustrated on page 125

One of the most popular Szechwan pork dishes, it is cleverly produced by combining two very different cooking methods: boiling and stir-frying.

1 Neatly remove the spareribs, if any, from the pork. Put the whole piece, rind and all, in a saucepan, cover with boiling water and simmer over a moderate heat for about 20-25 minutes. The pork is not expected to be thoroughly cooked. Remove and leave to cool. Store in the refrigerator for about 2 hours to firm up the meat. It can be left overnight, covered.

2 When ready to cook, remove the rind and slice crosswise into very thin pieces not more than 2mm (¹⁄₁₀ inch) thick, if possible.

3 Cut the leek lengthwise into 2 and wash thoroughly to remove any grit caught between the leaves. Cut diagonally into 1cm (½ inch) sections.

4 *Prepare the sauce:* mix together the paste, soy sauce, salt, sugar and wine or sherry in a small bowl and put aside. (Those who like it really hot and spicy can use more hot soy bean paste.)

5 Heat a wok over a moderate heat until hot. Add 15ml (1tbsp) of the oil and swirl it around. Add the leek and stir-fry with the wok scoop or metal spatula for about 2 minutes. Season with salt to taste and remove to a warm plate. The leek should be moist but not swimming in liquid. Drain if there is any excess water.

6 Dry the wok and reheat over a high heat until smoke rises. Add the remaining oil and swirl it around. Add the garlic and, as soon as it sizzles and takes on colour, add the pork. Stir and spread the pieces into more or less a single layer so that the fat fries in the oil. Turn over, pressing gently to fry until the fat is transparent. Lower the heat if necessary; if excess fat oozes out, spoon off from the wok and discard.

7 Pour in the sauce and stir to let it permeate the pork. Add the leek and stir until the sauce is almost absorbed. Remove to a warm serving plate. Serve immediately.

Sweet and Sour Pork

To many people, sweet and sour pork is synonymous with bad Chinese take-away food: lumps of chewy pork wrapped in thick batter, covered with a gluey and sickening sweet and sour sauce. However, when well made – crisp outside yet tender inside, topped with a well-balanced sweet and sour sauce – this is one of the most appetizing Cantonese dishes.

1 Cut the pork into pieces, about 2.5 x 3 x 2cm (1 x 1¼ x ¾ inches). Put into a bowl.

2 Add the salt and soy sauce and leave to marinate for 30-60 minutes. Stir in the egg to coat thoroughly.

3 Dredge the pork, piece by piece, through the cornflour, making sure it is evenly coated. It is not necessary to use up all the flour.

4 Half fill a wok or deep-fryer with oil. Heat to a temperature of 180°C (350°F) or until a cube of stale bread browns in 60 seconds. Add the pork and deep-fry for about 1 minute in 1 or 2 batches; separate the pieces with a pair of chopsticks or a wooden spoon if they stick together. Drain on kitchen paper. This step can be done ahead of time.

5 *Prepare the sauce:* in a bowl dissolve the potato flour in the water and pineapple juice. Add the vinegar, sugar, salt, soy sauce, tomato ketchup and Worcestershire sauce and stir to blend.

6 Heat a frying pan or saucepan (unless you have another wok) until hot. Add 22.5ml (1½tbsp) oil and swirl it around. Add the garlic and onion, stir a few times and then add the green pepper. Stir-fry for about 2 minutes over a medium heat and season with salt, if desired. Add the pineapple chunks. Pour in the well-stirred sauce and bring to the boil slowly, stirring constantly. (This sauce can be made in advance.)

7 Reheat the oil for deep-frying to a higher temperature of 190°C (375°F) or until a cube of stale bread browns in 50 seconds. Add the pork and again deep-fry in one batch for about 2-3 minutes to ensure that the outside is crisp and golden without the pork inside getting dry. Drain on kitchen paper and remove to a warm serving plate. Reheat the sweet and sour sauce and stir in the remaining 15ml (1tbsp) of oil. This prevents the sauce from being gluey. Pour the sweet and sour sauce over the pork. Serve immediately.

Note: when reheated, sweet and sour pork will be soggy but it will still taste good.

INGREDIENTS

450g (1lb) lean belly pork, skinned and trimmed of excess fat
2.5ml (½tsp) salt
5ml (1tsp) thin soy sauce
½ egg, lightly beaten
45ml (3tbsp) cornflour
groundnut or corn oil for deep-frying
37.5ml (2½tbsp) groundnut or corn oil
1 clove garlic, peeled and minced
1 onion, skinned and roughly chopped
1 green pepper, halved, seeded and diced
100g (4oz) canned pineapple chunks, drained, juice reserved

FOR THE SAUCE
10ml (2tsp) potato flour
60ml (4tbsp) water
60ml (4tbsp) pineapple juice
45ml (3tbsp) rice or wine vinegar
60-67.5ml (4-4½tbsp) sugar
1.25ml (¼tsp) salt
10ml (2tsp) thin soy sauce
30ml (2tbsp) tomato ketchup
7.5ml (1½tsp) Worcestershire sauce

Serves 4-6 with 2-3 other dishes

Illustrated on page 125

Braised Beef with Garlic

INGREDIENTS
1.1kg (2½lb) beef, shin and
    chuck steak, trimmed
60ml (4tbsp) groundnut or corn
    oil
225g (8oz) cloves garlic, peeled
45ml (3tbsp) Shaohsing wine or
    medium dry sherry
1.25ml (¼tsp) salt
5ml (1tsp) sugar
30ml (2tbsp) thick soy sauce
15ml (1tbsp) thin soy sauce
600ml (1 pint) clear stock
2.5-5ml (½-1tsp) potato flour,
    dissolved in 15ml (1tbsp) water
8 spring onions, cut into 2.5-cm
    (1-inch) sections

Serves 6 as a main course

Illustrated opposite

Do not be put off by the large amount of garlic used in this recipe: the Chinese way of sizzling the garlic in hot oil burns off the garlic odour, and instead produces a heavenly aroma which is absorbed by the beef.

1 Cut the beef into cubes of about 4cm (1½ inches).

2 Heat a wok over a high heat until smoke rises. Add the oil and swirl it around. Add the garlic, turn and toss until it takes on colour. Add the beef, turn and flip with a wok scoop or metal spatula to brown it with the garlic for 2-3 minutes. Splash in the wine or sherry around the side of the wok, stirring continuously as it sizzles and reduces to about half. Remove from the heat.

3 Transfer the wok contents to a large, heavy saucepan or flameproof casserole, scraping all the juices from the wok as well. Season with the salt, sugar and soy sauces, and pour in the stock. Bring to the boil, reduce the heat to maintain a moderate simmer and continue to cook, covered, for 1½-1¾ hours or until the beef is tender and most of the garlic has been assimilated into the sauce. Check the water level from time to time and replenish whenever necessary; also stir thoroughly a few times to make sure that the beef has not stuck to the bottom. When ready, there should be more than 300ml (½ pint) sauce. (This dish can be prepared and cooked to this stage several hours or even a day in advance. The taste actually improves overnight.)

4 Just before serving, bring to the boil, then add the well-stirred, dissolved potato flour to thicken the sauce slightly. Add the spring onions, replace the lid and cook for a few seconds more. Remove to a warm serving dish and serve.

Facing page, clockwise from the top: Braised beef with garlic (see above); Beef in oyster sauce (see page 130); Beef with preserved tangerine peel (see page 131)

Beef in Oyster Sauce

Whilst the Cantonese enjoy pork as much as all the other Chinese, they tend to eat more beef than many of their compatriots. Beef in oyster sauce is perhaps the most basic of all the Cantonese beef dishes. Delicious even without the asparagus, other vegetables such as mushroom, celery, bamboo shoots or bean sprouts can also be used. In stir-frying beef, the Cantonese believe that it is most important to make it tender and "velvety" and to achieve this they add bicarbonate of soda to the marinade. However, this part of the tenderizing process is unnecessary in the West, where the meat is generally well hung.

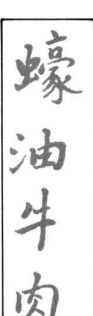

INGREDIENTS
450g (1lb) beef, rump, fillet or best skirt
225g (8oz) asparagus
75-90ml (5-6tbsp) groundnut or corn oil
3-4 cloves garlic, peeled and finely chopped
5mm (¼ inch) fresh ginger root, peeled and finely chopped
3-4 spring onions, cut into 2.5-cm (1-inch) sections, white and green parts separated
15ml (1tbsp) Shaohsing wine or medium dry sherry
sesame oil to taste (optional)

FOR THE MARINADE
1.25ml (¼tsp) salt
1.25ml (¼tsp) sugar
10ml (2tsp) thick soy sauce
6 turns pepper mill
10ml (2tsp) Shaohsing wine or medium dry sherry
5ml (1tsp) potato flour
15-30ml (1-2tbsp) water
10ml (2tsp) groundnut or corn oil

FOR THE SAUCE
5ml (1tsp) potato flour
90ml (6tbsp) clear stock or water
37.5-45ml (2½-3tbsp) oyster sauce

Serves 4 with 2 other dishes

Illustrated on page 129

1 Pat the beef dry. Cut across the grain into rectangular slices, about 2.5 x 4cm (1 x 1½ inches) and 6mm (¼ inch) thick. Put into a fairly large, deep bowl.

2 *Prepare the marinade:* add the salt, sugar, soy sauce, pepper, wine or sherry to the beef. Stir to blend. Sprinkle with the potato flour. Add 15ml (1tbsp) of the water and stir in the same direction to coat the beef until it is too difficult to continue. Add the remaining water and stir again. This process will make the beef velvety and tender when cooked. Leave to marinate in the refrigerator for 30 minutes. Blend in the oil.

3 *Prepare the sauce:* put the potato flour in a small bowl, stir in the water or stock to blend thoroughly and then add the oyster sauce.

4 Wash and trim the asparagus. Cut diagonally into thin slices so that they can be cooked quickly and can absorb the sauce easily.

5 Heat a wok over a high heat until smoke rises. Add 60-75ml (4-5tbsp) of the oil and swirl it around. Add the garlic, ginger and white spring onion in rapid succession. Stir several times to release their aroma and then add the beef. Sliding the wok scoop or metal spatula to the bottom of the wok, flip and toss for up to 1 minute. Splash in the wine or sherry around the side of the wok, just above the beef and, while it sizzles, continue to stir. Remove to a warm plate as soon as the sizzling is over but leave some oil behind.

6 Without washing the wok, add 15ml (1tbsp) oil. Add the asparagus and stir-fry for 1 minute. Season with salt, sprinkle with drops of water, lower the heat, cover and steam for about 1 more minute.

7 Push the asparagus around the sides of the wok and pour the well-stirred sauce into the centre. As soon as it bubbles, return the beef, add the green spring onion and stir together with the asparagus until hot. Remove to a warm serving plate. Serve immediately. Sprinkle with sesame oil at the table if desired.

Beef with Preserved Tangerine Peel

True to form, this Hunan dish is spicy hot, savoury and slightly sweet. As if these flavours are not complex enough, tangy tangerine peel is added to provide a further dimension in taste. The orange rind is not a traditional ingredient for the dish, but it is used here since it complements rather than detracts from the tangerine peel.

1 Soak the tangerine peel in cold water for about 2 hours or until soft. Drain and slice into strips about 5mm (⅕ inch) wide.

2 Peel the orange rind lengthwise and blanch in boiling water for 5 minutes to remove its bitterness. Drain and rinse in cold water. Slice into strips similar to the tangerine strips.

3 Cut the beef into thickish slices, about 2.5 x 4cm (1 x 1½ inches) and put into a bowl.

4 *Prepare the marinade:* add the salt, sugar, soy sauces, wine or sherry and potato flour to the meat. Add the water, 15ml (1tbsp) at a time, and stir in the same direction until all is absorbed. Mix in the chopped chilli and leave to marinate for 30-60 minutes. Blend in the hot chilli oil.

5 Heat a wok over a high heat until smoke rises. Add the oil and swirl it around. Add the ginger, stir, then add the white spring onion and let it sizzle. Add the tangerine and orange peel and fry for a few seconds. Put in the beef and, sliding the wok scoop or metal spatula to the bottom of the wok, flip and turn for 1-2 minutes or until very hot. Splash in the wine or sherry around the side of the wok, continuing to stir. When the sizzling dies down, add the chilli sauce. Cover, lower the heat and cook for about 2 minutes so that the flavour of the tangerine peel can permeate the beef.

6 *Prepare the sauce:* mix together the potato flour, water or stock and soy sauce.

7 Dribble the sauce into the wok and stir as the sauce thickens. Add the green spring onion and stir to mix. Remove to a warm serving dish. Serve immediately.

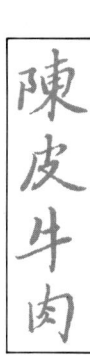

INGREDIENTS

5-6 pieces preserved tangerine peel

1 sweet orange

700g (1½lb) beef, rump, fillet or skirt steak, trimmed

60ml (4tbsp) groundnut or corn oil

2.5cm (1 inch) fresh ginger root, peeled and cut into silken threads (see page 00)

6 spring onions, cut into 5-cm (2-inch) sections, white and green parts separated

15ml (1tbsp) Shaohsing wine or medium dry sherry

30-45ml (2-3tbsp) chilli sauce

FOR THE MARINADE

4ml (¾tsp) salt

5ml (1tsp) sugar

10ml (2tsp) thin soy sauce

10ml (2tsp) thick soy sauce

10ml (2tsp) Shaohsing wine or medium dry sherry

7.5ml (1½tsp) potato flour

30ml (2tbsp) water

1 dried red chilli, seeded and chopped

15ml (1tbsp) hot chilli oil (see page 00)

FOR THE SAUCE

2.5ml (½tsp) potato flour

30ml (2tbsp) water or clear stock

15ml (1 tbsp) thick soy sauce

Serves 4 with 2 other dishes

Illustrated on page 129

White-cut Pork

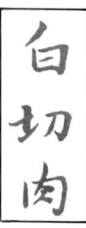

INGREDIENTS
450-550g (1-1¼lb) lean or thick end belly pork

SZECHWAN-STYLE SAUCE
12.5ml (2½tsp) very finely chopped garlic

30ml (2tbsp) fresh coriander leaves, chopped

2 large spring onions, cut into small rounds

1 fresh green or red chilli, about 7.5cm (3 inches) long, seeded and chopped

45ml (3tbsp) thick soy sauce

15ml (1tbsp) sesame oil

7.5ml (1½tsp) rice or wine vinegar

4ml (¾tsp) sugar

7.5ml (1½tsp) hot chilli oil

PEKING-STYLE SAUCE
20ml (4tsp) very finely chopped garlic

37.5ml (2½tbsp) thick soy sauce

10ml (2tsp) sesame oil

Serves 4-6 with 2-3 other dishes

Illustrated opposite

This dish, popular in both Szechwan and Peking cuisines, either as a family fare or for entertaining, can be made one day ahead. It is so called because the pork is simply boiled in a pot of clear tap water, or "white water", as the Chinese term goes. True to form, the Szechwan-style sauce evokes a wide range of tastes and aftertastes while its Peking counterpart is laden with garlic.

1 Put the piece of pork in a large saucepan and cover with water. Bring to the boil.

2 Lower the heat and simmer gently for 1 hour or until the pork is thoroughly cooked. To test, insert a chopstick or fork into the thickest part; if no pink juices run out, the pork is cooked.

3 Remove the pork to a colander, saving the water, however, for the stockpot. Rinse under cold water for 10 minutes to firm up the texture.

4 Refrigerate, covered, for several hours or overnight.

5 *Prepare the sauce:* mix together the chosen sauce ingredients and put aside.

6 Put the chilled pork on the chopping board. Slide a sharp knife between the rind and the fat and slice off the rind. Discard.

7 Slice the pork along the grain into paper-thin pieces, about 6.5cm (2½ inches) wide. Arrange on a round serving plate, overlapping each other. Pour the sauce over and serve.

Facing page, clockwise from the top: White-cut pork (see above); Pearly pork balls (see page 135); Char-siu (see page 134)

Char-siu: Cantonese Roast Pork

INGREDIENTS

1-1.25kg (2-2½lb) pork without
  bone or rind, neck end,
  blade-bone or leg joint
about 30ml (2tbsp) runny honey

FOR THE MARINADE

30ml (2tbsp) hoisin sauce
30ml (2tbsp) ground yellow bean
  sauce
60ml (4tbsp) thin soy sauce
60ml (4tbsp) sugar
15ml (1tbsp) Shaohsing wine or
  medium dry sherry
5ml (1tsp) salt

*Serves 4 as a main course; 8 with
  4 other dishes*

Illustrated on page 133

As a contribution towards Chinese gastronomy, this dish is arguably as notable as Peking Duck (see page 209), and it's certainly easier to make. When roasted, this fragrant and succulent pork looks reddish brown with slightly burned edges, especially around the fat. Delicious served hot or cold, it's a versatile ingredient and can be stir-fried with vegetables, or mixed with fried rice and used as a topping on noodles.

1 Divide the pork into 4 strips (a). Leave any fat on because it is delicately succulent when roasted.

2 Make 3-4 diagonal cuts from opposite directions, cutting three-quarters through the width of a strip without cutting it into pieces (b). This allows for better absorption of the marinade and gives the pork the traditional char-siu look.

 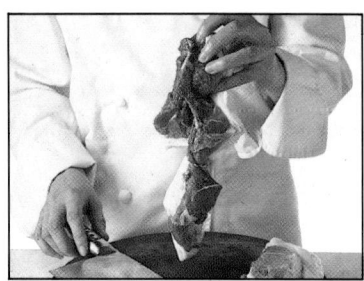

a   b

3 *Prepare the marinade:* in a large bowl mix together the sauces, sugar, wine, sherry and salt. Put in the pork and leave to marinate for 4 hours, turning it over every 30 minutes.

4 Place the strips of pork side by side on a wire rack in the top third of the oven with a tray of water 1cm (½ inch) deep underneath to catch the drippings. (The water prevents the juices that drip from the pork from burning; steam from it also keeps the pork from drying up.) Roast in a preheated oven at 190°C (375°F) mark 5 for 25-30 minutes, at the end of which time the top side will be reddish brown. Remove from the oven, dip each piece into the marinade and return to the rack with the bottom side up. Reduce the oven temperature to 180°C (350°F) mark 4 and continue to roast for another 25-30 minutes. Insert a chopstick or fork into the thickest part of one piece: if no pink juices run out, the pork is cooked.

5 Remove to a wire rack. Immediately brush all over with honey, making sure not to neglect the crevices.

6 Carve into slices and serve immediately.

Note: this dish can be frozen. To reheat, place on a rack in a preheated oven at 180°C (350°F) mark 4 for about 12 minutes. The left-over marinade can be cooked to make a dipping sauce for the pork. If it is too sweet, add more salt to it.

Variation: Roast spareribs
Use one whole side of spareribs (about 1.4kg [3lb]), divide it in half and roast in the same manner as char-sui.

Pearly Pork Balls

It is a misconception to think that every Hunan dish is spicy hot. On the contrary, many are not, and this dish, which derives its name from the glutinous rice which shines like little pearls on the pork balls, is one of them.

1 Rinse the rice, rubbing gently with your fingers in 3-4 changes of water or until it is no longer milky. Drain.

2 Soak in plenty of cold water for about 4 hours. Drain well and spread out on a tray.

3 Drain and squeeze out excess water from the mushrooms but leave damp. Chop into the size of matchstick heads.

4 Soak the shrimps in just enough boiling water to cover them for 10-15 minutes. Drain them, reserving the soaking liquid.

5 Finely chop or mince the dried shrimps and water chestnuts.

6 Chop the fat and lean pork by hand or mince coarsely.

7 Combine the mushroom, dried shrimp, water chestnut and pork in a large bowl. Add the salt, pepper and potato flour. Stir in, a spoonful at a time, 45ml (3tbsp) water and the soaking liquid from the shrimps.

8 Cut up the ham into the size of matchstick heads and mix with the rice on the tray.

9 Pick up about 15ml (1tbsp) pork mixture, roll it between your palms into a ball about the size of a ping-pong ball. Roll this ball over the rice and ham, making sure they stick all over the ball, and put it on a heatproof plate. Repeat until all the pork mixture is used up. The pork balls will fill up more than one plate.

10 Steam the pork balls in a wok or steamer for 15 minutes (see page 44).

11 Serve the pearly balls hot, either piled up neatly in a bowl or arranged on a warm serving plate.

INGREDIENTS
150g (5oz) white glutinous rice
4 medium dried Chinese mushrooms, reconstituted (see page 39)
30ml (2tbsp) dried shrimps, rinsed
4 water chestnuts, fresh peeled or canned drained
350g (12oz) pork, about 75g (3oz) fat and 275g (9oz) lean
2.5ml (½tsp) salt
8 turns white pepper mill
15ml (1tbsp) potato flour
50g (2oz) lean ham

Serves 6 with 3 other dishes

Illustrated on page 133

Stir-fried Pork with Szechwan Preserved Vegetable

INGREDIENTS
225g (8oz) pork fillet
50g (2oz) Szechwan preserved
    vegetable, rinsed
60ml (4tbsp) groundnut or corn
    oil
1 large clove garlic, peeled and
    cut into silken threads (see
    page 35)
5-6 spring onions, halved
    lengthwise, then cut into 5-cm
    (2-inch) sections

FOR THE MARINADE
large pinch salt
2.5ml (½tsp) sugar
2.5ml (½tsp) thin soy sauce
5ml (1tsp) Shaohsing wine or
    medium dry sherry
2.5ml (½tsp) potato flour
15ml (1tbsp) water
5ml (1tsp) sesame oil

Serves 2 with 1 other dish

Illustrated opposite

As preserved Szechwan vegetable is a regional product and pork is the national Chinese meat, it is hardly surprising that a standard Szechwan dish combines the two. In fact, this simple stir-fried dish is popular family fare all over China, eaten as much in the South as in the North.

1 Slice the pork into matchstick-sized strips. Put into a bowl.

2 *Prepare the marinade:* add the salt, sugar, soy sauce, wine or sherry, potato flour and water to the pork. Stir in the same direction until absorbed. Leave to marinate for about 15 minutes. Blend in the sesame oil.

3 Slice the preserved vegetable into the thinnest pieces, stack them up and slice them into very thin strips.

4 Heat a wok over a high heat until smoke rises. Add the oil and swirl it around. Add the garlic and, as it sizzles, add the preserved vegetable and stir a few times. Before it begins to "bounce", add the pork. Sliding the wok scoop or metal spatula to the bottom of the wok, turn and toss in rapid succession for about 1 minute, separating the strips at the same time. Splash in the wine or sherry around the side of the wok and continue to stir as it sizzles. Add the spring onion and stir together for another minute or until the pork is cooked and has become opaque. Remove to a warm serving plate. Serve immediately.

Facing page, clockwise from the top: Stir-fried pork with Szechwan preserved vegetable (see above); Mu-shu pork (see page 139); Stir-fried beef with pickled mustard green (see page 138)

Stir-fried Beef with Pickled Mustard Green

INGREDIENTS
225g (8oz) canned pickled
    mustard green, rinsed
34ml (2¼tbsp) sugar
350g (12oz) beef, skirt, rump or
    fillet
5ml (1tsp) potato flour
90ml (6tbsp) water
75ml (5tbsp) groundnut or corn
    oil
4-5 cloves garlic, peeled and
    finely chopped
4 spring onions, cut into 2.5-cm
    (1-inch) sections, white and
    green parts separated
15ml (1tbsp) Shaohsing wine or
    medium dry sherry
6mm-1cm (¼-½ inch) fresh
    ginger root, peeled and finely
    chopped or sliced

FOR THE MARINADE
1.25ml (¼tsp) salt
scant 15ml (1tbsp) thick soy
    sauce
8 turns black pepper mill
10ml (2tsp) Shaohsing wine or
    medium dry sherry
5ml (1tsp) potato flour
30ml (2tbsp) water
5ml (1tsp) sesame oil

Serves 4 with 2 other dishes

Illustrated on page 137

This Cantonese dish, with its mouth-watering combination of pungent, savoury, sweet and sour tastes, comes from the area along the Eastern River in Kwangtung province.

1 Shred the pickled mustard green thinly. Put into a bowl, add the sugar and mix well. Leave to stand at room temperature for up to 1 hour.

2 Cut the beef across the grain into slices about 2.5 x 4cm (1 x 1½ inches) and 6mm (¼ inch) thick. Put into a bowl.

3 *Prepare the marinade:* add the salt, soy sauce, pepper and wine or sherry to the beef. Sprinkle with the potato flour and add the water, 15ml (1tbsp) at a time, stirring in the same direction until it is difficult to continue before adding another spoonful. This process will make the beef velvety and tender. Leave in the refrigerator for 30 minutes. Blend in the sesame oil.

4 Mix the 5ml (1tsp) potato flour and 90ml (6tbsp) water in a small bowl and put aside.

5 Heat a wok over a high heat until smoke rises. Add 60ml (4tbsp) of the oil and swirl it around. Add the garlic and, as soon as it takes on colour, add the white spring onion and stir. Add the beef. Sliding the wok scoop or metal spatula to the bottom of the wok, turn and toss vigorously for 30-60 seconds or until partially cooked. Splash in the wine or sherry around the side of the wok, continuing to turn and toss until the sizzling dies down. Remove to a warm plate.

6 Add the remaining 15ml (1tbsp) oil to the wok and swirl it around. Tip in the ginger, stir, and then add the pickled mustard green. Stir and turn until piping hot and then push to the edge, leaving a well in the middle.

7 Return the beef to the middle and immediately pour in the well-stirred dissolved potato flour. Continue to toss the beef until this thickening has cooked. Stir in the green spring onion. Remove to a warm serving plate. Serve immediately.

Mu-shu Pork

Some Chinese dishes have a time-honoured formula for the ingredients and this Northern dish, consisting of golden needles, cloud ears, pork and egg, is one of them. Mu-shu is the Chinese name for golden needles which, in this dish, rank in equal importance with the pork. Mu-shu is also said to refer to the egg pieces because they, being yellow in colour, remind one of the tinge of the golden needles.

1 Drain the cloud ears (for extra slipperiness, soak in boiling water for another 20-30 minutes). Squeeze out excess water but leave damp.

2 Drain the golden needles; soak in boiling water for another 20-30 minutes for extra tenderness. Drain and squeeze out excess water but leave damp. Split each one lengthwise with the fingers.

3 Slice the pork into thin, even-sized rectangular pieces. Put into a bowl.

4 *Prepare the marinade:* add the salt, sugar, soy sauces, pepper, wine or sherry, potato flour and water to the pork. Stir in the same direction to coat. Leave to marinate for about 20 minutes. Stir in the oil.

5 Beat the eggs lightly with 15ml (1tbsp) of the oil and 1.25ml (¼tsp) of the salt.

6 Heat a wok over a high heat until smoke rises. Add 30ml (2tbsp) of the oil and swirl it around. Add the cloud ears and stir for about 30 seconds, lowering the heat if they jump in the air and make popping noises. Add the golden needles and continue to stir and turn until very hot. Season with 1.25ml (¼tsp) salt, the soy sauce and sugar. Remove to a warm dish and keep nearby.

7 Wipe the wok and reheat until hot. Add 30ml (2tbsp) of the oil and swirl it around. Pour in the egg and, sliding the wok scoop or metal spatula to the bottom of the wok, fold and turn until the egg forms into lumps. Remove to a warm plate and keep nearby. Wash and dry the wok.

8 Reheat the wok until smoke rises. Add the remaining oil and swirl it around. Add the white spring onion, stir and let it sizzle for a few seconds. Add the pork and turn and toss in rapid succession for about 1 minute or until partially cooked and turning opaque. Splash in the wine or sherry around the side of the wok, continuing to stir and turn as it sizzles. Return all the other ingredients to the wok. Stir and mix for another minute so that the pork is thoroughly cooked, the egg firmer and all the ingredients piping hot. Add the green spring onion. Remove to a warm serving dish. Sprinkle on the sesame oil and serve immediately.

INGREDIENTS

15g (½oz) cloud ears, reconstituted (see page 39)
25g (1oz) golden needles, reconstituted (see page 39)
275-350g (10-12oz) lean pork
4 eggs
120ml (8tbsp) groundnut or corn oil
2.5ml (½tsp) salt
15ml (1tbsp) thick soy sauce
1.25ml (¼tsp) sugar
3-4 large spring onions, sliced diagonally, white and green parts separated
15ml (1tbsp) Shaohsing wine or medium dry sherry
10ml (2tsp) sesame oil or to taste

FOR THE MARINADE

1.25ml (¼tsp) salt
2.5ml (½tsp) sugar
5ml (1tsp) thin soy sauce
5ml (1tsp) thick soy sauce
6 turns white pepper mill
5ml (1tsp) Shaohsing wine or medium dry sherry
5ml (1tsp) potato flour
15ml (1tbsp) water
15ml (1tbsp) groundnut or corn oil

Serves 6 with 3 other dishes

Illustrated on page 137

Stir-fried Pork with Red-in-snow

INGREDIENTS
350g (12oz) lean pork
100g (4oz) canned red-in-snow, drained
2.5ml (½tsp) sugar
100g (4oz) canned bamboo shoots, drained
60-75ml (4-5tbsp) groundnut or corn oil
15ml (1tbsp) Shaohsing wine or medium dry sherry
5ml (1tsp) sesame oil

FOR THE MARINADE
10ml (2tsp) thin soy sauce
6 turns white pepper mill
5ml (1tsp) Shaohsing wine or medium dry sherry
5ml (1tsp) cornflour
15ml (1tbsp) egg white
5ml (1tsp) sesame oil

Serves 4 with 2 other dishes

Illustrated opposite

The preserved vegetable, red-in-snow, lends a special fragrance to the pork in this dish. As in many other Shanghai or Eastern stir-fried dishes, neither garlic nor spring onion are used.

1 Slice the pork into matchstick-sized strips. Put into a bowl.

2 *Prepare the marinade:* add the soy sauce, pepper, wine or sherry, cornflour and egg white to the pork. Stir in the same direction until absorbed. Leave to marinate for about 15 minutes. Blend in the sesame oil.

3 Roughly chop the red-in-snow. Mix in the sugar.

4 Slice the bamboo shoots into matchstick-sized strips.

5 Heat a wok over a high heat until smoke rises. Add the oil and swirl it around. Add the red-in-snow and stir a few times to enhance its fragrance. Add the bamboo shoots and stir a few more times. Add the pork and turn and toss for about 1 minute, separating the strips as you do so. Splash in the wine or sherry around the side of the wok, continuing to stir as it sizzles. When the pork, having turned opaque, is cooked, remove to a warm serving plate. Serve immediately.

Facing page, clockwise from the top: Dry-fried beef (see page 143); Stir-fried pork with red-in-snow (see above); Green pepper beef in black bean sauce (see page 142)

Green Pepper Beef in Black Bean Sauce

INGREDIENTS

450g (1lb) beef, rump, skirt or
    fillet, trimmed
5ml (1tsp) potato flour
90ml (6tbsp) water
75ml (5tbsp) groundnut or corn
    oil
225g (8oz) green pepper, seeded
    and roughly chopped
salt to taste
5 cloves garlic, peeled and finely
    chopped
4 spring onions, cut into 2.5-cm
    (1-inch) sections, white and
    green parts separated
37.5ml (2½tbsp) fermented black
    beans, rinsed and mashed with
    1.25ml (¼tsp) sugar and 5ml
    (1tsp) oil
½-1 fresh red chilli, seeded and
    sliced (optional)
15ml (1tbsp) Shaohsing wine or
    medium dry sherry

FOR THE MARINADE

1.25ml (¼tsp) salt
1.25ml (¼tsp) sugar
10ml (2tsp) thick soy sauce
8 turns black pepper mill
10ml (2tsp) Shaohsing wine or
    medium dry sherry
7.5ml (1½tsp) potato flour
45ml (3tbsp) water
5ml (1tsp) groundnut or corn oil
5ml (1tsp) sesame oil

Serves 4 with 2 other dishes

Illustrated on page 141

This is one of the most celebrated Cantonese dishes using the versatile black bean as an essential ingredient. It is served as much at home as in restaurants.

1 Cut the beef across the grain into rectangular slices, about 2.5 x 4cm (1 x 1½ inches) and 6mm (¼ inch) thick. Put into a fairly large mixing bowl.

2 *Prepare the marinade:* add the salt, sugar, soy sauce, pepper and wine or sherry to the meat. Sprinkle with the potato flour (a) and add the water, 15ml (1tbsp) at a time, stirring in the same direction (b), until it is difficult to continue before adding another spoonful. This process will make the beef velvety and tender. Leave covered in the refrigerator for 30 minutes. Blend in the oils.

a   b

3 Mix the 5ml (1tsp) potato flour and 90ml (6tbsp) water together in a small bowl and put aside.

4 Heat a wok until hot. Add 15ml (1tbsp) oil and swirl it around. Add the green pepper and stir-fry for about 2 minutes, lowering the heat if the pieces begin to burn. Season with salt to taste and remove to a warm plate.

5 Reheat the wok over a high heat until smoke rises. Add the remaining 60ml (4tbsp) oil and swirl it around. Add the garlic and, as soon as it takes on colour, add the white spring onion and stir. Add the black bean paste and chilli, and stir. Tip in the beef. Sliding the wok scoop or metal spatula to the bottom of the wok, turn and toss vigorously for 1-2 minutes or until the beef is partially done. Splash in the wine or sherry around the side of the wok, continuing to turn and toss until the sizzling dies down. Still stirring, pour in the well-stirred, dissolved potato flour, add the green pepper and green spring onion and mix until this thickening has cooked. Remove to a warm serving plate. Serve immediately.

Dry-fried Beef

The traditional preparation of this Szechwan dish calls for great patience as the beef is stir-fried over a low heat for about an hour until it becomes shrivelled and quite crisp. However, the same effect can be achieved in less than half that time by using the combined techniques of deep-frying and stir-frying. The beef should taste spicy hot, sweet and savoury at the same time. Besides rice, it goes equally well with silver-thread buns (see page 201).

1 Shred the beef into long thread-like strips, about 6-7.5cm (2½-3 inches) long, 5mm (⅕ inch) thick and wide. Put into a bowl.

2 *Prepare the marinade:* add the soy sauce, sugar, wine or sherry, oil and peppercorns to the beef. Mix well. Leave to marinate at room temperature for 45-60 minutes.

3 Put the carrots into a small bowl and add 1.25ml (¼tsp) salt to draw out the water. Drain after 20-30 minutes. Pat dry, if necessary.

4 Put the celery into another bowl and add 1.25ml (¼tsp) salt to draw out the water. Drain after 20-30 minutes. Pat dry, if necessary.

5 Seed the red chillies but leave whole, if possible.

6 *Prepare the sauce:* mix together the cornflour, sugar and water in a small bowl and put aside.

7 Half fill a wok or deep-fryer with oil. Heat to a temperature of about 200°C (400°F) or until a cube of stale bread browns in 40 seconds. While the oil is being heated, stir the cornflour into the beef to coat evenly. Add the beef gently to the oil and deep-fry for 4-5 minutes or until crisp. Turn off the heat and remove with a large hand strainer or perforated disc and drain on kitchen paper. Pour the oil into a container for future use. Wash and dry the wok.

8 Reheat the wok over a moderate heat until hot. Add 22.5-30ml (1½-2tbsp) oil and swirl it around. Add the red chillies and fry until they are dark in colour. Remove and discard. Add the carrots, stir and toss, and then add the celery. Stir for a few minutes until dry before adding the beef. Continue to stir over a gentle heat for another 3-4 minutes or until everything is quite dry and crisp.

9 Gradually add the well-stirred sauce, stirring continuously to coat the beef. Remove to a warm serving plate.

10 Sprinkle with the ground Szechwan peppercorns and sesame oil.

Note: this dish can be prepared several hours in advance up to step 8. When ready to serve, simply reheat thoroughly over a gentle heat and proceed with steps 9 and 10.

INGREDIENTS

450g (1lb) beef, lean cut buttock steak or topside, trimmed
75-100g (3-4oz) carrots, peeled and cut into thin strips
3-4 sticks celery, cut into thin strips
2.5ml (½tsp) salt
2-3 dried red chillies
groundnut or corn oil for deep-frying
4ml (¾tsp) cornflour
22.5-30ml (1½-2tbsp) groundnut or corn oil
2.5ml (½tsp) ground roasted Szechwan peppercorns (see page 21)
5ml (1tsp) sesame oil

FOR THE MARINADE

34ml (2¼tbsp) thin soy sauce
11.25ml (2¼tsp) sugar
15ml (1tbsp) Shaohsing wine or medium dry sherry
5ml (1tsp) sesame oil
2.5ml (½tsp) ground roasted Szechwan peppercorns (see page 21)

FOR THE SAUCE

5ml (1tsp) cornflour
4-5ml (¾-1tsp) sugar
60ml (4tbsp) water

Serves 4-6 with 2-3 other dishes

Illustrated on page 141

乾炒牛肉絲

Ants Climbing a Tree

INGREDIENTS

75g (3oz) cellophane noodles
175g (6oz) loin pork
60ml (4tbsp) groundnut or corn oil
3 cloves garlic, peeled and finely chopped
3-4 spring onions, cut diagonally into long slices, white and green parts separated
15-22.5ml (1-1½tbsp) hot soy bean paste or chilli sauce
10ml (2tsp) Shaohsing wine or medium dry sherry
250ml (8fl oz) clear stock
salt to taste
thin or thick soy sauce to taste

FOR THE MARINADE

2.5ml (½tsp) salt
15ml (1tbsp) thick soy sauce
4 turns black pepper mill
5ml (1tsp) Shaohsing wine or medium dry sherry
2.5ml (½tsp) potato flour
15ml (1tbsp) water
10ml (2tsp) sesame oil

Serves 6 with 3-4 other dishes or 4 as a first course

Illustrated opposite

Don't be put off by the name of this dish: it is characteristic of the Szechwanese sense of humour to visualize minced pork over cellophane noodles as ants climbing up a tree, even though you may not wish to conjure up the same image. Whatever the mental picture, the marinated pork cooked in a spicy sauce lends colour and flavour to the otherwise bland cellophane noodles which do, however, contribute an interesting texture to the overall effect.

1 Put the cellophane noodles in a large bowl and pour over about 1 litre (1¾ pints) boiling water. Leave to soak, preferably covered, for a minimum of 20 minutes.

2 Finely chop or mince the pork. Put into a bowl.

3 *Prepare the marinade:* add the salt, soy sauce, pepper, wine or sherry, potato flour and water to the pork. Stir vigorously in the same direction for 1-2 minutes in order to give the pork the right consistency. Leave to marinate for about 15 minutes. Blend in the sesame oil.

4 Drain the cellophane noodles and make a few cuts with a pair of scissors to make them shorter and easier to handle.

5 Heat a wok over a high heat until smoke rises. Add the oil and swirl it around. Add the garlic, then the white spring onion. As they sizzle, add the soy bean paste or chilli sauce and stir a couple of times. Add the pork and, sliding the wok scoop or metal spatula to the bottom of the wok, turn and toss for about 1 minute, breaking up any lumps at the same time. Splash in the wine or sherry around the side of the wok, continuing to stir and break up any lumps.

6 When the sizzling dies down, add the noodles, stir and fold to blend. Add the stock, bring to the boil, add the salt and soy sauce to taste, then lower the heat and continue to cook, covered, for about 5 minutes.

7 Remove the wok cover. Most of the stock should have been absorbed. Add the green spring onion, then scoop on to a warm serving dish.

8 Arrange the pork on top of and around the noodles. Serve hot.

Note: if you cannot tolerate hot soy bean paste or chilli sauce, use thick soy sauce instead. This dish reheats well over a low heat.

Facing page, clockwise from the top: Red-braised ox-tongue (see page 147); Ants climbing tree (see above); Roast belly pork (see page 146); Hoisin sauce for pork

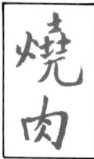

INGREDIENTS
1.4kg (3lb) belly pork in one
    piece, without spareribs
about 2.5ml (½tsp) salt
10ml (2tsp) red food colouring
    (optional)

FOR THE MARINADE
5ml (1tsp) salt
5ml (1tsp) sugar
15ml (1tbsp) ground yellow bean
    sauce
15ml (1tbsp) hoisin sauce
2.5ml (½tsp) thin soy sauce
5ml (1tsp) five-spice powder

FOR THE DIPS
thick soy sauce
hoisin sauce

Serves 4-6 as a main course

Illustrated on page 145

Roast Belly of Pork

In special Cantonese establishments, a whole pig is roasted to a rich red colour in a specially built oven. A similar effect can be achieved at home using a piece of pork from the middle section of the belly, with the skin or rind left on. Never score the skin and never use pork which has been frozen as the skin will not crisp up to form the distinctive crackling of the dish.

1 Wipe the pork skin or rind dry. Using an onion fork with 10 close-set, sharp tines, or a similar metal piercing instrument, pierce the skin rind vigorously and repeatedly (a), for about 15-20 minutes or until it is entirely covered with fine holes. Rub the salt all over the skin.

2 Lightly brush some of the food colouring over the skin (b), if used.

a   b

3 Make horizontal cuts on the flesh side, about 2.5cm (1 inch) apart and 1cm (½ inch) deep.

4 *Prepare the marinade:* mix together the salt, sugar, yellow bean sauce, hoisin sauce, thin soy sauce and five-spice powder in a small bowl.

5 Using a clean brush, smear as much marinade as possible on the flesh side, particularly the grooves. Do not smear any marinade along the sides of the pork otherwise they will be burned when roasted.

6 Using 2 butcher's meat hooks, hang the pork up in a windy place for about 8 hours or overnight until the skin is very dry. The drier the skin, the better the crackling when roasted.

7 Place the pork, skin side up, on a rack in the top half of the oven over a tray of hot water to catch the drippings. Roast in a preheated oven of 200°C (400°F) mark 6 for 15 minutes and then reduce the oven temperature to 190°C (375°F) mark 5 for about 1 hour. Do not open the oven door at all until it is time to test whether the pork is done. Test by piercing the meat with a skewer or chopstick; if it goes in easily and the juices that run out are clear and not pink, the pork

is done. The skin will have turned into excellent crackling.

8 Remove the pork to rest on a carving board for a few minutes. Carve into 1-2.5-cm (½-1-inch) pieces with a cleaver or a sharp, serrated meat carver. Transfer to a warm serving dish and serve.

Red-braised Ox Tongue

A very down-to-earth dish, especially good during the autumn and winter. Ox tongue may be more readily available and cheaper but calf tongue has a more delicate flavour and texture, so by all means use 3 or 4 calves' tongues if you prefer them.

1 Place the ox tongue in a large saucepan of water and bring to the boil. Reduce the heat to a fast simmer for 1 hour. Drain and rinse in cold water. Peel and discard the hard skin which covers the tongue (this should not be difficult after boiling).

2 Heat a large heavy saucepan (an enamelled casserole with a cast iron bottom is ideal) until hot. Add 30ml (2tbsp) of the oil and swirl it around. Add the garlic, spring onions and tongue, and brown for about 1 minute on each side. Add the star anise, peppercorns, tangerine peel, stock, soy sauce, sugar, salt and wine or sherry. Cover and gradually bring to the boil. Reduce the heat and simmer fast for about 2 hours. Check the water level from time to time and add more stock or water, if necessary. There should be about 400ml (14fl oz) sauce when ready and the ox tongue should be very tender. (This can be done several hours in advance or overnight).

3 Remove the tongue and slice into thin pieces of uniform thickness.

4 Strain the sauce through a sieve. Discard the solids.

5 Blanch the petits pois or garden peas in boiling salted water with 15ml (1tbsp) oil for about 2 minutes. Drain and refresh under cold running water.

6 Just before ready to serve, return the tongue, sauce and peas to the saucepan and gradually bring to a simmer. Add the well-stirred, dissolved potato flour. Continue to stir as it thickens.

7 Transfer to a large warm serving plate and serve.

Note: the cooked ox tongue freezes well, either whole or in sections. Step 2 can be cooked in a preheated oven at 200°C (400°F) mark 6 for 20 minutes, then at 170°C (325°F) mark 3 for 1¾ hours.

INGREDIENTS

1 ox tongue, about 1.4kg (3lb), unsalted
45ml (3tbsp) groundnut or corn oil
3 cloves garlic, peeled and crushed
3 large spring onions, white parts only
2 whole star anise or 16 segments
5ml (1tsp) Szechwan peppercorns
1 piece (¼ of whole) dried tangerine peel
600ml (1 pint) clear stock
75ml (5tbsp) thick soy sauce
7.5ml (1½tsp) brown sugar
2.5ml (½tsp) salt
22.5ml (1½tbsp) Shaohsing wine or medium dry sherry
225g (8oz) petits pois or garden peas
15ml (1tbsp) potato flour, dissolved in 30ml (2tbsp) water

Serves 6 as a main course

Illustrated on page 145

An Eastern or Shanghai Menu

上海菜

This menu for eight reflects the cuisines of the two eastern gastronomic provinces: Kiangsu and Chekiang. Between them, they boast of several of the best products in China: Chinhua ham,

Shaohsing wine and Chinkiang vinegar. In this menu, the decorative and delicate dishes are balanced by more down-to-earth dishes.

雪菜肉絲湯 **Red-in-snow soup with pork**
Tasty soup with pork, cellophane noodles and crisp red-in-snow as main ingredients (see page 213).

芙蓉蛋片 **Fu-yung egg slices**
Tender pieces of egg served in a nourishing and tasty stock (see page 213).

揚州炒飯 **Yangchow fried rice**
Fried rice cooked with ham, shrimps, peas and onions, garnished with strips of egg (see page 216).

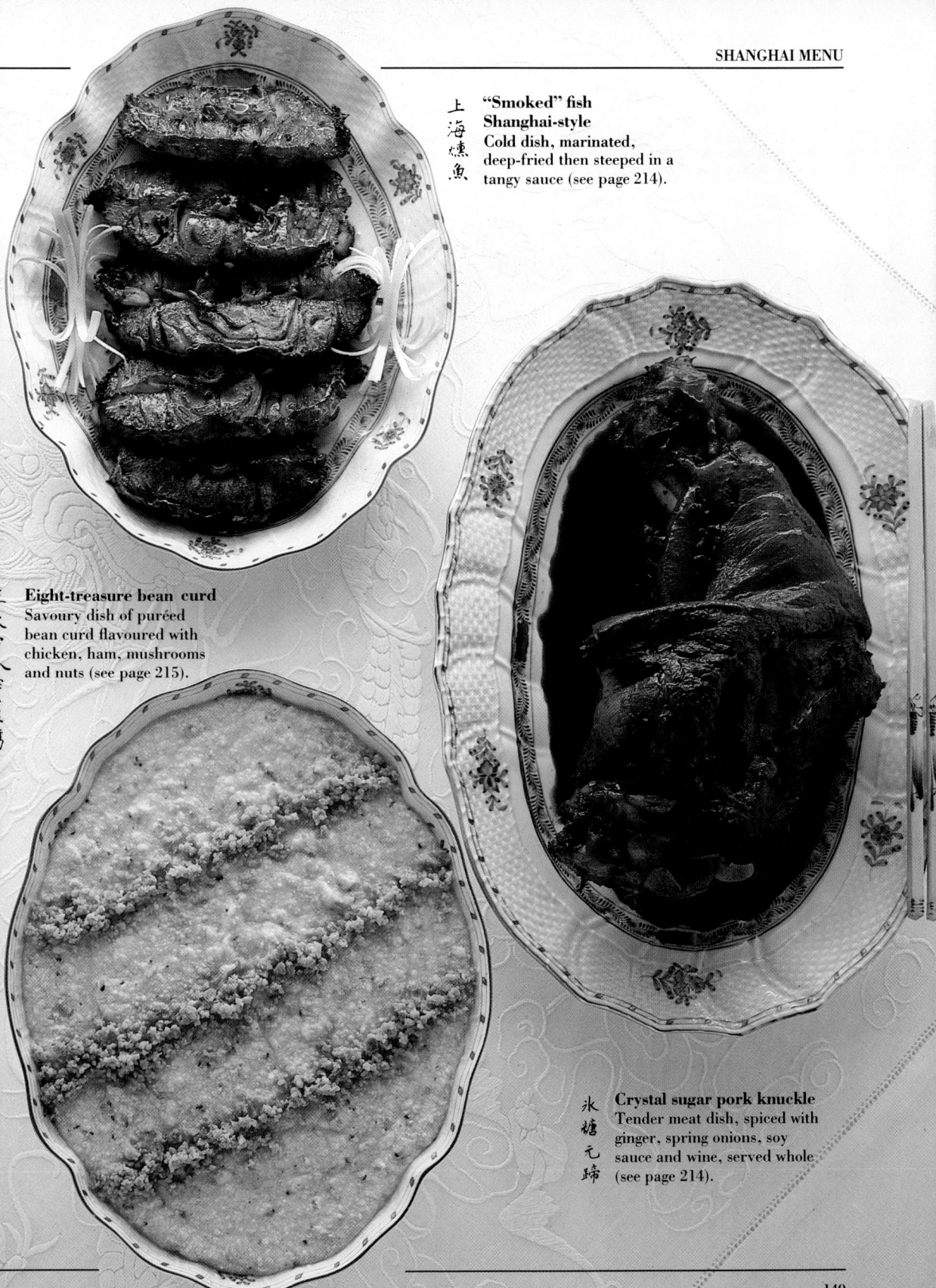

上海燻魚 **"Smoked" fish Shanghai-style**
Cold dish, marinated, deep-fried then steeped in a tangy sauce (see page 214).

Eight-treasure bean curd
Savoury dish of puréed bean curd flavoured with chicken, ham, mushrooms and nuts (see page 215).

冰糖元蹄 **Crystal sugar pork knuckle**
Tender meat dish, spiced with ginger, spring onions, soy sauce and wine, served whole (see page 214).

VEGETABLES

Fish Fragrant Aubergine

INGREDIENTS

15g (½oz) cloud ears,
    reconstituted (see page 39)
2 aubergines, about 700g (1½lb)
groundnut or corn oil for
    deep-frying
22.5ml (1½tbsp) groundnut or
    corn oil
4-5 cloves garlic, peeled and
    finely chopped
6mm (¼ inch) fresh ginger root,
    peeled and finely chopped
3 spring onions, cut into 2.5-cm
    (1-inch) sections, white and
    green parts separated
15-22.5ml (1-1½tbsp) Szechwan
    chilli paste (see page 226)
15ml (1tbsp) Shaohsing wine or
    medium dry sherry
5ml (1tsp) salt
7.5ml (1½tsp) sugar
15ml (1tbsp) thin soy sauce
2.5ml (½tsp) potato flour,
    dissolved in 45ml (3tbsp) water
15ml (1tbsp) rice or white wine
    vinegar

Serves 6 with 3 other dishes

Illustrated opposite

In Szechwan, there is a range of dishes which emulate the fragrance of fish because the condiments used to flavour them are the same as those traditionally used to flavour fish. This flavour is achieved by blending Szechwan chilli paste with garlic, ginger and spring onion in oil and then allowing this sauce to impregnate the main ingredients cooked in it. The finishing touch is the addition of wine, sugar and vinegar which enhance the tastes and aftertastes, the hallmark of Szechwanese cooking. It is delicious served either hot or cold.

1 Drain the cloud ears and cut up into narrow strips.

2 Peel alternate strips of the aubergine skin, lengthwise. (If all the skin is peeled, the aubergine shrinks too much when cooked.) Slice each aubergine lengthwise into 4-5 pieces according to diameter, then lengthwise again into strips and then cut crosswise into pieces the size of potato chips.

3 Half fill a wok or deep-fryer with oil. Heat to a temperature of 180°C (350°F) or until a cube of stale bread browns in 60 seconds. Put in all the aubergine chips and deep-fry for 2 minutes. Remove and drain well on kitchen paper. (This step can be done a few hours ahead.)

4 Heat a wok over high heat until smoke rises. Add 22.5ml (1½tbsp) oil and swirl it around. Add the garlic, which will sizzle and takes on colour almost instantly, then add the ginger and white spring onion, stirring a few times. Stir in the chilli paste and add the aubergine and cloud ears. If the cloud ears make a cracking sound, reduce the heat. Spinkle with the wine or sherry and stir in the salt, sugar and soy sauce to mix. Add the well-stirred dissolved potato flour and the green spring onion, stirring as the sauce thickens. Remove from the heat. Sprinkle with the vinegar and quickly stir thoroughly before removing to a warm serving plate. Serve immediately.

Facing page, clockwise from the top: Fish fragrant aubergine (see above); Dry-braised bamboo shoots and Chinese mushrooms (see page 152); Eight-treasure vegetarian assembling (see page 153)

Dry-braised Bamboo Shoots and Chinese Mushroom

INGREDIENTS
12-16 medium dried Chinese
  mushrooms, reconstituted (see
  page 39)
700g (1½lb) canned bamboo
  shoots (winter bamboo shoots
  are ideal), drained
groundnut or corn oil for
  deep-frying
1.25ml (¼tsp) salt
2.5ml (½tsp) sugar
22.5ml (1½tbsp) thick soy sauce
10ml (2tsp) thin soy sauce
30ml (2tbsp) mushroom water

Serves 4 with 2 other dishes

Illustrated on page 151

*This is a classic Eastern vegetarian dish with a play-on-word
Chinese title which, literally translated, is Dry-braised Two Tung.
The two tungs of the pun are tung-sun (winter bamboo shoots) and
tung-ku (dried Chinese mushrooms).*

1 Squeeze out excess water from the Chinese mushrooms but leave
damp. Save the soaking liquid.

2 Either roll cut the bamboo shoots into fairly large pieces or cut
into wedges. Pat dry with kitchen paper.

3 Half fill a wok or deep-fryer with oil. Heat to a temperature of
190°C (375°F) or until a cube of stale bread browns in 50 seconds.
Carefully add the bamboo shoots to the oil and deep-fry for about
1½ minutes or until the edges have turned brownish. Remove with a
hand strainer or perforated disc and put on to kitchen paper.
Empty all but about 45ml (3tbsp) of the oil into a container and save
for later use.

4 Reheat the oil over a high heat. When hot, add the Chinese
mushrooms and, going to the bottom of the wok with a wok scoop or
metal spatula, flip and toss for about 1 minute to enhance the
fragrance of the mushrooms. Return the bamboo shoots to the wok
and continue to stir-fry together for another minute.

5 Season with the salt, sugar, soy sauces and mushroom water.
Lower the heat to medium and cook until all the liquid is absorbed,
leaving only oil around the mushrooms and bamboo shoots. Remove
to a warm serving plate and serve immediately.

Bean Curd Puffs

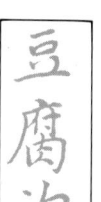

INGREDIENTS
4 cakes bean curd
groundnut or corn oil for
  deep-frying

Makes 16

Used in recipe on page 153

*Once deep-fried, the puffs, unlike fresh bean curd which will perish
within 2-3 days even when refrigerated, can be kept for up to 2
weeks in the refrigerator. They are a useful ingredient to use with
meat, fish and vegetables as they soak up sauces and add an
interesting dimension to the dish.*

1 Quarter each bean curd. Put the 16 cubes on changes of kitchen
paper or cloths to drain excess water.

2 Half fill a wok or deep-fryer with oil. Heat to a temperature of
200°C (400°F) or until a cube of stale bread browns in 40 seconds.
Gently immerse the bean curd in the oil and deep-fry for about 15
minutes or until golden and crisp. Remove with a hand strainer or
perforated disc and drain on kitchen paper.

Eight-treasure Vegetarian Assembling

Eight is a significant number for the Chinese, for in Buddhism, which for many centuries exerted great influence in China, there are eight treasures in life: the pearl, lozenge, stone chime, rhinoceros horn, coin, mirror, books and leaf. The symbolism of these eight treasures is not lost in Chinese food: any dish comprising eight or more main ingredients can term itself "eight-treasure".

1 Drain the cloud ears and golden needles but leave damp. Break up the large pieces of cloud ears.

2 Soak the cellophane noodles in plenty of boiling water for 30 minutes. They will expand and become pliable. Drain. Cut with scissors to shorten.

3 Bring a saucepan of water to the boil and add 2.5ml (½tsp) of the salt and 7.5ml (½tbsp) of the oil. Add the mange tout and, as soon as the water returns to the boil, drain in a colander. Refresh under cold running water and drain again.

4 Heat a wok over a high heat until smoke rises. Add the remaining oil and swirl it around. Add the ginger, then the spring onion and stir for a few seconds, then add the red bean curd cheese and stir to blend. Add the cloud ears, toss and stir, then adjust the heat to moderate. Add the cellophane noodles, golden needles, bean curd puffs, baby corn, straw mushrooms and ginkgo nuts, and mix together. Season with the remaining salt, sugar and soy sauce. Pour in the stock and cook, covered or uncovered, until much of the stock has been absorbed. Add the mange tout, mix well and heat through. Sprinkle with sesame oil to taste. Remove to a warm serving dish. Serve hot.

INGREDIENTS

35ml (2 heaped tbsp) cloud ears, reconstituted (see page 39)
15g (½oz) golden needles, reconstituted (see page 39)
50g (2oz) cellophane noodles
5ml (1 tsp) salt
67.5ml (4½tbsp) groundnut or corn oil
100g (4oz) mange tout, trimmed
6 thin slices fresh ginger root, peeled
6 spring onions, sliced diagonally
15ml (1tbsp) fermented red bean curd cheese, mashed with 5ml (1tsp) own juice or water
8 bean curd puffs, halved (see page 152)
8 canned baby corn on the cobs, halved lengthwise
100g (4oz) canned straw mushrooms
75-100g (3-4oz) canned ginkgo nuts
175ml (6fl oz) vegetable or clear stock, mixed with 2.5ml (½tsp) potato flour
2.5ml (½tsp) sugar
30-37.5ml (2-2½tbsp) thin soy sauce
sesame oil to taste

Serves 6 with 3 other dishes

Illustrated on page 151

Sautéed Stuffed Pepper

INGREDIENTS

5 medium peppers, green and red, seeded and quartered
4-5 medium dried Chinese mushrooms, reconstituted (see page 39)
350g (12oz) pork with a little fat
30ml (2tbsp) dried shrimps, rinsed
4-5 spring onions, cut into tiny rounds
50g (2oz) canned bamboo shoots, finely chopped
1 small egg white, lightly beaten
60ml (4 tbsp) groundnut or corn oil
30ml (2tbsp) Shaohsing wine or medium dry sherry

FOR THE MARINADE

2.5ml (½tsp) salt
2.5ml (½tsp) sugar
5ml (1tsp) thick soy sauce
5ml (1tsp) thin soy sauce
10ml (2tsp) Shaohsing wine or medium dry sherry
7.5ml (1½tsp) potato flour
90ml (6tbsp) water
5ml (1tsp) sesame oil

FOR THE SAUCE

7.5ml (1½tsp) potato flour
135ml (9tbsp) stock and mushroom water
22.5ml (1½tbsp) groundnut or corn oil
5 cloves garlic, peeled and finely chopped
37.5ml (2½tbsp) fermented black beans, rinsed and mashed with 2.5ml (½tsp) sugar and 5ml (1tsp) oil
2-3 small fresh chillies, seeded and cut into small rounds (optional)

Serves 5-6 as a main course

Illustrated opposite

Tender yet still crisp pepper stuffed with pork with a suggestion of the taste of shrimps. The black bean sauce, especially with chilli, adds another dimension in taste.

1 Plunge the peppers into boiling water to blanch for 1-2 minutes. Drain and immediately rinse under cold running water to retain their crispness. Drain and pat dry.

2 Drain and squeeze out excess water from the mushrooms but leave damp. Shred into the thinnest possible strips and then dice. Reserve soaking water.

3 Chop or mince the pork together with the shrimps. Put into a large bowl.

4 *Prepare the marinade:* add the salt, sugar, soy sauces, wine or sherry, potato flour and half of the water to the pork. Stir vigorously in the same direction to coat the meat. Add the remaining water, a little at a time, stirring vigorously in between each addition. This lightens the texture of the pork.

5 Stir in the mushroom, spring onion and bamboo shoots. Leave to marinate for 15-30 minutes. Blend in the sesame oil and egg white.

6 Fill the hollow of each piece of pepper with the stuffing until level with the edges.

7 Heat a frying pan or wok over a high heat until smoke rises. Add 30ml (2tbsp) oil and swirl it around. Put in half the peppers, stuffing side down, and brown for 1 minute. Reduce the heat to moderate or low, cover and continue to sauté for 2 more minutes. Turn and sauté for 1-2 more minutes.

8 Turn up the heat to high and splash in 15ml (1tbsp) of the wine or sherry, which will sizzle. As soon as the sizzling dies down, remove to a warm serving plate and keep warm.

9 Wash and dry the frying pan or wok and repeat the process of sautéing the remaining pepper. Wash and dry the pan or wok again.

10 *Prepare the sauce:* in a small bowl, dissolve the potato flour by gradually stirring in the stock and mushroom water. Heat the wok or pan until smoke rises, add 22.5ml (1½tbsp) oil and swirl it around. Add the garlic, which will sizzle. Add the black bean paste and chilli and stir to blend. Pour in the well-stirred, dissolved potato flour and stir to blend over a low heat. As soon as the sauce bubbles, pour over the pepper on the serving plate, scraping every drop from the frying pan or wok. Serve immediately.

Facing page, clockwise from the top: Red-braised gluten (see page 157); Sautéed stuffed peppers (see above); Wheat gluten – boiled and deep-fried (see page 156)

Wheat Gluten

INGREDIENTS
900g (2lb) strong flour
15ml (1tbsp) salt
500-550ml (18-19fl oz) cold or
    tepid water
groundnut or corn oil for
    deep-frying

Yields about 275-350g (10-12oz)
gluten

Illustrated on page 155

In Chinese, wheat gluten literally means the "sinewy essence" of wheat flour dough. For Buddhist vegetarians in China, it is the substitute for meat and is thus an indispensable ingredient for their vegetarian dishes. In China, Taiwan and Hong Kong, wheat gluten is sold in its cooked state but as yet it is not available elsewhere; neither is a satisfactory canned product. Fortunately, it is not difficult to make, so do try it.

1 Sift the flour into a large deep bowl. Add the salt. Gradually add the water and work into a dough which should be firm but not hard.

2 Knead the dough. If you use your hands, knead, punch, throw and pull it as much as possible. If you use a dough hook fitted to a food mixer, knead for about 4-6 minutes or the maximum amount of time directed in the instructions. In either case, knead until the dough is very, very smooth and elastic so that the maximum amount of gluten can be produced.

3 Cover the dough and leave to rest for about 1 hour.

4 Put the dough in a colander and stand it in the sink with the plug in. Turn on the cold tap and start pressing and squeezing the dough with both hands. The idea is literally to wash off all the floury substance. When the water becomes too milky, change it and continue washing. At the end of about 12 minutes, the water will become almost clear, being slightly cloudy rather than milky. The dough will have become a soft and spongy mass in the colander – this is the wheat gluten. Wash for 1-2 more minutes, then squeeze out excess water. The dough is now ready to use (a).

5 Pull with your fingers to break up the gluten lump into 4 portions. Pull each portion into 10 pieces (b) – making 40 pieces in total. Put them on a plate with a little space between each one so that they will not stick together.

a

b

6 To cook the gluten pieces, either boil or deep-fry. To boil: bring plenty of water in a large saucepan to the boil. Add 20 gluten pieces, continue to boil for about 4-5 minutes until they float to the surface indicating that they are cooked (c). To deep-fry: half fill a wok or

deep-fryer with oil. Heat to a temperature of 190°C (375°F) or until a cube of stale bread browns in 50 seconds. Put in the gluten, 1 piece at a time (10 can be deep-fried together). They will sink to the bottom, then come up to the surface, puffing bubbles all over. Turn them over repeatedly for about 2 minutes until light brown in colour (d). Remove and drain on kitchen paper.

c   d

Note: boiled gluten keeps well in the refrigerator for about 2 days; deep-fried gluten for 7 days. Both freeze well.

Red-braised Gluten

During the slow braising of this dish, the dark soy sauce, enriched by sugar, permeates the boiled gluten and dyes it red. The bamboo shoots give a contrasting texture to the spongy gluten and tender mushrooms. In keeping with the Buddhist tradition of vegetarian food, neither ginger, garlic, spring onion nor wine are used.

1 Drain and squeeze out excess water from the mushrooms but leave damp. Reserve the soaking liquid.

2 Squeeze excess water from the boiled gluten.

3 Heat a wok over a high heat until smoke rises. Add 30ml (2tbsp) of the oil and swirl it around. Add the mushrooms, flip and turn with a wok scoop or metal spatula until very hot. Add another 15ml (1tbsp) oil and put in the bamboo shoots, continuing to fold and turn until very hot and fragrant. Add the remaining oil and the gluten. Stir to mix.

4 Pour in the mushroom water. Add the salt, soy sauce and sugar. Bring to the boil then lower the heat. Cover and simmer for 30 minutes.

5 Turn up the heat and flip and turn the ingredients continuously to absorb the remaining liquid. This adds richness to the dish.

6 Remove to a warm serving dish. Sprinkle on the sesame oil and serve hot.

INGREDIENTS

20 small dried Chinese mushrooms, reconstituted in 450ml (16fl oz) boiling water (see page 39)
20 pieces boiled gluten (see page 156)
60ml (4tbsp) groundnut or corn oil
175g (6oz) canned bamboo shoots, thinly sliced
1.25ml (¼tsp) salt
37.5ml (2½tbsp) thick soy sauce
5ml (1tsp) sugar
10-15ml (2-3tsp) sesame oil

Serves 4 with 3 other dishes

Illustrated on page 155

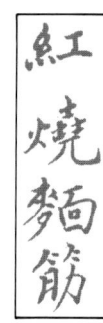

Pi Pa Bean Curd

INGREDIENTS

6 medium dried Chinese
   mushrooms, reconstituted (see
   page 39)
4 cakes bean curd, drained
2ml (⅓tsp) salt
1 egg yolk
30ml (2tbsp) self-raising flour
groundnut or corn oil for
   deep-frying
30-37.5ml (2-2½tbsp) groundnut
   or corn oil
2 cloves garlic, peeled and finely
   chopped
6mm (¼ inch) fresh ginger root,
   peeled and cut into silken
   threads (see page 34)
4 spring onions, cut diagonally
   into long slivers, white and
   green parts separated
50g (2oz) char-siu (Cantonese
   roast pork, see page 134) or
   ham, cut into matchstick-sized
   pieces

FOR THE SAUCE

7.5ml (1½tsp) potato flour
135ml (9tbsp) mushroom water
22.5ml (1½tbsp) oyster sauce
7.5ml (½tbsp) thick soy sauce

Serves 4-6 with 2-3 other dishes

Illustrated on page 161

So-called because the mashed bean curd is shaped into halved pear-shape pieces resembling the celebrated Chinese musical instrument, the pi pa.

1 Drain and squeeze out excess water from the mushrooms but leave damp. Slice into the thinnest possible slivers. Reserve the soaking liquid.

2 Using a wooden spoon, mash the bean curd and force it through a sieve into a dry, clean bowl. Discard the coarse dregs.

3 Add the salt, egg yolk and self-raising flour, and blend to a smooth paste. Leave for about 10 minutes.

4 *Prepare the sauce:* mix together the potato flour, reserved mushroom water, oyster and soy sauce.

5 Half fill a wok or deep-fryer with oil. Heat to a temperature of 190°C (375°F) or until a cube of stale bread browns in 50 seconds.

6 Before the oil is ready, dip 5-6 Chinese soup spoons into the oil then pack them with the bean curd paste (a), levelling it off with a palette knife or the back of a knife. When the oil is ready, hold the handles of the spoons, lower them one by one into the oil (b) and let the paste slip out, forming a halved pear shape or *pi pa* as it enters the oil. If necessary, use a knife to loosen the paste.

7 Deep-fry the pieces for about 3-4 minutes, turning them over periodically (c) until they are golden in colour and floating in the oil. As they are cooked, remove with a perforated disc or spoon (d) and

a

b

c

d

drain on kitchen paper. Arrange on a warm serving dish.

8 Pour the oil into a container for later use. Wash and dry the wok.

9 Reheat the wok over a high heat until smoke rises. Add about 30ml (2tbsp) oil and swirl it around. Add the garlic, ginger and white spring onion. As they sizzle, add the mushrooms, stir a few times, then add the char-siu or ham and stir a few more times.

10 Pour the well-stirred sauce into the wok and continue to stir over a moderate heat as it thickens. Add the green spring onion, then scoop the mixture over the bean curd. Serve immediately.

Pock-ma Bean Curd

This internationally famous Szechwan dish was the creation of a woman, wife of chef Ch'en Shen-fu, who worked in the capital, Ch'eng-tu, during the second half of the 19th century. If the pock-marks on her face earned her this rather derogatory nickname, "Pock-ma" or "Pock-woman", they also immortalized her bean curd dish.

1 Mince the pork and put into a bowl.

2 *Prepare the marinade:* add the salt, sugar, soy sauces, wine or sherry and oil to the pork. Stir to coat well. Leave to marinate for 15-30 minutes.

3 Chop the Szechwan vegetable into the size of matchstick heads. Dice the bean curd into 1-cm (½-inch) cubes. Transfer to a strainer, handling gently.

4 Mix together the potato flour and water for the thickening and put aside.

5 Heat a wok over a high heat until smoke rises. Add the oil and swirl it around. Add the garlic and pork and, using a wok scoop or metal spatula, flip and toss until partially cooked. Add the Szechwan vegetable, bean paste, soy sauce and sugar, continuing to turn and toss to let the sauce permeate the meat. Pour in the stock and slowly bring to the boil over a moderate heat.

6 Add the bean curd and stir gently so as not to break it up. Cook for about 2 minutes to absorb the flavours of both the pork and the sauce. Pour in the well-stirred potato flour mixture and blend well. Remove to a warm serving dish.

7 Add the hot oil and sesame oil; sprinkle with the ground Szechwan peppercorns and spring onion. This garnish adds a pretty red and green contrast as well as subtle flavouring. Serve piping hot.

INGREDIENTS
100g (4oz) lean pork
15-20g (½-¾oz) Szechwan preserved vegetable, well rinsed and dried
4 cakes bean curd, drained
5ml (1tsp) potato flour
15ml (1tbsp) water
60ml (4tbsp) groundnut or corn oil
3 cloves garlic, peeled and finely chopped
15ml (1tbsp) hot soy bean paste or broad bean paste (for moderately-hot flavour)
5ml (1tsp) thin soy sauce
5ml (1tsp) sugar
150ml (5fl oz) prime or clear stock (see page 225)
5ml (1tsp) hot chilli oil (see page 225)
5ml (1tsp) sesame oil
2.5ml (½tsp) ground roasted Szechwan peppercorns (see page 21)
2 spring onions, green parts only, cut into tiny rounds

FOR THE MARINADE
1ml (⅛tsp) salt
1.25ml (¼tsp) sugar
5ml (1tsp) thin soy sauce
5ml (1tsp) thick soy sauce
7.5ml (1½tsp) Shaohsing wine or medium dry sherry
5ml (1tsp) sesame oil

Serves 4-6 with 2-3 other dishes

Illustrated on page 161

麻婆豆腐

Stir-fried Chinese Broccoli with Beef

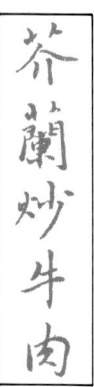

INGREDIENTS
100-175g (4-6oz) beef, fillet, rump or skirt, trimmed
450-700g (1-1½lb) Chinese broccoli, trimmed
60-67.5ml (4-4½tbsp) groundnut or corn oil
4 thin slices fresh ginger root, peeled
1.25-2ml (¼-⅓tsp) salt
1.25-2ml (¼-⅓tsp) sugar
1-2 cloves garlic, peeled and cut diagonally into slivers
2 spring onions, cut into 2.5-cm (1-inch) sections, white and green parts separated
7.5ml (½tbsp) Shaohsing wine or medium dry sherry

FOR THE MARINADE
1.25-2ml (¼-⅓tsp) salt
1.25-2ml (¼-⅓tsp) sugar
5ml (1tsp) thick soy sauce
3-4 turns black pepper mill
5ml (1tsp) Shaohsing wine or medium dry sherry
2.5ml (½tsp) potato flour
15ml (1tbsp) water
5ml (1tsp) groundnut or corn oil

FOR THE SAUCE
2.5-4ml (½-¾tsp) potato flour
45-75ml (3-5tbsp) water
15-22.5ml (1-1½tbsp) oyster sauce
7.5ml (½tbsp) thick soy sauce

Serves 4 with 3 other dishes

Illustrated opposite

As is so often the case in Chinese cooking, meat is used here to complement the vegetables: the Chinese broccoli in this dish, with its distinctive flavour similar to asparagus, goes especially well with the velvety beef slices. If it is not available, use plain broccoli as a substitute.

1 Cut the beef across the grain into slices, about 2.5 x 4cm (1 x 1½ inches) and 5mm (⅕ inch) thick. Put into a bowl.

2 *Prepare the marinade:* add the salt, sugar, soy sauce, pepper, wine or sherry, potato flour and water to the beef. Stir in the same direction until well coated. Leave to marinate for 15-30 minutes. Blend in the oil.

3 Cut the Chinese broccoli into pieces, about 7.5-10cm (3-4 inches) long.

4 *Prepare the sauce:* mix together the potato flour, water, oyster sauce and soy sauce.

5 Heat a wok until hot. Add 22.5-30ml (1½-2tbsp) of the oil and swirl it around. Add the ginger, stir and add the Chinese broccoli. Sliding the wok scoop or metal spatula to the bottom of the wok, turn and toss in rapid succession for about 1 minute, adjusting the heat if the broccoli begins to burn. Add the salt and sugar. Now add about 60-75ml (4-5tbsp) water, bring to the boil, then continue to cook, covered, over a moderate heat for about 4-5 minutes. The broccoli should be tender yet crunchy. Remove with a perforated disc to a warm serving plate and keep warm nearby.

6 Wash and dry the wok. Reheat over a high heat until smoke rises. Add the remaining oil and swirl it around. Add the garlic, then stir in the white spring onion. Add the beef and turn and toss for about 30 seconds to brown. Splash in the wine or sherry around the side of the wok, continuing to stir as it sizzles. Add the well-stirred sauce to the wok. Toss and stir as the sauce thickens. Add the green spring onion and remove from the heat.

7 Scoop the beef mixture over the Chinese broccoli. Serve immediately.

Facing page, clockwise from the top: Stir-fried Chinese broccoli with beef (see above); Pi pa bean curd (see page 158); Deep-fried bean curd in earthen pot (see page 162); Pock-ma bean curd (see page 159)

Deep-fried Bean Curd in Earthen Pot

INGREDIENTS

4 large or 6 medium dried
   Chinese mushrooms,
   reconstituted (see page 39)
4 cakes bean curd, drained
4 large leaves Chinese celery
   cabbage
37.5-45ml (2½-3tbsp) groundnut
   or corn oil
2 thin slices fresh ginger root,
   peeled
salt to taste
groundnut or corn oil for
   deep-frying

FOR THE SAUCE

5ml (1tsp) potato flour
75ml (5tbsp) mushroom water or
   clear stock
10ml (2tsp) thick soy sauce
30ml (2tbsp) oyster sauce
1-2 cloves garlic, peeled and
   finely chopped
2-3 spring onions, cut into 2.5-cm
   (1-inch) sections, white and
   green parts separated

Serves 4 with 2 other dishes

Illustrated on page 161

It is very popular in South China and Hong Kong to serve certain dishes in a flameproof earthen pot, especially in the winter. This range of dishes, comprising meat, offal, fish, seafood, vegetables and bean curd, is known as Earthen-pot dishes. The main ingredient is often deep-fried and then assembled with the other ingredients in the pot which, being flameproof, can be heated up just before being brought to the table. Instead of an earthen pot, an enamelled casserole or a copper pot can also be used.

1 Drain and squeeze out excess water from the mushrooms but leave damp. Slice into thin strips.

2 Cut each cake of bean curd into 3 rectangular pieces, taking care to keep them whole. Lay on several changes of kitchen paper to drain excess water.

3 Cut the cabbage crosswise into 2.5-cm (1-inch) lengths.

4 Heat a wok over a high heat until smoke rises. Add 15ml (1tbsp) of the oil and swirl it around. Add the ginger and, as it sizzles, add the cabbage. Sliding the wok scoop or spatula to the bottom of the wok, turn and toss for about 30 seconds. Season with a little salt, lower the heat and continue to cook, covered, for 2-3 minutes or until tender yet still crisp. Remove and drain, if necessary. Put into the warm earthen pot.

5 *Prepare the sauce:* mix together the potato flour, mushroom water or stock, soy sauce and oyster sauce. Heat a saucepan (or another wok if you have a second one) until hot. Add the remaining 22.5-30ml (1½-2tbsp) oil and swirl it around. Add the garlic, let it sizzle and take on colour, then add the white spring onion and then the Chinese mushroom. Stir and turn for about 30 seconds. Pour the well-stirred potato flour mixture into the saucepan or wok. Lower the heat, continuing to stir as it thickens. Remove from the heat.

6 Half fill a wok or deep-fryer with oil. Heat to a temperature of 200°C (400°F) or until a cube of stale bread browns in 40 seconds. Lower the bean curd into the oil, piece by piece, and deep-fry for about 4 minutes or until golden, turning over with a pair of long bamboo chopsticks or tongs halfway through cooking. Remove with a large hand strainer or perforated disc and drain on kitchen paper.

7 Lay the bean curd on the cabbage in the pot. Add the green spring onion. Reheat the sauce and pour over the bean curd.

8 Heat the pot up for 1-2 minutes, then bring to the table and serve immediately.

Stuffed Chinese Mushrooms

A delicately flavoured steamed dish much enjoyed by the Cantonese and Fukienese. The egg white lightens the pork, and the bamboo shoots or water chestnuts add just a bite to the otherwise smooth texture; the sauce glistens on the stuffing, giving the dish a transparent effect.

1 Chop the pork by hand or mince coarsely. Put into a bowl.

2 *Prepare the marinade:* add the ginger, salt, sugar, soy sauce, pepper, wine or sherry, potato flour and water to the pork. Stir vigorously in the same direction for about 30 seconds or until well coated. Add the egg white and stir again in the same direction for another 30 seconds or until smooth and light. Leave to marinate for about 15 minutes.

3 Mix the bamboo shoots or water chestnuts with the pork. Mix in the spring onion. Stir in the 15ml (1tbsp) oil. The stuffing is now ready.

4 Drain and squeeze out the excess water from the mushrooms but leave damp. Reserve the soaking liquid.

5 Hold a mushroom cap in one hand with the hollow side up. Using a small knife, fill the hollow generously with stuffing, shaping it into a slightly sloping mound to give an attractive appearance. Repeat until all are done. Put on to a heatproof dish, stuffing side up, preferably in one layer.

6 Put the dish in a wok or steamer and steam, tightly covered, for 10 minutes over a high heat (see page 44).

7 *Prepare the sauce:* a few minutes before the end of the steaming time mix together the flour, mushroom water, oyster sauce and soy sauce. Pour into a wok or a saucepan. Bring to the boil, stirring continuously as it thickens. Blend in the oil which will give a sheen.

8 Remove the mushrooms from the steamer. Arrange them in 2 layers, either in the same heatproof dish or on a warm serving dish. Pour the sauce over. Serve piping hot.

INGREDIENTS

28 thick medium dried Chinese mushrooms, with slightly curled edges, reconstituted (see page 39)

100g (4oz) pork, shoulder or leg

50g (2oz) canned bamboo shoots, or 3-4 fresh or canned water chestnuts, finely chopped

5 spring onions, cut into tiny rounds

15ml (1tbsp) groundnut or corn oil

FOR THE MARINADE

2-4 thin slices fresh ginger root, peeled and finely minced

2.5ml (½tsp) salt

2.5ml (½tsp) sugar

10ml (2tsp) thin soy sauce

6 turns white pepper mill

5ml (1tsp) Shaohsing wine or medium dry sherry

2.5ml (½tsp) potato flour

15ml (1tbsp) water

15ml (1tbsp) egg white

FOR THE SAUCE

7.5ml (1½tsp) potato flour, dissolved in 15ml (1tbsp) water

175ml (6fl oz) mushroom water

15ml (1tbsp) oyster sauce

15ml (1tbsp) thick soy sauce

22.5-30ml (1½-2tbsp) groundnut or corn oil

Serves 6 with 3-4 other dishes

Illustrated on page 165

Braised Bamboo Shoots

INGREDIENTS
8 medium dried Chinese
    mushrooms, reconstituted (see
    page 39)
25g (1oz) dried shrimps, rinsed
450g (1lb) canned bamboo shoots
30ml (2tbsp) thin soy sauce
10ml (2tsp) sugar
75ml (5tbsp) groundnut or corn
    oil
100g (4oz) lean pork, cut into
    matchstick-sized pieces
150ml (¼ pint) clear stock,
    including shrimp water
5ml (1tsp) potato flour, dissolved
    in 15ml (1tbsp) water
10-15ml (2-3tsp) sesame oil

Serves 6 with 3 other dishes

Illustrated opposite

In Fukien, this dish is made from fresh winter bamboo shoots, but in the West we have to be content with the canned product which, fortunately, retains much of its characteristic crispness.

1 Drain and squeeze out excess water from the mushrooms but leave damp. Slice into thin strips.

2 Soak the shrimps in just enough boiling water to cover them for about 15 minutes. Drain them, reserving the soaking liquid.

3 Slice the bamboo shoots into strips, about 5cm (2 inches) long, 1cm (½ inch) wide and 6mm (¼ inch) thick. Put into a bowl and mix in the soy sauce and sugar and leave for 3-5 minutes.

4 Heat a wok over a high heat until smoke rises. Add the oil and swirl it around. Lift the bamboo shoots with a perforated spoon, leaving in the bowl as much soy sauce as possible, and add to the oil. Immediately put the pork into the bowl to soak up the soy sauce. Sliding the wok scoop or metal spatula to the bottom of the wok, turn and toss the bamboo shoots so that each piece is coated with the oil. Remove with a perforated spoon.

5 Add the shrimps to the wok, stir a few times and add the mushroom. Stir, then add the pork. Continue to turn and toss for about 1 minute until the pork is almost cooked.

6 Return the bamboo shoots to the wok, stir to mix and add the stock. As soon as the stock comes to the boil, cover, reduce the heat and simmer for about 10 minutes or until all but 75-90ml (5-6tbsp) stock has been absorbed.

7 Add the well-stirred, dissolved potato flour to the wok and stir to thicken the sauce.

8 Remove to a warm plate. Sprinkle the sesame oil on top and serve.

Facing page, clockwise from the top: Stir-fried bean sprouts with shredded pork (see page 166); Braised bamboo shoots (see above); Stuffed mushrooms (see page 163); Stir-fried Chinese celery with dried shrimps (see page 167)

Stir-fried Bean Sprouts with Shredded Pork

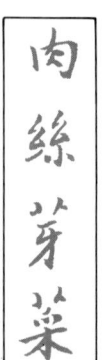

INGREDIENTS

175g (6oz) lean pork
1 small green pepper, halved lengthwise and seeded
90ml (6tbsp) groundnut or corn oil
3 thin slices fresh ginger root, peeled and cut into silken threads (see page 35)
450g (1lb) bean sprouts
2.5ml (½tsp) salt
2-3 cloves garlic, peeled and finely chopped
3 spring onions, halved lengthwise, cut into 5-cm (2-inch) sections, white and green parts separated
10ml (2tsp) Shaohsing wine or medium dry sherry

FOR THE MARINADE

1.25ml (¼tsp) salt
1.25ml (¼tsp) sugar
10ml (2tsp) thin soy sauce
4 turns white pepper mill
5ml (1tsp) Shaohsing wine or medium dry sherry
2.5ml (½tsp) potato flour
15ml (1tbsp) water

FOR THE SAUCE

2.5ml (½tsp) potato flour
45ml (3tbsp) water
30ml (2tbsp) oyster sauce

Serves 4 with 2 other dishes

Illustrated on page 165

The combination of meat and vegetables is a regular occurrence in Chinese cooking. Even though a small amount of meat is used, it nevertheless adds so much taste and interest to the vegetables that it is worth the effort.

1 Cut the pork into matchstick-sized pieces. Put into a bowl.

2 *Prepare the marinade:* add the salt, sugar, soy sauce, pepper, wine or sherry, potato flour and water to the pork. Stir in the same direction to coat. Leave to marinate for about 20 minutes.

3 Slice the green pepper lengthwise into thin strips.

4 *Prepare the sauce:* mix together the potato flour, water and oyster sauce.

5 Heat a wok over a high heat until smoke rises. Add 45ml (3tbsp) of the oil and swirl it around. Add the ginger and, as it sizzles, add the bean sprouts and green pepper. Season with the salt. Sliding the wok scoop or spatula to the bottom of the wok, turn and toss continuously over a high heat for about 2½-3 minutes. The bean sprouts and green pepper will be cooked but still crunchy. Remove to a warm serving plate and keep warm nearby.

6 Wash and dry the wok. Reheat over a high heat until smoke rises. Add the remaining oil and swirl it around. Add the garlic and, as it sizzles and takes on colour, add the white spring onion. Stir a few times, then put in the pork. Turn and toss for about 30 seconds or until the pork begins to turn opaque. Splash in the wine or sherry around the side of the wok. As it sizzles, continue to stir and turn for another 30-60 seconds or until the pork is cooked. Lower the heat. Pour the well-stirred sauce on to the pork, stirring as it thickens. Add the green spring onion and stir a few more times. Scoop the pork mixture on to the bean sprouts. Serve immediately.

Stir-fried Chinese Celery Cabbage with Dried Shrimps

An economical and healthy day-to-day dish that is easy to make. It is as popular with the Cantonese as with the Shanghaiese but whereas the Cantonese use spring onions, ginger and shrimps to heighten the flavour, the Shanghaiese prefer just dried shrimps.

INGREDIENTS

25g (1oz) dried shrimps, rinsed
1 Chinese celery cabbage, about
 900g (2lb)
45-60ml (3-4tbsp) groundnut or
 corn oil
4 spring onions, cut into 2.5-cm
 (1-inch) sections, white and
 green parts separated
4 thin slices fresh ginger root,
 peeled
1.25-2.5ml (¼-½tsp) salt

Serves 4-6 with 2-3 other dishes

Illustrated on page 165

1 Soak the shrimps (a) in just enough boiling water to cover them for 30 minutes or longer (b). Drain them, reserving the soaking liquid.

a   b

2 Discard any wilted or hard outer leaves of the cabbage then put together similarly sized leaves (c). Chop crosswise into thin strips (d). Remove and discard the hard core.

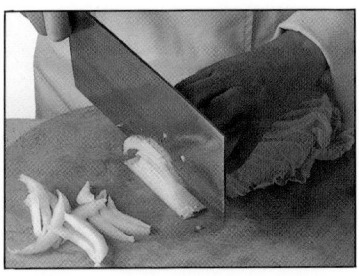

c   d

3 Heat a wok over a high heat until smoke rises. Add the oil and swirl it around. Add the white spring onion, stir a couple of times, then add the ginger. As they sizzle, add the shrimps which will "explode" as they touch the oil, releasing a mouth-watering fragrance. Stir the shrimps for a few seconds.

4 Add the cabbage and, sliding the wok scoop or metal spatula to the bottom of the wok, turn and toss for about 1 minute so that the cabbage will absorb the fragrance of the other ingredients. Adjust the heat if the cabbage begins to burn. Pour in the shrimp water, season with the salt, cover and continue cooking for 1-2 minutes or until the cabbage is tender yet still crunchy. Add the green spring onion. Remove to a warm serving plate and serve immediately.

素菜

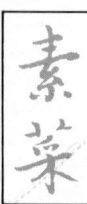

A Vegetarian Menu

Vegetarian food need not be dull and tasteless and this menu for eight is a fine example of the point. For non-vegetarians, as well as the less strict vegetarians, the addition of oyster sauce to vegetables does wonders, so be sure to follow the suggestion.

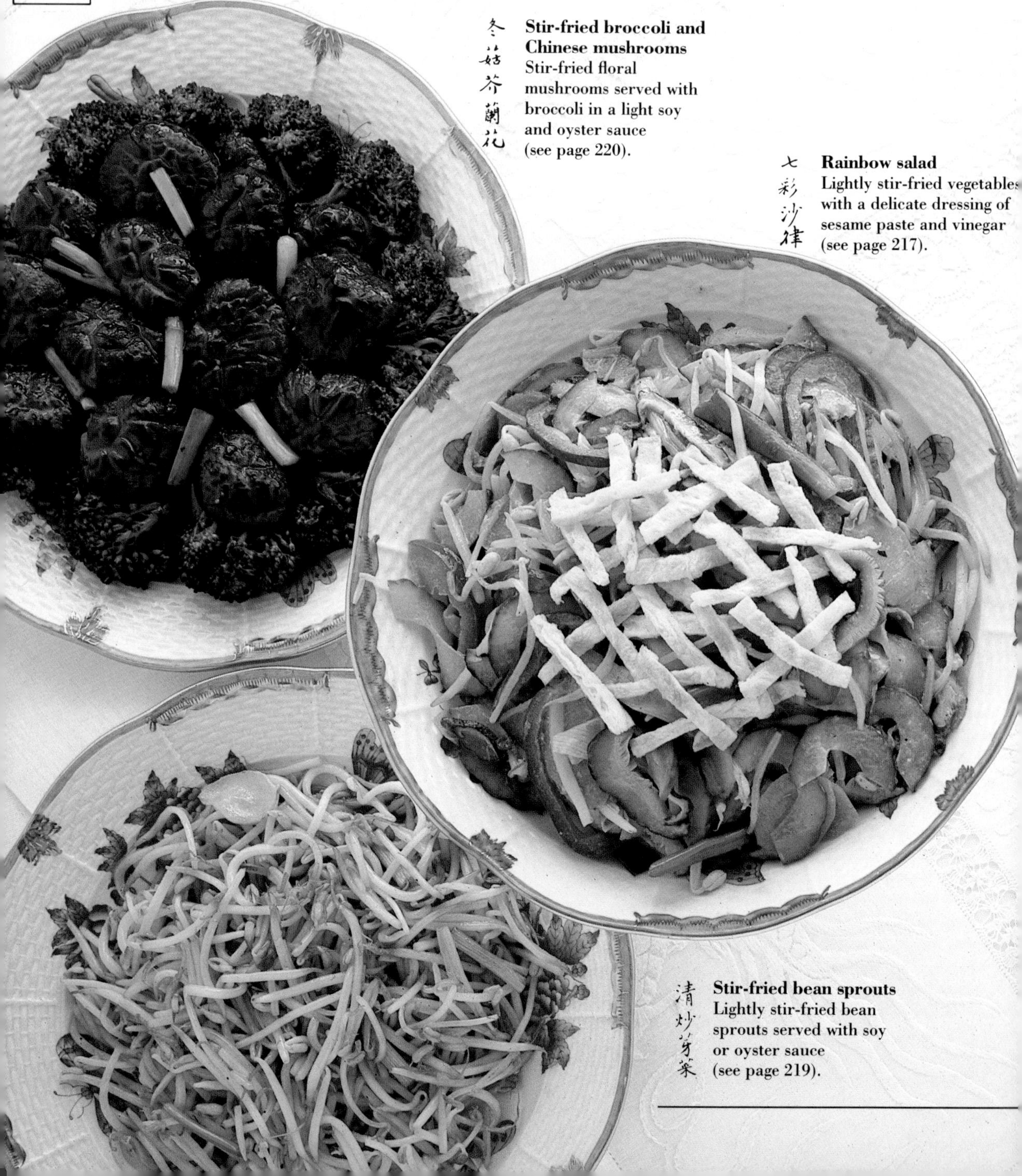

冬菇芥蘭花 **Stir-fried broccoli and Chinese mushrooms**
Stir-fried floral mushrooms served with broccoli in a light soy and oyster sauce (see page 220).

七彩沙律 **Rainbow salad**
Lightly stir-fried vegetables with a delicate dressing of sesame paste and vinegar (see page 217).

清炒芽菜 **Stir-fried bean sprouts**
Lightly stir-fried bean sprouts served with soy or oyster sauce (see page 219).

腐乳椒絲炒菠菜 **Stir-fried spinach in bean curd "cheese" sauce**
Spinach stir-fried with garlic and chilli, made all
the more special by the addition of bean curd
"cheese" (see page 220).

羅漢齋 **Lohan's delight**
Buddhist dish, therefore
none of the usual Chinese
condiments – ginger, garlic
and spring onions – are
used (see page 218).

醬油豆腐 **Bean curd in a simple sauce**
Cubed bean curd, briefly
stir-fried and served with soy
sauce and spring onions
(see page 219).

RICE, NOODLES AND DUMPLINGS

Boiled Rice

INGREDIENTS

1 cup or 190g (6½oz) long grain white rice
10ml (2tsp) groundnut or corn oil
1½ cups or 350ml (12fl oz) water

Serves 4-5 with other dishes

Illustrated opposite

Cooked rice, served with other dishes, is the Chinese staple. The general Chinese yardstick for measuring the water required to cook the rice is to put the rice in a pan, then stand an index finger on the surface of the rice and let the water come up to the first joint. However, for those who are less experienced, or who are cooking a smaller amount of rice, the chart below is recommended as a guideline. The rice should be cooked thoroughly, and be tender but not mushy.

Rice	Water	Oil	Cooked rice
1 cup or 190g (6½oz)	1½ cups or 350ml (12fl oz)	10ml (2tsp)	3 cups
2 cups or 375g (13oz)	2½ cups or 600ml (20fl oz)	20ml (4tsp)	6 cups
3 cups or 540g (19½oz)	3¼ cups or 800ml (26fl oz)	30ml (6tsp)	9 cups

1 Wash the rice in 3-4 changes of cold or tepid water, rubbing the grains gently with the fingers to get rid of excess starch. Drain.

2 Put the rice into a saucepan, preferably with a copper bottom. Add the oil and water. (The oil prevents the rice from boiling over and from sticking to the bottom of the saucepan; it also enhances the natural flavour of the rice.)

3 Cover and bring to the boil. Stir thoroughly with a wooden spoon and continue to boil, either covered or uncovered, until most of the water is absorbed, leaving only tiny droplets around the rice. Reduce the heat to a minimum.

4 Place a metal heat diffuser under the saucepan (the French *diffuseur/mijoteur* with a flexible handle is ideal), and leave the rice to simmer with the lid on for 12-15 minutes.

5 Before serving, fluff up the rice with a spoon. Either scoop all the rice into a large communal bowl from which everyone takes his or her portion, or scoop some rice into individual rice bowls.

Facing page, clockwise from the top: Beef-fried rice (see page 172); Plain fried rice (see page 172); Boiled rice (see above); Stir-fried glutinous rice (see page 173)

Plain Fried Rice

INGREDIENTS

3 cups or 400g (14oz) boiled rice, cooked at least 3-4 hours in advance (see page 170)

30ml (2tbsp) groundnut or corn oil

2 spring onions, cut into small rounds, white and green parts separated

1 large egg, lightly beaten with 10ml (2tsp) oil and 1.25ml (¼tsp) salt

1.25ml (¼tsp) salt or to taste

10ml (2tsp) thick soy sauce

30ml (2tbsp) clear stock (optional)

Serves 2 with 1 other dish

Ilustrated on page 171

When cooked rice is stir-fried with egg, but without meat or seafood, it is called plain fried rice, and it often has greater appeal than boiled rice to those who are not used to eating rice as a staple as the stir-frying process adds so much taste and fragrance. As the best result is obtained from cooked rice it is also a way to turn any left-over rice into an appetizing dish.

1 Loosen the rice grains as much as possible.

2 Heat a wok over a high heat until smoke rises. Add the oil and swirl it around. Add the white spring onion, stir a few times, then pour in the egg. Leave for 5-10 seconds so that the egg sets at the bottom but remains runny on the surface.

3 Add the rice. Sliding the wok scoop or metal spatula to the bottom of the wok, turn and toss continuously for 3-4 minutes or until thoroughly hot. Season with the salt and soy sauce. If the rice is very hard, add the stock and stir for a few more seconds. Add the green spring onion. Put in a warm serving bowl and serve immediately.

Stir-fried Glutinous Rice

INGREDIENTS

450g (1lb) white glutinous rice

25g (1oz) dried shrimps, rinsed

10 medium dried Chinese mushrooms, reconstituted in 250ml (8fl oz) water (see page 39)

1 large pork wind-dried Chinese sausage

1 large duck liver wind-dried Chinese sausage

30ml (2tbsp) groundnut or corn oil

5ml (1tsp) salt

4-6 spring onions, cut into small rounds, white and green parts separated

175g (6oz) fatty roast belly pork, diced (see page 146)

15ml (1tbsp) thick soy sauce

small bunch coriander leaves, torn up

Serves 4-5 as a main course

Illustrated on page 171

Glutinous rice is usually steamed or boiled but, as it is very starchy, these methods of cooking can make it into a rather stodgy food. Stir-frying glutinous rice from its raw state until cooked through, however, makes the rice much lighter and more fragrant in taste.

1 Wash the glutinous rice 3-4 times, rubbing with the fingers. Drain, then soak in plenty of cold water for 5-6 hours. Drain just before ready to use.

2 Soak the shrimps in just enough boiling water to cover them for about 20 minutes. Drain them, reserving the soaking liquid.

3 Drain and squeeze out excess water from the mushrooms but leave damp. Reserve the soaking liquid. Dice the mushrooms.

4 Rinse the wind-dried sausages and dice.

5 Heat a wok over a high heat until smoke rises. Add the oil and swirl it around. Add the wind-dried sausages and shrimps, and turn and toss for about 1 minute. Then add the mushrooms, continuing to stir-fry for a few seconds.

6 Add the glutinous rice and, sliding the wok scoop or metal spatula

to the bottom of the wok, turn and toss about 12 times, adjusting the heat if the rice begins to burn. Sprinkle on about 60-90ml (2-3fl oz) shrimp/mushroom water, cover and continue to cook over a medium to low heat for 2 minutes. Sprinkle on the same amount of liquid again, fold and turn the rice 5-6 times, then cover once more. Repeat this procedure 4 times, using ordinary water when the shrimp/mushroom water is used up.

7 Add the salt, white spring onion and roast belly pork. Flip and turn to mix and repeat the sprinkling of water and simmering another 3-4 times, each time for about 4-5 minutes. The rice should be cooked through by this time but, if not, continue to simmer and add more water if necessary.

8 Remove from the heat. Add the soy sauce, green spring onion and coriander leaves. Fold and turn to mix, then remove to a warm serving plate. Serve hot.

Beef Fried Rice

Much of the attraction of this dish lies in the fact that the flavour of the beef and spices permeate the rice while it is being stir-fried.

1 Chop or mince the beef. Put into a bowl.

2 *Prepare the marinade:* add the salt, sugar, soy sauces, pepper, wine or sherry and potato flour to the beef. Add the water, one spoonful at a time, stirring vigorously in the same direction between additions until too difficult to continue. This makes the beef fluffy and velvety. Leave to marinate for 15 minutes. Blend in the oil.

3 Loosen the rice grains as much as possible.

4 Heat a wok over a high heat until smoke rises. Add 45ml (3tbsp) of the oil and swirl it around. Add the garlic and, when it sizzles, add the ginger and the white spring onion. Stir a few times. Add the beef and, sliding the wok scoop or metal spatula to the bottom of the wok, flip and toss, breaking up any lumps at the same time. When partially cooked, splash in the wine or sherry around the side of the wok, continuing to stir as it sizzles. Pour in the beaten egg, tip in the rice, turn and toss for about 2 minutes or until all the ingredients are very hot and well mixed. Stream in the remaining oil around the side of the wok, turning the rice to incorporate it. Remove from the heat.

5 Add half of the lettuce and the green spring onion. Scoop on to a warm serving dish. Top with the remaining lettuce and serve hot.

INGREDIENTS

400g (14oz) or 3 cups boiled rice, cooked at least 3-4 hours in advance (see page 170)
225g (8oz) beef, rump or skirt
60-75ml (4-5tbsp) groundnut or corn oil
4 cloves garlic, peeled and finely chopped
6mm (¼ inch) fresh ginger root, peeled and finely chopped
4 spring onions, cut into small rounds, white and green parts separated
1 egg, lightly beaten
2-4 leaves lettuce, Cos, Iceberg, Webb, thinly shredded

FOR THE MARINADE

2.5ml (½tsp) salt
2.5ml (½tsp) sugar
10ml (2tsp) thin soy sauce
10ml (2tsp) thick soy sauce
6 turns black pepper mill
5ml (1tsp) Shaohsing wine or medium dry sherry
2.5ml (½tsp) potato flour
45-60ml (3-4tbsp) water
15ml (1tbsp) groundnut or corn oil

Serves 2 as a main course

Illustrated on page 171

生炒牛肉飯

Yin-yang Rice

INGREDIENTS
450g (1lb) lean pork
900g (2lb) tomatoes
80ml (12tbsp) groundnut or corn oil
1 clove garlic, peeled and finely chopped
2.5ml (½tsp) salt
2.5ml (½tsp) sugar
about 550g (1¼lb) or 4½ cups boiled rice, freshly cooked (see page 170)
3-4 cloves garlic, peeled and cut into silken threads (see page 35)
15ml (1tbsp) Shaohsing wine or medium dry sherry
6 large egg whites, beaten with 2.5ml (½tsp) salt
2 garden peas, blanched (optional)

FOR THE MARINADE
2.5ml (½tsp) salt
1.25ml (¼tsp) sugar
15ml (1tbsp) thin soy sauce
5ml (1tsp) Shaohsing wine or medium dry sherry
10 turns white pepper mill
5ml (1tsp) potato flour
15-30ml (1-2tbsp) water
15-30ml (1-2tbsp) groundnut or corn oil

FOR THE SAUCE
juice from the tomatoes
10ml (2tsp) potato flour
15ml (1tbsp) thin soy sauce
15ml (1tbsp) oyster sauce

Serves 3-4 as lunch or as last course for 8-10

Illustrated opposite

Yin-yang is the all-pervading dual principle of Chinese philosophy, symbolizing the sun and the moon, man and woman, good and evil, light and darkness. In this dish, the egg white and the red tomato are used decoratively to form the yin-yang symbol.

1 Cut the pork into matchstick-sized strips. Put into a bowl.

2 *Prepare the marinade:* add the salt, sugar, soy sauce, wine or sherry, pepper and potato flour to the pork. Stir in the same direction to coat, adding the water to make the pork lighter. Leave to marinate for 20-30 minutes. Stir in the oil.

3 Submerge the tomatoes in boiling water for a few minutes, then peel. Deseed and cut into cubes. Put into a wire sieve over a bowl to drain, saving the juice for the sauce.

4 Heat a wok over a high heat until smoke rises. Add 30ml (2tbsp) of the oil and swirl it around. Add the chopped garlic and when it sizzles, add the tomato and stir a few times. Season with the salt and sugar. Cook over a medium heat, covered, for about 5 minutes. Remove to the sieve and drain, saving the juice for the sauce and then transfer to a bowl and keep warm in a cool oven.

5 *Prepare the sauce:* mix together the tomato juice, potato flour, soy sauce and oyster sauce.

6 Spread the rice on to a round serving dish. Keep warm.

7 Wash and dry the wok. Reheat over a high heat until smoke rises. Add 60ml (4tbsp) of the oil and swirl it around. Add the shredded garlic and when it sizzles and takes on colour, add the pork. Sliding the wok scoop or metal spatula to the bottom of the wok, turn and toss for about 1 minute or until the pork, turning whitish in colour, is partially cooked. Splash in the wine or sherry around the side of the wok, continuing to turn and fold until the sizzling dies down. Add the well-stirred sauce to the pork, stirring as it thickens. Scoop all over the rice.

8 Wash and dry the wok. Reheat until hot, add the remaining 90ml (6tbsp) oil and swirl it around. Pour in the egg white and fold continuously with the wok scoop or spatula so that the runny egg white goes to the bottom while the set layers are turned to the surface; lower the heat if necessary. Scoop up the tender flaky egg white and spread on to the right or yin half of the rice, making a curvy yin-yang motif in the middle.

9 Spread the tomato on to the yang or left side. Garnish with the 2 garden peas if desired. Serve hot.

Facing page, clockwise from the top: Spring onion cake (see page 178); Yin-yang rice (see above); Boiled dumplings (see page 176); Sauteed dumplings (see page 177)

Boiled Northern Dumplings

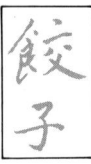

INGREDIENTS

FOR THE DOUGH
575g (1¼lb) plain flour
about 350ml (12fl oz) cold water

FOR THE FILLING
25g (1oz) dried shrimps, rinsed
5ml (1tsp) Shaohsing wine or
    medium dry sherry
900g (2lb) Chinese celery
    cabbage, trimmed
10ml (2tsp) salt
450g (1lb) pork with a little fat,
    finely chopped
12 spring onions, cut into small
    rounds

FOR THE MARINADE
7.5ml (1½tsp) salt
8 turns pepper mill
10ml (2tsp) Shaohsing wine or
    medium dry sherry
45ml (3tbsp) sesame oil
45ml (3tbsp) groundnut or corn
    oil

FOR THE DIPS
soy sauces, thin or thick, vinegar,
    Chinkiang wine or hot chilli oil
    (see page 225)

Serves 10 as first course
Yields about 100 dumplings

Illustrated on page 175

Northern Chinese people adore these dumplings, chiao-tzu, especially during the Chinese New Year. They sometimes eat them as the only course of a meal, and a man may consume more than 50 at a sitting. To wrap them is an exciting family activity in which everyone lends a hand. The filling can be a variety of different vegetables, such as Chinese chives and winter melon, with either pork or beef or sometimes fish. The size can also vary, but chiao-tzu, when cooked, should always contain a small amount of liquid (soup) inside the wrapper.

1 *Prepare the dough:* sift the flour into a mixing bowl. Gradually stir in the water and start kneading. Knead for 1-2 minutes or until smooth. The dough should be firm but pliable and not dry. Cover the bowl with a towel and leave for about 30 minutes at room temperature.

2 *Prepare the filling:* soak the shrimps in enough boiling water to just cover them, for 15-20 minutes. Drain them, reserving the soaking liquid. Chop the shrimps into the size of matchstick heads (see page 38) and add the wine or sherry.

3 Shred the cabbage crosswise as thinly as possible and then chop roughly, cutting out the hard core. Put the cabbage into a bowl. Mix in the salt and leave for about 30 minutes.

4 *Prepare the marinade:* add the salt, pepper, wine or sherry and oils to the pork. Also add 45ml (3tbsp) of the shrimp water (if insufficient, make up with cold water), and stir vigorously in the same direction for about 1 minute. Mix in the shrimps and spring onions and leave to marinate until the dough is ready.

5 Squeeze out the excess water from the cabbage but leave damp. Add to the pork mixture. Mix thoroughly.

6 Divide the dough into 4 pieces. On a lightly floured board, roll out one piece with both hands into a long cylindrical roll, about 2cm (¾ inch) in diameter and then cut into pieces about 1.5cm (⅗ inch) long. Cover spare dough with a towel.

7 One by one, stand each piece upright on the heel of your hand; slightly round off the dough then flatten with the other hand. Flour them lightly. Using a narrow rolling pin, roll out each piece into a circular wrapper about 7.5cm (3 inches) in diameter. Make the centre slightly thicker than the edge by rotating the dough anti-clockwise as you roll.

8 Place a wrapper in the palm of one hand and put about 7.5ml (1½tsp) of the filling in the middle. Pinch tightly to seal the 2 edges (a). Now hold the dumpling between the thumbs and index fingers of both hands, seal the right edges by squeezing the thumb and index

finger together (b), pinching and pleating to make one or two tucks simultaneously, then seal the left edges in the same way. Put the dumpling on a floured tray. Repeat until all áre made.

a   b

9 To boil the dumplings in a wok, bring about 1.7 litres (3 pints) of water to a fast boil. Put in 5 or 6 dumplings and stir so that they do not stick to the bottom of the wok. Add another 14 or 15 and stir again. Cover the wok and return to the boil. Stir, then cover again, lower the heat and continue to simmer gently for another 8-10 minutes or until the dumplings have floated to the surface. (If the cooking is done on an electric burner where the temperature cannot be controlled instantly, about 250ml (8fl oz) cold water should be added twice during cooking to prevent the dumplings from bursting.)

10 Serve hot. To eat, dip them in soy sauce, vinegar and hot chilli oil, mixing them to individual taste.

Sautéed Northern Dumplings

A combination of cooking methods is used to produce these delicious dumplings which are crisply sautéed underneath but lightly steamed on top. Steps 2-7 are as Boiled Northern Dumplings.

8 Turn the floured side of a wrapper towards you, make 6 straight pleats, each about 1cm (½ inch) deep, along the top edge of just under half the circle, forming a little pouch (a). Add about 10ml (2tsp) of the filling to the pouch. Fold up the unpleated edge (b) and pinch together the 2 edges of the dumpling, making it into a crescent. Repeat until all are made.

INGREDIENTS
as for Boiled Northern
 Dumplings

FOR THE DOUGH
follow step 1 of Spring Onion
 Cake dough (see page 178)

**FOR SAUTÉEING EACH
 PANFUL**
30ml (2tbsp) groundnut or corn
 oil
120ml (4fl oz) hot water mixed
 with 10ml (2tsp) oil and 5ml
 (1tsp) rice or white wine
 vinegar
5ml (1tsp) plain flour, dissolved
 in 30ml (2tbsp) water

Serves 10 as first course
Yields about 100 dumplings

Illustrated on page 175

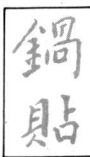

a   b

9 To cook the dumplings, heat a heavy (20-25cm [8-10 inch]) frying pan, with a lid, for about 30 seconds or until hot. Add the oil and swirl to cover the entire surface. Lower the heat and put in about 12 dumplings, in 2 parallel rows, with the dumplings just touching each other. Cover and cook for 3 minutes. Pour in the hot water mixture carefully, cover and continue to cook over a higher heat for about 7 minutes or until the water is almost absorbed and the bottoms of the dumplings are turning golden. Pour the dissolved flour along the sides of the dumplings. Cover and cook for 1-2 more minutes; the flour forms a crisp film linking the dumplings.

10 With a spatula, remove as many dumplings in a row as possible and turn them, brown side up, on to a warm serving plate. Either serve straight away while you continue to cook the other dumplings or keep them warm and serve all together.

Spring Onion Cakes

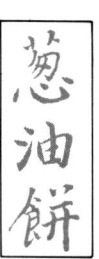

INGREDIENTS
550g (1¼lb) plain white flour
350ml (12fl oz) boiling water
15-30ml (1-2tbsp) cold water
5-10ml (1-2tsp) sesame oil
7.5ml (1½tsp) salt
about 100g (4oz) margarine
35 spring onions, about 350g
    (12oz), cut into small rounds
groundnut or corn oil for frying

Serves 6 for lunch; 10-12 as a
    first course or more as hors
    d'oeuvres

Illustrated on page 175

When the biting wind howls in Peking, people tuck into these hearty, oily cakes, made all the more appetizing by the spring onion trapped within their layers. They are often served with tea or Chinese wine as a meal on their own. Traditionally, lard or rendered duck's fat is used but margarine is a very satisfactory and healthier substitute.

1 Sift the flour into a large bowl. Pour in the boiling water gradually and mix with a pair of chopsticks or a fork as you do so. Rub together with the fingers while the flour is still warm. Add the cold water and knead to form a dough which should be firm but not hard. Continue to knead for about 2-3 more minutes and then leave, covered, for at least 30 minutes.

2 Oil a flat surface with 5ml (1tsp) sesame oil. Also oil a rolling pin with a little sesame oil.

3 Place the dough on the surface. Knead a few times and shape into a roll. Divide into 6 pieces.

4 With the oiled rolling pin, roll out 1 piece into a circular shape about 16-17.5cm (6½-7 inches) in diameter, with the edges slightly thinner than the centre.

5 Sprinkle with a good 1.25ml (¼tsp) salt all over and press it in with the fingers.

6 Generously spread about 15g (½oz) margarine all over, stopping just short of the edges.

7 Spread about 75ml (5tbsp) chopped spring onion, adding slightly more to the centre.

8 With both hands, pick up the sides nearest you and roll up the cake away from you, taking care not to let the spring onion fall out.

9 Pinch in both ends (a). Then, holding one end in each hand, roll in towards the middle until the ends meet (b). Lift one end and put on top of the other and twist, in opposite directions (c), and then press down to make into a ball (d).

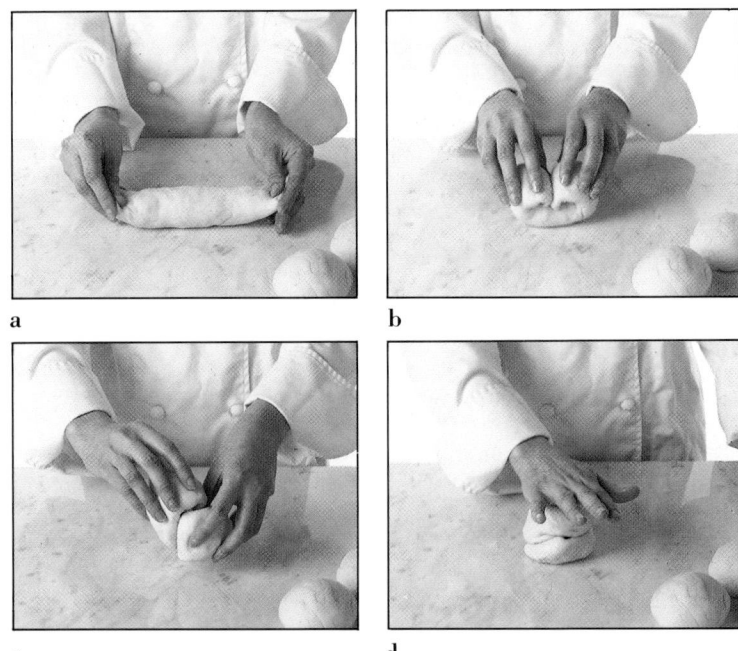

a

b

c

d

10 Gently roll out the ball, turn over and roll out the other side. Repeat this process until it forms a circular shape about 15cm (6 inches) in diameter. If the surface of the cake should burst during rolling, do not worry for it does not make much difference when cooked.

11 Heat a heavy frying pan until hot then add 30ml (2tbsp) oil. Put in one cake, lower the heat and fry, covered, for about 4-5 minutes or until spotted golden brown. Turn over and fry the other side, covered, for about the same length of time, checking to make sure it does not burn. Remove, drain on kitchen paper and keep warm on a warm serving plate.

12 Repeat steps 4 to 10 to prepare another cake while the first cake is being fried. Replenish the oil in the frying pan before frying the second cake. Repeat until all 6 cakes are cooked.

13 Cut each cake into 6 or 8 pieces and serve hot. If served as an hors d'oeuvre, cut into bite-sized pieces.

Note: spring onion cakes can be made ahead of time. They can be reheated either in a frying pan with a little oil or on a rack with margarine spread over them in a preheated oven at 180°C (350°F) mark 4 for 15 minutes, or until hot and crisp again. They also freeze well.

Dry-braised Yi Noodles

INGREDIENTS

2 Yi noodle cakes, 225g (8oz)
    (each cake is usually 25cm
    [10inches] in diameter)
25g (1oz) dried shrimps, rinsed
52.5ml (3½tbsp) groundnut or
    corn oil
3 cloves garlic, peeled and finely
    chopped
6mm (¼ inch) fresh ginger root,
    peeled and finely chopped
225g (8oz) cooked white crabmeat
1.25ml (¼tsp) salt
450-600ml (¾-1 pint) prime or
    clear stock (see page 225)
6 spring onions, sliced into 5-cm
    (2-inch) sections and cut into
    silken threads (see page 34)
7.5ml (½tbsp) thin soy sauce
45ml (3tbsp) oyster sauce

*Serves 8 as the last dish to end a
    dinner of 5-6 dishes*

Illustrated opposite

*Called in Chinese, "Noodles of the Yi Mansion," this dish is believed
to have been invented by the scholar-official, Yi Ping-shou, in the
18th century. Yi, with his gourmet palate for noodles, wanted them
kneaded only with egg, no water, then deep-fried before being
braised in the best stock. The Yi noodle cakes sold in Chinese stores
are already deep-fried.*

1 Put 2-2.3 litres (3½-4 pints) water in a large saucepan and bring
to the boil. Break each noodle cake into 3-4 pieces and submerge
them in the water. Return to the boil and continue to boil for about
1 minute or until the noodles are tender but not soggy. Drain in a
colander and leave aside. (If prepared several hours in advance,
rinse under cold running water.)

2 Soak the shrimps in just enough boiling water to cover them for
about 15 minutes. Drain them, reserving the soaking liquid. Chop
the shrimps into the size of matchstick heads.

3 Heat a wok over a high heat until smoke rises. Add 7.5ml (½tbsp)
of the oil and swirl it around. Add the shrimps, toss and stir for 1-2
minutes or until dry. Remove to a small dish.

4 Rinse and dry the wok and reheat over a high heat until smoke
rises. Add the remaining oil and swirl it around. Add the garlic and,
when it takes on colour, add the ginger and stir a few times. Add the
crabmeat and stir with the wok scoop or metal spatula. Season with
the salt.

5 Pour in the stock and bring to the boil. Add the noodles, mix with
the crabmeat and continue to cook over a moderate heat until most
of the stock has been absorbed. Add the spring onion, season with
the soy sauce and oyster sauce, and check for taste.

6 Remove to a warm serving dish. Sprinkle the shrimp on top and
serve.

Note: left-over noodles reheat well when a little stock is added to
them.

*Facing page, clockwise from the top: Deep-fried bean paste sauce with
noodles (see page 185); Tossed noodles with ginger and spring onion (see
page 183); Double-faced brown rice noodles with pork (see page 182);
Dry-braised Yi noodles (see above); Singapore fried rice sticks (see page
184)*

Double-faced Brown Noodles with Pork

INGREDIENTS
225g (8oz) dried or 350g (12oz) fresh Chinese egg noodles
225g (8oz) lean pork, boneless pork chop, shoulder, leg or fillet
6 dried medium Chinese mushrooms, reconstituted (see page 39)
180ml (12tbsp) groundnut or corn oil
2-3 cloves garlic, peeled and finely chopped
6 spring onions cut into 2.5-cm (1-inch) sections, white and green parts separated
15ml (1tbsp) Shaohsing wine or medium dry sherry
225g (8oz) bean sprouts
Chinese red vinegar (optional)

FOR THE MARINADE
2.5ml (½tsp) salt
2.5ml (½tsp) sugar
5ml (1tsp) thin soy sauce
5ml (1tsp) thick soy sauce
4 turns black pepper mill
5ml (1tsp) Shaohsing wine or medium dry sherry
4ml (¾tsp) potato flour
15ml (1tbsp) water

FOR THE SAUCE
12.5ml (2½tsp) potato flour
300ml (½ pint) stock and mushroom water
1.25ml (¼tsp) salt
15ml (1tbsp) thick soy sauce
10ml (2tsp) thin soy sauce
22.5ml (1½tbsp) oyster sauce

Serves 3 for lunch; 8 with 4 other dishes

Illustrated on page 181

A toasted noodle dish, crisp and golden brown on both sides – hence the name – but moist and soft in the middle. The contrast of texture in the noodles themselves is enhanced by the topping of stir-fried ingredients and a sauce which permeates the noodles; a delight to the palate! You can also make up your own toppings, for example chicken, prawn, fish or vegetables.

1 Plunge the noodles into 1.4 litres (2½ pints) boiling water in a large saucepan, bring back to the boil and continue to boil uncovered until they are *al dente*. (Generally 4 minutes for dried noodles, 1-1½ minutes for fresh noodles, but use your discretion or follow instructions on the packet.) Separate them with a pair of chopsticks or a fork while boiling.

2 Drain in a colander and immediately rinse thoroughly under cold running water. Leave to dry for 1 hour, turning them over once to ensure even drying.

3 Cut the pork into matchstick-sized pieces. Put into a bowl.

4 *Prepare the marinade:* add the salt, sugar, soy sauces, pepper, wine or sherry and potato flour to the pork. Stir in the water in the same direction to coat the meat thoroughly. Leave to marinate for 15-30 minutes.

5 Drain and squeeze out excess water from the mushrooms but leave damp. Slice into the thinnest possible strips. Reserve the soaking liquid.

6 *Prepare the sauce:* dissolve the potato flour with a little stock in a bowl. Add the salt, soy sauces and oyster sauce and the remaining stock and mushroom water. Put aside.

7 Heat a large flat frying pan over a high heat until hot. Add 105ml (7tbsp) of the oil to cover the surface and heat until smoke rises. Add the noodles and arrange them evenly to the edges like a pancake. Shallow fry for about 1 minute or until golden brown but not burned. Slip the wok scoop or a metal spatula underneath to check the colour and loosen edges. Adjust the heat if necessary. Either turn the cake over with the spatula or toss. Fry the other side until golden brown. Remove to a warm serving plate and keep warm in a cool oven with the door open.

8 Heat a wok over a high heat until smoke rises. Add 45ml (3tbsp) oil and swirl it around. Add the garlic, which will take on colour instantly, then add two-thirds of the white spring onion, and stir a couple of times. Put in the pork and flip and toss until it turns whitish. Pour in the wine or sherry and continue to stir while it

sizzles. Add the mushrooms and two-thirds of the green spring onion; flip and toss some more and remove to a warm plate.

9 Wash and dry the wok. Reheat over a high heat until smoke rises. Add 30ml (2tbsp) oil and swirl it around; add the remaining white spring onion and then the bean sprouts. Flip and toss vigorously and constantly for about 2 minutes or until just cooked and yet still crunchy and firm. Add the remaining green spring onion. Remove to a warm plate.

10 Lower the heat and pour in the well-stirred sauce. Slowly bring to the boil, stirring to prevent lumps. Pour in the cooked pork and bean sprouts, stirring to blend with the sauce. When hot, scoop evenly on to the noodle cake.

11 To facilitate serving, cut up the noodles with a pair of scissors or a knife and fork. Traditionally, red Chinese vinegar is served at the table to make digestion easier.

Tossed Noodles with Ginger and Spring Onion

If you wish to have a quick and simple yet appetizing bowl of noodles, here is the answer for you. They make an ideal lunch dish.

1 Plunge the noodles into 1.4 litres (2½ pints) of boiling water in a large saucepan, bring back to the boil and continue to boil uncovered until *al dente*. Generally, allow 1-1½ minutes for fresh noodles and 4 minutes for dried noodles. Separate the noodles with a pair of chopsticks or a fork while boiling.
2 Drain in a colander and then remove to a warm dish.
3 Heat a wok over a high heat until smoke rises. Add the oil and swirl it around. Add the ginger, stir for a few seconds, then add the spring onions and stir until thoroughly hot. Season with the salt. Remove from the heat.
4 Return the noodles to the wok and toss them with a pair of chopsticks or a fork. Add the oyster sauce and toss again. Remove to a warm serving dish and serve.

Variation: Tossed noodles with cucumber and ham.
Cut up ½ of a long cucumber and 100-175g (4-6oz) ham into matchstick-sized pieces. Cook the noodles as above. Add about 45ml (3tbsp) oil and the cucumber and ham. Toss together and serve.

INGREDIENTS
225g (8oz) fresh or 150g (5oz) dried Chinese egg noodles
45ml (3tbsp) groundnut or corn oil
5cm (2 inches) fresh ginger root, cut into silken threads (see page 35)
8 spring onions, cut into 5-cm (2-inch) sections and then into silken threads (see page 34)
2.5ml (½tsp) salt
30ml (2tbsp) oyster sauce

Serves 2

Illustrated on page 181

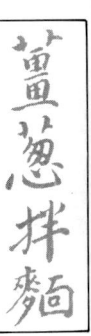

Singapore Fried Rice Sticks

It is always interesting to note how cuisines influence each other: fried rice sticks is a favourite Fukienese dish and when they emigrated to Singapore during the 19th century they took this dish with them. As time went by, curry spices were added to suit local taste, and they still remain as a distinctive element now that the dish has been readopted by the Southern Chinese.

INGREDIENTS

100g (4oz) fresh or frozen raw
  shrimps or prawns shelled
175g (6oz) dried rice sticks
150ml (¼ pint) groundnut or
  corn oil
1 egg, lightly beaten
1 small onion, skinned and
  shredded lengthwise
1 small green pepper, seeded and
  cut into matchstick-sized
  pieces
100g (4oz) char-siu (Cantonese
  roast pork, see page 134), cut
  into matchstick pieces
5ml (1tsp) curry powder

FOR THE MARINADE

1ml (⅕tsp) salt
2.5ml (½tsp) cornflour
15ml (1tbsp) egg white

FOR THE SAUCE

60ml (2fl oz) clear stock or water
4ml (¾tsp) salt
2.5ml (½tsp) sugar
15ml (1tbsp) thin soy sauce

Serves 3-4 as a snack

Illustrated on page 181

1 If frozen shrimps are used, defrost thoroughly, then pat dry. Put into a bowl. If prawns are used, devein and quarter.

2 *Prepare the marinade:* add the salt and cornflour to the shrimps and stir to mix. Add the egg white and stir vigorously in the same direction until the shrimps are well coated. Leave to marinate for 2-3 hours in the refrigerator.

3 Submerge the rice sticks in sufficiently hot but not boiling water to cover them completely. Soak for about 30 minutes until soft and pliable. Drain. Make several cuts with scissors to shorten their length so that they can be handled more easily.

4 *Prepare the sauce:* mix together the stock or water, salt, sugar and soy sauce.

5 Heat a frying pan until hot. Add 15ml (1tbsp) of the oil and swirl it to the edges. Turn the heat down, pour in the egg and, tilting the pan, spread it to the edges to make a crêpe. As soon as it is set, turn it over, fry the other side for a few seconds and remove to a plate. Slice into narrow strips about 5cm (2 inches) long.

6 Heat a wok over a high heat until smoke rises. Add 60ml (4tbsp) of the oil and swirl it around. Add the onion and turn and stir for about 30 seconds. Add the shrimps and toss and turn in rapid succession for about 1 minute or until cooked and turning pinkish. Scoop up on to a dish, leaving as much oil behind as possible.

7 Tip the green pepper into the wok and stir for about 30 seconds. Add the char-siu and stir together for another minute or until piping hot. Scoop up on to a dish.

8 Add another 60ml (4tbsp) of the oil to the wok and swirl it around. Add the curry powder and let it sizzle for a few seconds. Add the rice sticks and sauce. Holding 2 pairs of chopsticks or 2 large wooden spoons with both hands, lift and toss the rice sticks until they have absorbed almost all the sauce. Also add the remaining oil around the side of the wok to prevent the rice sticks from sticking. Taste, and if they are hard rather than *al dente*, add 30-45ml (2-3tbsp) stock or water and cook for 1-2 minutes over a low heat with the wok cover on. Return the onion, shrimps, green pepper, char-siu and egg to the wok, toss and mix with the rice sticks. Remove to a warm serving dish. Serve immediately.

Deep-fried Bean-paste Sauce with Noodles

Because wheat is grown in such large quantities in the north of China, noodles form an important part of the staple diet for the people of that area. On the whole, unlike the Southern Chinese, they do not put their noodles in soup; they prefer them dressed in a sauce. This is a celebrated Peking sauce.

1 *Prepare the bean-paste:* chop the pork by hand or mince coarsely. Heat a wok over a high heat until smoke rises. Add the oil and swirl it around. Tip in the spring onion, turn and toss for about 20-30 seconds to release its fragrance. Add the pork and, sliding the wok scoop or metal spatula to the bottom of the wok, flip and toss for about 1 minute, separating any lumps. Splash in the wine or sherry around the side of the wok, continuing to stir for another 1-2 minutes. Remove to a dish and keep nearby. If water oozes from the mixture, drain.

2 Add the 350ml (12fl oz) oil to a deep heavy saucepan (or a wok). Heat until just hot (about 170°C [325°F]). Gently add the yellow bean sauce and hoisin sauce and lower the heat as there will be fierce sizzling and splashing when the sauces touch the oil. The oil must cover the sauces. Deep-fry for about 6-7 minutes or until the sauce becomes thicker, stirring gently with a wooden spoon to prevent it from sticking, turning the heat up again if necessary.

3 Add the pork and continue to deep-fry for another 12-15 minutes or until most of the steam has evaporated. Stir all the time and adjust the heat accordingly to prevent the sauce from burning.

4 Remove from the heat and leave to cool. Scoop the bean-paste into glass jars or earthenware pots. Cover it with at least 2.5cm (1 inch) of the oil. The bean-paste, if stored in the larder or refrigerator, can be kept for several months.

5 *Prepare the bean-paste with noodles:* put about 450ml (16fl oz) water with 2.5ml (½tsp) of the salt and 7.5ml (1½tsp) oil in a saucepan and bring to the boil. Add the bean sprouts and return to the boil. Pour immediately into a colander and refresh under cold running water. Drain thoroughly.

6 Bring a large pan of water to the boil with the remaining salt added. Add the noodles and boil for about 4 minutes or until just cooked. Pour into a colander and drain.

7 Transfer to a serving bowl or a platter. Sprinkle with the bean sprouts and cucumber.

8 To eat, each person helps themselves to a bowl of noodles and some topping, then mixes some bean-paste, starting with no more than 15ml (1tbsp), into the noodles.

INGREDIENTS

FOR THE BEAN-PASTE
450g (1lb) pork, leg or shoulder, with about 50g (2oz) fat
45ml (3tbsp) groundnut or corn oil
350g (12oz) spring onions, cut into small rounds
15ml (1tbsp) Shaohsing wine or medium dry sherry
350ml (12fl oz) groundnut or corn oil
700g (1½lb) ground yellow bean sauce
350g (12oz) hoisin sauce

FOR THE BEAN-PASTE WITH NOODLES
7.5ml (1½tsp) salt
7.5ml (1½tsp) groundnut or corn oil
225g (8oz) bean sprouts
450g (1lb) dried Chinese noodles or thin spaghetti, Korean or Japanese U-Dong
½ long cucumber, about 350g (12oz) cut into matchstick-sized pieces
deep-fried bean-paste (above)

Serves 4 as a light meal

Illustrated on page 181

A Mixed Regional Menu

In planning your own menu, I urge you to mix the different regional dishes so that you can get the full benefit of the various tastes and flavours from the four corners of China. This menu for eight should be but a starting point for you.

獅 **Lion's head**
子 Tender pork meatballs
頭 offset by the crisp cabbage
and water chestnuts
(see page 222).

八 **Eight-treasure rice**
寶 **pudding**
飯 Decorative dessert
combining boiled rice and
dried fruits – served with a
sweet syrup (see page 224).

麻辣子雞 **Yu-ling's hot and numbing chicken**
An intriguing dish, deriving its heat from chillies and Szechwan peppercorns (see page 223).

蠔豉燉菜 好市發財 **Dried oysters and hair algae**
An unusual New Year dish combining stir-fried pork, oysters and mushrooms with algae (see page 221)

葱爆羊肉 **Paper-thin lamb with spring onions**
Tender pieces of lamb stir-fried with plenty of spring onions rightly make this one of Peking's most famous dishes (see page 223).

白灼時菜 **Plain boiled vegetables**
Chinese flowering cabbage, briefly boiled and served with oyster sauce (see page 222).

Almond Bean Curd

INGREDIENTS

1 litre (1¾ pints) water
about 130ml (8 heaped tbsp) or
7g (¼oz) cut-up agar-agar
75ml (5 tbsp) sugar
175ml (6fl oz) evaporated milk
15ml (1tbsp) almond essence
1 large can lychees

Serves 6

Illustrated opposite

In cookery, the Chinese often enjoy making up a dish to resemble the looks, if not also the taste, of a particular ingredient, giving the dish the same name. This very light and delightful summer dessert, which looks like bean curd is, in fact, not bean curd at all!

1 Put the water in a saucepan and bring to the boil. Add the agar-agar, reduce the heat and simmer to dissolve for 20-25 minutes, stirring occasionally.

2 Add the sugar and stir until completely dissolved.

3 Remove the saucepan from the heat. Pour in the evaporated milk and stir once.

4 Strain the mixture through a fine sieve into a serving bowl, discarding any dregs from the agar-agar.

5 Stir in the almond essence. Leave to cool and set, then put into the refrigerator to chill.

6 Cut the "bean curd" into diamond-shaped pieces. Put into a serving dish and top with lychees. Serve cold.

Note: other fruits, fresh or canned, like kiwi, peaches, grapes, pineapple, mangoes, etc. can also be used. Instead of agar-agar, about 30ml (6 tsp) powdered gelatin can be used.

Facing page, clockwise from the top: Apples or bananas pulling golden threads (see page 190); Almond bean curd (see above); Red bean paste pancakes (see page 191)

Apples or Bananas Pulling Golden Threads

INGREDIENTS

3 apples, Granny Smith or
   Golden Delicious or 3 fairly
   large bananas, on the unripe
   side
15ml (1tbsp) plain flour
groundnut or corn oil for
   deep-frying
90ml (6tbsp) fresh groundnut or
   corn oil
135ml (9tbsp) sugar
6ml (1 heaped tsp) white sesame
   seeds

FOR THE BATTER

100g (4oz) self-raising flour
1 large egg, lightly beaten
about 120ml (8tbsp) water
15ml (1tbsp) groundnut or corn
   oil

Serves 6-8

Illustrated on page 189

In this recipe, an ingenious and foolproof Chinese method of caramelizing sugar in a few tablespoonfuls of hot oil is used in the preparation of this delicious dessert. What's more, the oil is then separated from the caramel and can be reused for other cooking.

1 *Prepare the batter:* sift the flour into a mixing bowl and stir in the egg. Add the water gradually and stir to blend into a smooth batter, like thick cream in consistency. Leave to stand for about 15 minutes, then blend in the oil.

2 Peel and core the apples or peel the bananas and remove any strings. Divide each apple or roll-cut each banana into 8 pieces (see page 34). Sprinkle on the plain flour and toss well to mix.

3 Half fill a wok or deep-fryer with oil. Heat to a temperature of 180°C (350°F) or until a cube of stale bread browns in 60 seconds. One by one, dip the fruit pieces into the batter. Add to the oil and deep-fry for about 2-3 minutes or until pale golden. Remove with a pair of chopsticks or perforated disc and drain on kitchen paper. (This can be done several hours in advance.) Reheat the oil to the same temperature. Deep-fry the fruits for a second time for about 1 minute or until crisp and golden in colour. Remove with a hand strainer or perforated disc and drain on kitchen paper.

4 Fill a large bowl with water and ice cubes and keep nearby.

5 Heat a well-cleaned and salt-free wok or heavy saucepan over a high heat. Add the fresh oil, swirl it around and heat until smoke rises. Add the sugar and let it dissolve in the oil over a moderately high heat, stirring all the time (a). Almost as soon as the sugar has completely dissolved, it will turn light brown in colour. Immediately add all the fruit pieces (b) and sprinkle on the sesame seeds (c). Using two wok scoops or spatulas, toss the pieces around to coat them with the caramelized syrup (d). This must be done with care and speed. Remove to a large plate (e) then immediately dip them, one by one, into the bowl of iced water so that the caramel sets. As they are put into the bowl you will see the threads being pulled (f).

a

b

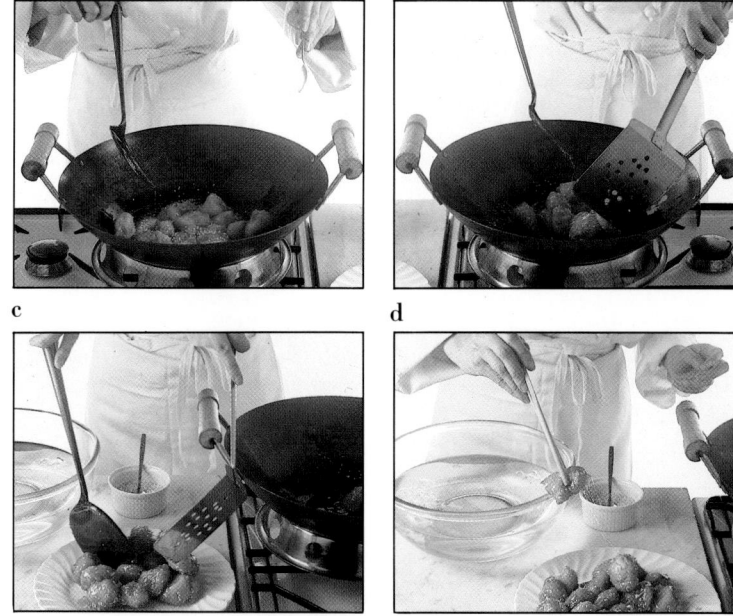

c

d

e

f

6 Quickly lift the pieces from the iced water and put on to a serving plate. Serve immediately.

Red Bean Paste Pancakes

This Northern pudding, consisting of two sweet, stuffed pancakes, is both crisp and soft to the bite.

1 In a mixing bowl blend the egg and flour together to a paste. Stir in the water, gradually diluting the paste to a thin, runny consistency. Divide the mixture into 2 equal portions.

2 Put a smear of oil on a 20-cm (8-inch) flat, non-stick frying pan and wipe all over with kitchen paper. Pour all but 5ml (1tsp) of one portion of the mixture into the frying pan and tilt it to let the mixture run evenly to the edges, forming a thin layer.

3 Cook over a low heat for about 2 minutes or until it becomes a thin pancake but without any brown spots. Do not turn the pancake over.

4 Loosen the edges and, using a palette knife, lift the pancake on to a lightly-oiled plate or a flat surface.

5 Make the other pancake the same way.

INGREDIENTS
1 large egg, lightly beaten
75ml (5 tbsp) plain flour
60ml (4tbsp) water
a little groundnut or corn oil
60ml (4tbsp) canned red bean
   paste
groundnut or corn oil for
   deep-frying

Serves 4-6

Illustrated on page 189

6 Spread 30ml (2tbsp) of the red bean paste across the middle third of each pancake, leaving about 2.5cm (1 inch) at either end. Fold the near flap over the bean paste (a), and the side flaps inwards (b). Smear a little beaten egg or water along the edge of the remaining flap (c), then fold the flap down towards the centre to seal the pancake (d).

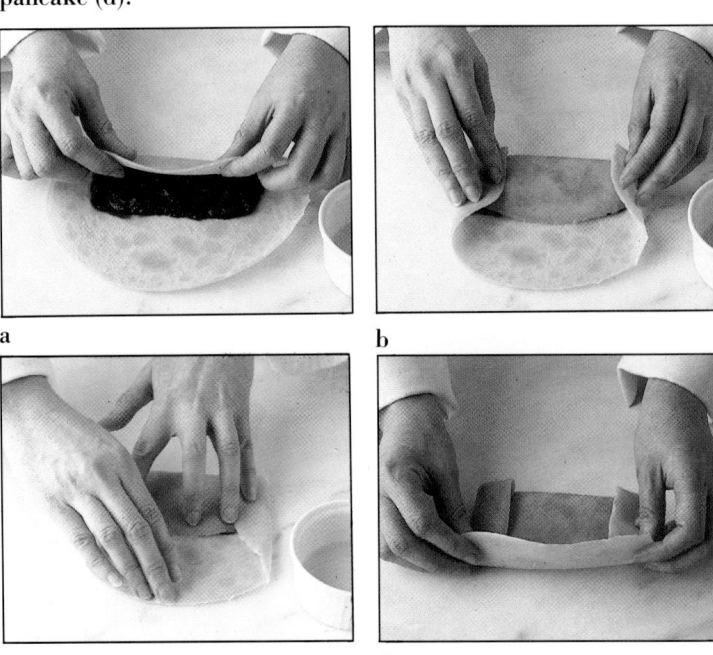

a

b

c

d

7 Half fill a wok or deep-fryer with oil. Heat to a temperature of 180°C (350°F) or until a cube of stale bread browns in 60 seconds. Add the pancakes, smooth side up first, and deep-fry for 3-4 minutes or until golden in colour, turning over periodically for even browning. The pancakes will puff up so take care they do not burst. Remove with a perforated disc.

8 Reheat the oil to 180°C (350°F) and fry the pancakes for a few seconds to recrisp. Remove and drain on kitchen paper.

9 Transfer the pancakes to a warm serving plate. Cut each across into 8 strips and serve immediately.

SPECIAL MENUS

DEEP-FRIED APPETIZERS

Deep-fried Wontons

A popular cold starter or a snack that is part and parcel of Cantonese dimsum.

INGREDIENTS

6 medium raw prawns in the shell, without heads
egg white, lightly beaten
72 wonton wrappers, each 7.5cm (3 inches) square
groundnut or corn oil for deep-frying

FOR THE SWEET AND SOUR SAUCE

300ml (½ pint) water
60ml (4tbsp) sugar
45ml (3tbsp) rice or wine vinegar
4ml (¾tsp) salt
30ml (2tbsp) tomato ketchup
12.5ml (2½tsp) potato flour, dissolved in 30ml (2tbsp) water
1.25 (¼tsp) red food colouring (optional)

Serves 8

1 *Prepare the sweet and sour sauce:* put the water, sugar, vinegar, salt and ketchup in a saucepan and bring to simmering point. Gradually add the dissolved potato flour, stirring as the sauce thickens. Stir in the food colouring. Pour into one or two serving bowls and leave to cool.

2 If frozen prawns are used, defrost thoroughly. Shell the prawns, devein (see page 39) and pat dry. Cut each one into 6 cubes.

3 *Prepare the wontons:* pick up 2 wrappers together, one on top of the other, and place them on the fingers of one hand in the shape of a diamond. Place 1 cube of prawn just above the lower triangular point (a). Fold the wrappers over the prawn and roll towards the centre, stopping just short of mid-way (b). Dip the index finger of the other hand into the egg white and then smear either the right or left corner of the bottom wrapper. Fold backwards towards the centre, then put on top of the other corner and pinch the two together to seal (c). Separate the 2 triangular flaps, turn one towards you, and the other away from

you (d). Turn it over and you will find the cube of prawn wrapped in the centre. Repeat until all are done.

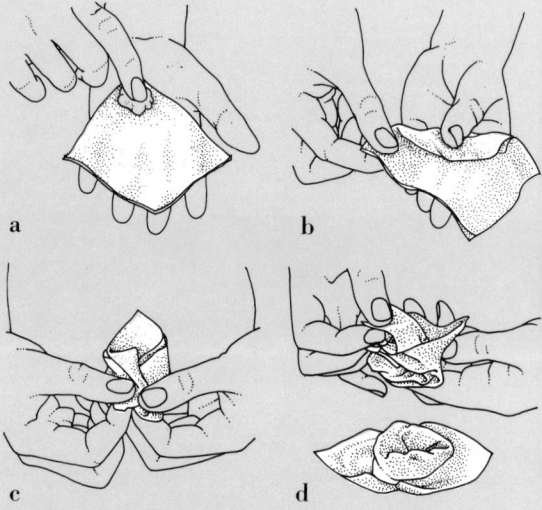

4 Half fill a wok or deep-fryer with oil. Heat to a temperature of 180°C (350°F) or until a cube of stale bread browns in 60 seconds. Tip in 8-10 wontons, or however many will float freely, and deep-fry for about 40-60 seconds or until golden in colour and crisp in the centre. Remove with a hand strainer or perforated disc and drain on kitchen paper. Repeat until all are fried.

5 The wontons will stay crisp for several hours and can be served either warm or cold.

6 To eat, spoon sweet and sour sauce on each wonton, then pick up with either chopsticks or fingers.

Note: if left overnight, deep-fried wontons will lose their crispness. They can, however, be turned into Wonton Wrapper Crisps Soup (see page 66).

Deep-fried Five-spice Rolls

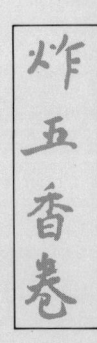

Five-spice powder lends this dish its name as well as its characteristic aroma. In Fukien, where this dish originates from, ducks' eggs, both the white and the yolk, are used because of their stronger taste.

INGREDIENTS

1 packet dried bean curd sheet (usually 225g [8oz] containing 8 sheets, each 32.5 x 15cm [13 x 6 inches])

12 spring onions, white parts only, cut into small rounds

175g (6oz) water chestnuts, fresh peeled or canned drained

700g (1½lb) pork with some fat

45ml (3tbsp) potato flour

2 egg yolks

groundnut or corn oil for deep-frying

FOR THE MARINADE

5ml (1tsp) salt

10ml (2tsp) thin soy sauce

12.5ml (2½ tsp) sugar

25ml (5tsp) Shaohsing wine or medium dry sherry

10ml (2tsp) sesame oil

10ml (2tsp) five-spice powder

1½ egg whites

FOR THE DIPS

tomato ketchup

chilli sauce

15ml (1tbsp) thick soy sauce mixed with 5ml (1tsp) hot made-up mustard

Serves 12

1 Soak the bean curd sheets in cold water for about 4 minutes or until the sheets are soft and pliable. Lift each sheet carefully with both hands to drain, blot excess water dry and place flat on a large tea towel, one on top of another. Put another tea towel on top to keep them moist. This step can be done 2-3 hours ahead.

2 Chop the water chestnuts by hand or mince coarsely.

3 Chop the pork by hand or mince coarsely. Put into a large bowl.

4 *Prepare the marinade:* add the salt, soy sauce, sugar, wine or sherry, oil, five-spice powder and egg whites to the pork. Stir in the same direction to coat well. Leave to marinate for 5 minutes. Add the spring onion and water chestnut. Stir in the potato flour, 15ml (1tbsp) at a time, to ensure smooth mixing.

5 Divide the pork filling into 16 portions.

6 Take one bean curd sheet out of the covered pile and put it on a flat surface with the 32.5cm (13 inch) wide side in front of you. Halve it.

7 Scoop up one portion of the filling and roll it between your palms into the shape of a sausage. Place the filling near the bottom edge of 1 piece of bean curd sheet and roll as tightly as possible away from you (a). Using either your fingers or a brush, smear some egg yolk on the opposite edge (b) and seal the roll. Leave the 2 ends open and place the roll on a tray, seam side down. Cover the tray with a damp cloth. Repeat steps 6 and 7 until all are made.

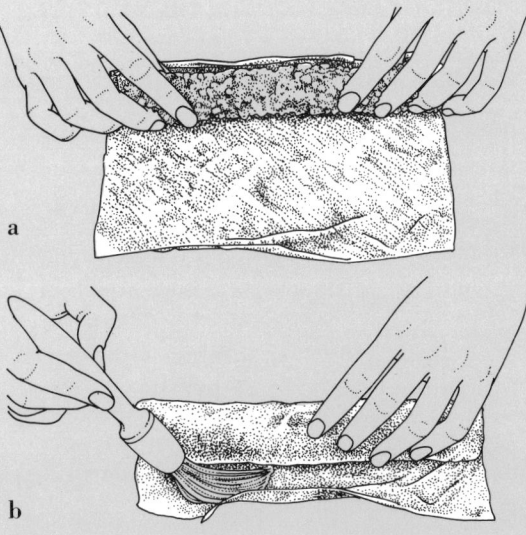

a

b

8 Half fill a wok or deep-fryer with oil. Heat to a temperature of 190°C (375°F) or until a cube of stale bread browns in 50 seconds. Put in 8 rolls or however many will float freely in the oil and deep-fry for about 8 minutes or until honey-brown in colour. Remove with a hand strainer or perforated disc and drain on kitchen paper. Repeat until all the rolls are done.

9 To serve, cut each roll into 5 pieces and put them on a large warm platter. The ketchup, chilli sauce and soy sauce with mustard dips can be put either on the table or in the middle of the platter.

Special Spring Rolls

特式春卷

Spring rolls, also known as egg rolls, comprise a filling wrapped in a thin dough, deep-fried until crispy. The more tasty the filling and the thinner the dough wrapper, the more delicious the spring roll.

INGREDIENTS

450g (1lb) carrots, peeled and cut into strips
175g (6oz) cellophane noodles
10 medium dried Chinese mushrooms, reconstituted (see page 39)
225g (8oz) lean pork
225g (8oz) raw shrimps or 300g (10oz) medium prawns in the shell but without heads
225g (8oz) mange tout or French beans, trimmed
75ml (5tbsp) groundnut or corn oil
4 cloves garlic, peeled and finely chopped
1-2cm (½-¾ inch) fresh ginger root, peeled and finely chopped
6-8 spring onions, cut into small rounds
15ml (1tbsp) Shaohsing wine or medium dry sherry
175g (6oz) canned bamboo shoots, cut into matchstick-sized strips
30ml (2tbsp) thin soy sauce
30-35 pieces large spring roll wrappers, about 21-23.5cm (8½-9½ inches) square
lightly beaten egg white
groundnut or corn oil for deep-frying

FOR THE MARINADE

2.5ml (½tsp) salt
1.25ml (¼tsp) sugar
10ml (2tsp) thin soy sauce
6 turns pepper mill
5ml (1tsp) Shaohsing wine or medium dry sherry
5ml (1tsp) sesame oil
5ml (1tsp) potato flour
22.5ml (1½tbsp) water

FOR THE SHRIMP MARINADE

1.25ml (¼tsp) salt
1.25ml (¼tsp) sugar
10ml (2tsp) thin soy sauce
4 turns pepper mill
5ml (1tsp) sesame oil

Serves 10-15

1 Put the carrots into a bowl and add 5ml (1tsp) salt to draw out the water. Drain after 30 minutes. Pat dry, if necessary.

2 Put the cellophane noodles into a large bowl and pour over 1.1 litres (2 pints) boiling water. Cover and leave to soak and expand for at least 30 minutes. Drain well. Cut up roughly.

3 Drain and squeeze out excess water from the mushrooms but leave damp. Shred into thin slivers (do not use a food processor).

4 Cut the pork into matchstick-sized pieces. Put into a bowl.

5 *Prepare the pork marinade:* add the salt, sugar, soy sauce, pepper, wine or sherry, oil, potato flour and water to the pork. Stir well to coat. Leave to marinate for 15-30 minutes.

6 Shell and devein the prawns if necessary (see page 39); slice into pieces similar in size to the pork. If shrimps are used, however, they can be left whole or halved. Put into a bowl.

7 *Prepare the shrimp marinade:* add the salt, sugar, soy sauce, pepper, and oil to the shrimps. Leave to marinate for 15 minutes.

8 Cut the mange tout or French beans diagonally into strips similar to the bamboo shoot.

9 Heat a wok over a high heat until smoke rises. Add 45ml (3tbsp) of the oil and swirl it around. Add the garlic, half the ginger and half the spring onion. When the garlic sizzles and takes on colour, add the pork and turn and toss with the wok scoop for about 30 seconds. Add the shrimps and continue to flip and turn for another minute. Splash in the wine along the edge of the wok and continue to flip and toss. When the sizzling dies down, put in the mushrooms and bamboo shoots. Stir until hot. Remove and cool.

10 Pour the remaining oil into the wok and swirl it around. Add the remaining ginger and spring onion. Add the mange tout and stir-fry for 1 minute. Stir in the carrots and then the cellophane noodles. Continue to stir until hot over a less fierce heat, letting any excess water evaporate. Season with 4ml (¾tsp) salt and the 30ml (2tbsp) thin soy sauce. Remove to a large dish and leave to cool.

11 Place a spring roll wrapper on a flat dish or a clear surface, arranging it in a diamond shape. Put about 30ml (2tbsp) of the vegetable filling just off the centre and top with about 15ml (1tbsp) of the other filling. Spread it out about 12.5cm (5 inches)

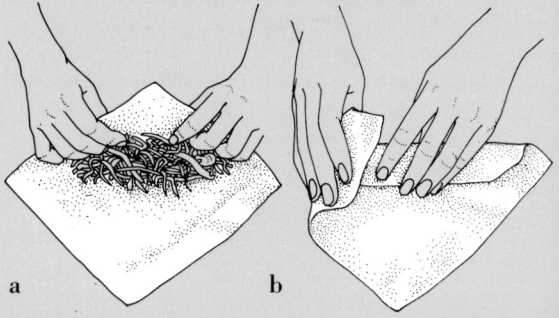

a   b

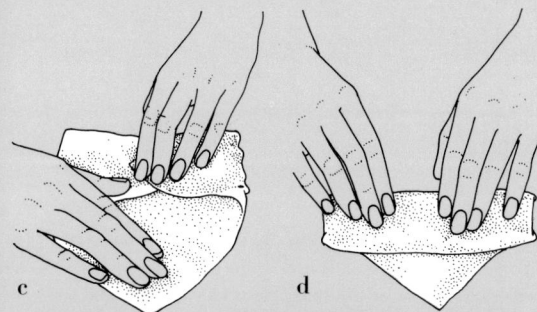

c   d

wide. Tucking in the filling, fold up the bottom flap (a) and start rolling. Midway, fold the 2 side flaps towards the centre (b), brush the remaining flap with the egg white (c) and fold it up (d) to seal the spring roll tightly. Repeat until all are done.

12 Half fill a wok or deep-fryer with oil. Heat to a temperature of 180°C (350°F) or until a cube of stale bread browns in 60 seconds. Carefully add about 6-8 spring rolls at a time or however many will float freely and deep-fry for about 4 minutes or until pale golden, turning over periodically. Remove with a hand strainer or perforated disc and drain on kitchen paper. To crisp, reheat the oil to 180°C (350°F) and deep-fry a second time for 1-2 minutes or until golden. Drain and serve hot.

Note: spring rolls can be frozen after the first deep-frying. The second deep-frying can therefore be done just before they are served.

Stuffed Crab Claws

Biting into crabmeat and prawn at the same time produces a rich and luxurious feeling. These crisp and juicy crab claws are as good to look at as they are to eat, so they are bound to be a successful starter for a dinner party. You can prepare in advance up to the end of step 6, and then simply recrisp the claws just before serving.

INGREDIENTS
550g (1¼lb) fresh or frozen medium raw prawns in the shell, without heads
75g (3oz) pork fat
60ml (4tbsp) cornflour
12 medium fresh or frozen cooked and shelled crab claws
groundnut or corn oil for deep-frying

FOR THE MARINADE
5ml (1tsp) salt
2.5ml (½tsp) sugar
5ml (1tsp) cornflour
1 egg white, lightly beaten
5ml (1tsp) sesame oil

FOR THE DIPS
chilli sauce
Worcestershire sauce

Serves 6

1 If frozen prawns and crab claws are used, defrost thoroughly. Shell and devein the prawns (see page 39). Pat dry with kitchen paper.

2 Chop the prawns and pork fat by hand or mince coarsely. Put in a bowl.

3 *Prepare the marinade:* add the salt, sugar and cornflour to the prawns and pork fat. Stir vigorously in the same direction for about 1 minute, or until the mixture becomes sticky. Add the egg white and stir again for about 1 minute or until the paste is firm and elastic. Cover and leave to marinate in the refrigerator for about 30 minutes. Blend in the sesame oil.

4 Put the 60ml (4 tbsp) cornflour in a bowl. Holding the pincers of one crab claw, dip the meaty part in the cornflour (a), shaking off any excess. Repeat with the rest of the claws.

5 *Stuff the claws:* divide the prawn paste into 12 portions. Lightly oil a plate. Holding the claw by the pincers, press a portion of the paste on to the meat, covering a small area of the shell to seal it (b). Place on the lightly oiled plate. Repeat with the rest of the claws. To prevent your fingers from getting too sticky, wet them with cold water.

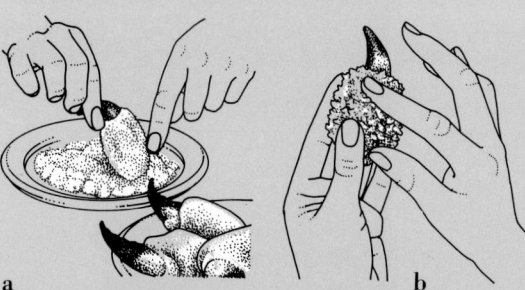

a   b

6 Half fill a wok or deep-fryer with oil. Heat to a temperature of 180°C (350°F) or until a cube of stale bread browns in 60 seconds. Carefully lower 6 claws into the oil, 1 at a time. Deep-fry for about 4 minutes or until golden, turning each one occasionally. Remove each claw with a perforated disc or tongs and drain on kitchen paper. Repeat with the remaining 6 claws.

7 Deep-fry all 12 claws together for a few seconds to crisp. Remove and drain. Serve the claws immediately. Pass the dips in separate saucers.

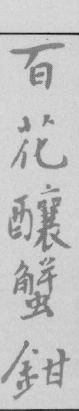

Deep-fried Milk

This is a very popular dish in Hong Kong: it satisfies the ever-present Chinese craving for a contrast between a crunchy and a tender texture in food. In the same mouthful, one can experience a smooth and creamy filling wrapped in a crispy batter coating. The recipe works equally well without the crabmeat.

INGREDIENTS
100g (4oz) solid creamed coconut
100g (4oz) cooked crabmeat (optional)
6.25ml (1¼tsp) salt
6 turns white pepper mill
75ml (5tbsp) cornflour
600ml (1 pint) milk
groundnut or corn oil for deep frying

FOR THE BATTER
150g (5oz) plain white flour
75ml (5tbsp) cornflour
7.5ml (1½tsp) baking powder
235ml (8½fl oz) water
30ml (2tbsp) groundnut or corn oil

Serves 8

1 Grate the creamed coconut and put the shavings into a saucepan.

2 Add the crabmeat, salt and pepper to the creamed coconut.

3 Stir in the cornflour and some of the milk and blend to a smooth paste. Then, over gentle heat, gradually add the remaining milk, stirring in the same direction all the time until the mixture has become well amalgamated and thickened.

4 Pour into a well-oiled shallow container 20cm (8 inches) square or 18-23cm (7-9 inches) rectangular and leave to set in the refrigerator for 2 hours. It can be left overnight covered with cling film.

5 *Prepare the batter:* sift the plain flour and cornflour into a large bowl, add the baking powder. Gradually stir in the water and blend to a smooth, runny consistency. Leave to stand at room temperature for a minimum of 30 minutes. Blend in the oil.

6 Loosen the well-set milk mixture with an oiled palette knife. Use an oiled knife to cut the mixture into about 32 diamond-shaped pieces.

7 Half fill a wok or deep-fryer with oil. Heat to a temperature of 190°C (375°F) or until a cube of stale bread browns in 50 seconds. Dip several pieces into the batter and, using either a pair of chopsticks or tongs, put the pieces one by one into the oil. Deep-fry about 12 at a time, or however many will float freely, for about 3 minutes or until pale golden. Remove with a hand strainer or perforated disc and drain on kitchen paper. Repeat until all are done. Remove the "bearded" excess batter with a pair of scissors.

8 To crisp, reheat the oil to 190°C (375°F) and deep-fry the pieces again briefly in 2 batches, each for about 1 minute. Remove and drain on kitchen paper. Serve immediately.

Deep-fried Phoenix-tail Prawns

This dish derives its name from the Chinese emblem of beauty, the phoenix, whose long and graceful tail the prawns are likened to.

INGREDIENTS
450g (1lb) fresh or frozen medium raw prawns in the shell, without heads
2.5ml (½tsp) salt
few turns white pepper mill
1 large green pepper, seeded
groundnut or corn oil for deep-frying

FOR THE BATTER
150g (5oz) plain flour
75ml (5tbsp) cornflour
7.5ml (1½tsp) baking powder
235ml (8½fl oz) water
2.5ml (½tsp) salt
30ml (2tbsp) groundnut or corn oil

Serves 6

1 *Prepare the batter:* sift the plain flour and cornflour into a large bowl, add the baking powder. Gradually whisk in the water and blend to a smooth consistency. Leave to stand for a minimum of 30 minutes. Just before using, add the salt and blend in the oil until the batter is smooth and shiny.

2 If frozen prawns are used, defrost thoroughly. Remove the shells but leave the tail intact. Devein (see page 39) and pat dry on kitchen paper.

3 Turn the prawns upside down, one by one, and make 3 slashes across the abdomen without cutting through completely. This prevents them from curling up when deep-fried. Add the salt and pepper.

4 Cut the green pepper into rectangular pieces.

5 Half fill a wok or deep-fryer with oil. Heat to a temperature of 190°C (375°F) or until a cube of stale bread browns in 50 seconds.

6 Hold the prawn by its tail and coat the rest of its body in the batter. Lift by the tail and let some of the runny batter drip off. Put into the oil. Add about half of the prawns at a time or as many as will float freely. Deep-fry for about 3 minutes or until the batter is pale golden in colour. Remove with a hand strainer or perforated disc and drain on kitchen paper. Snip off any "bearded" excess batter with a pair of scissors.

7 While the prawns are in the oil, put half of the green pepper in the batter and add to the oil to fry with the prawns. Remove them when they look pale golden in colour and drain on kitchen paper.

8 Deep-fry the remaining prawns and green pepper.

9 To serve, pile the green pepper in the middle of a platter and arrange the prawns around it with their tails facing outwards.

Note: to reheat, either deep-fry the prawns and green pepper for about 30 seconds until the batter is crisp again or put under a preheated grill.

Prawns Wrapped in Rice Paper

This classic dish is one of the Cantonese dimsum delicacies.

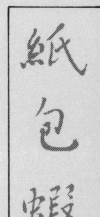

INGREDIENTS
450g (1lb) fresh or frozen medium raw prawns in the shell, without heads
1 egg white, lightly beaten
5ml (1tsp) salt
2.5ml (½tsp) sugar
10ml (2tsp) cornflour
50g (2oz) pork fat, chopped into size of matchstick heads
75g (3oz) lean ham, chopped into size of matchstick heads
100g (4oz) canned bamboo shoots, chopped into size of matchstick heads
4-6 spring onions, cut into tiny rounds
15 sheets rice paper
groundnut or corn oil for deep-frying
chilli sauce to serve

Makes about 28 rolls

1 If frozen prawns are used, defrost thoroughly. Shell and devein the prawns (see page 39). Pat dry with kitchen paper.

2 Chop the prawns roughly. Put into a bowl.

3 Add the egg white, salt, sugar and cornflour to the prawns. Stir in the same direction until well coated.

4 Add the pork fat, ham and bamboo shoots to the prawns and stir well. Mix in the spring onion.

5 Cut the rice paper sheets into 30 squares, each 10cm (4 inches).

6 Have some cold water in a dish nearby. Put 1 rice paper square on a plate or work surface. Spread on about 15ml (1tbsp) of the filling, almost to the edges. Fold over and roll into a small cigar, leaving both ends open. Seal with a little water smeared on the edge.

7 Half fill a wok or deep-fryer with oil. Heat to a temperature of 190°C (375°F) or until a cube of stale bread browns in 50 seconds. Using a pair of chopsticks or tongs, lower half of the prawn rolls into the oil. Deep-fry for about 3 minutes until the filling is cooked and the rice paper crisp. Remove with a hand strainer or perforated disc and drain on kitchen paper. Deep-fry the remainder.

8 Reheat the oil to about 180°C (350°F). Put in all the prawn rolls and deep-fry a second time for a few seconds, then remove and drain on kitchen paper. This makes them extra crisp and fragrant.

9 Serve hot with chilli sauce.

SZECHWAN MENU

Fragrant and Crispy Duck

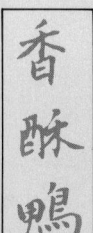

Deep-fried to golden brown, the meat is nevertheless so tender that it comes away from the bones merely with the help of a pair of chopsticks. And therein lies the secret of this Szechwan duck.

INGREDIENTS
1 oven-ready duck,
  1.8-2.3kg (4-5lb)
30ml (2tbsp) thin soy
  sauce
30-45ml (2-3tbsp) plain
  white flour
groundnut or corn oil for
  deep-frying
12 lotus leaf buns (see
  below)
ground roasted Szechwan
  peppercorns and salt
  to serve (see page 52,
  omitting the five-spice
powder)

FOR THE MARINADE
30ml (2tbsp) Shaohsing
  wine or medium dry
  sherry
15ml (1tbsp) salt
scant 5ml (1tsp) five-spice
  powder
4 slices fresh ginger root,
  peeled
3 spring onions, halved

Serves 6 with 3 other dishes

1 *Prepare the marinade:* rub the wine or sherry, salt and five-spice powder all over the duck skin and inside the cavity. Put the ginger and spring onion inside the cavity. Leave to marinate for at least 6 hours or overnight.

2 Put the duck in a heatproof bowl or dish with raised sides. Steam in a wok or steamer for 1¾-2 hours (see page 45). Quite a lot of fat and juice will collect in the bowl. (The juice, after the fat has been skimmed off, can be used as a tasty stock.)

3 Remove the duck from the bowl and stand it on a rack to let all the juice run out. Place the duck on another dish or stand it up to dry for 30 minutes or longer. Care must be taken to keep the duck whole at this stage.

4 Remove all the ginger and spring onion from the cavity.

5 Brush the duck skin with the soy sauce. Dust all over with flour.

6 Half fill a wok or deep-fryer with oil. Heat to a temperature of 190°C (375°F) or until a cube of stale bread browns in 50 seconds. Place the duck in the oil and deep-fry over a low to moderate heat for about 2 minutes. With a wooden spoon or spatula held in one hand and another put inside the cavity, turn the duck over and deep-fry the other side for 2 more minutes. Repeat this process for a total of 8 minutes, after which time the skin should be golden brown. Drain on kitchen paper.

7 Steam the lotus leaf buns for about 5 minutes or until hot.

8 Place the duck on a warm serving plate and put the buns around it. Serve at the table with either a fork and knife or a pair of chopsticks. The skin of the duck should be so crisp and the meat so tender that they come away easily from the bones as pressure from the chopsticks is applied. Dip in ground peppercorns and salt and eat with the buns. Silver thread buns also go well with the duck.

Bun Accompaniments

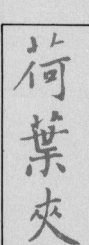

So called because they resemble lotus leaves and silver threads, these buns are the standard accompaniment to the Szechwan fragrant and crispy duck.

Lotus Leaf Buns

INGREDIENTS
2.5ml (½tsp) dried yeast
5ml (1tsp) sugar
175ml (6 fl oz) tepid water
275g (10oz) plain flour

7g (¼oz) lard
little extra flour
15ml (1tbsp) groundnut
  or corn oil
Makes 24 buns

1 Put the dried yeast and sugar in a small bowl, add the water and stir. Leave in a warm place until the yeast froths on the surface.

2 Sift the flour into a mixing bowl. Rub in the lard. Stir in the yeast liquid and work it into a dough. Knead lightly for 1-2 minutes until the dough is smooth. Either cover the dough with a damp cloth or cover the bowl with cling film. Leave in a warm place for at least 1 hour so that the dough will rise to more than double in size.

3 Knead the risen dough on a lightly floured board for a few seconds until smooth. Divide into 2 equal portions.

4 With both hands, roll each portion into a cylindrical roll 30cm (12 inches) long. Using a ruler as a guide, divide into 12 equal pieces.

5 One by one, stand each piece upright on the heel of your hand: slightly round off the dough with the other hand, then flatten it.

6 Using a lightly floured rolling pin, roll each into a circle 5cm (2 inches) in diameter, making the edges slightly thinner than the centre.

7 With one finger, smear a little oil on half of the surface of each circle. Fold the other half over to form a semi-circle (a).

8 Using an unserrated table knife, make a criss-cross pattern on the surface of each semi-circle. Then, using the blunt side of the knife, make

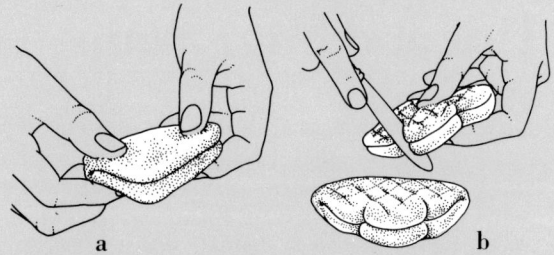

2 indents, 1cm (½ inch) deep, along the edge (b).

9 Space the buns out in one layer on a very wet cloth on a steaming rack. Steam in a wok or steamer over a high heat for about 12 minutes (see page 45). Remove from the heat.

10 Remove the buns to a wire rack for a few seconds, then put on to a warm plate and serve.

Silver-thread Buns

INGREDIENTS

4ml (¾tsp) dried yeast	85g (3⅓oz) lard
10ml (2tsp) sugar	little extra flour
270g (9fl oz) tepid water	37.5ml (2½tbsp) sugar
425g (15oz) plain flour	

Makes about 18-20 buns

1 Put the dried yeast and sugar in a small bowl, add the water and stir. Leave in a warm place until the yeast froths on the surface.

2 Sift the flour into a mixing bowl. Rub in 10g (⅓oz) of the lard with the fingertips. Stir in the yeast liquid and work it into a dough. Knead lightly for 1-2 minutes until the dough is smooth. Either cover the dough with a damp cloth or cover the bowl with cling film. Leave in a warm place for at least 1 hour so that the dough will rise to more than double in size.

3 Cream the remaining lard and sugar.

4 Knead the risen dough on a lightly floured board for a few seconds until smooth.

5 Roll out the dough with a lightly floured rolling pin into a thin circular or oblong sheet about 50cm (20 inches) across. Spread evenly with the sugar and lard mixture using a palette knife. Fold the sheet over and over at 7.5-cm (3-inch) intervals. Slice crosswise into thin "silver" threads about 3mm (⅛ inch) wide (a).

6 Group 7-8 strings of silver threads together and, using both hands, pull them slowly across into a 30cm (12 inch) long rope (b).

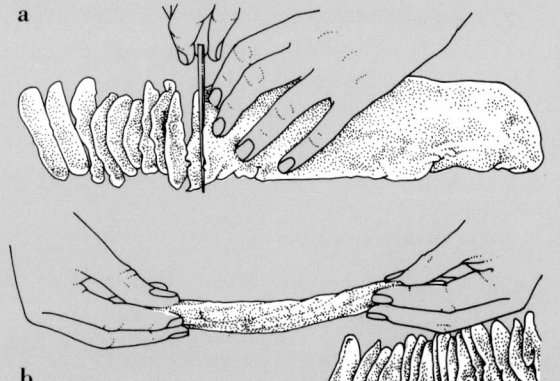

銀
絲
卷

7 Lay the rope on the floured board, turn one end away from you (c), and roll towards the other end to make a spiral tower, the base being about 5cm (2 inches) in diameter (d). Repeat until all are done.

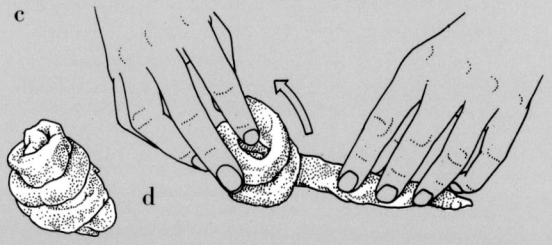

8 Space them out in one layer on a very wet cloth on a steaming rack. Steam over a high heat for 15 minutes (see page 45). Put buns on a wire rack for a few seconds, then serve.

Hot and Sour Soup

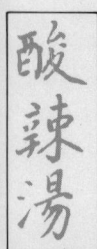

Pungent, peppery hot and slightly glutinous in consistency, this Szechwan and Peking peasant soup surprises the palate with its tastes and aftertastes. Now so popular with Westerners, it originally called for a special ingredient: fresh chicken's or duck's blood. I must confess, however, that I am quite happy to do without it. Indeed, in restaurants outside China this soup is invariably made without blood.

INGREDIENTS
100g (4oz) lean pork
6 dried Chinese mushrooms, reconstituted (see page 39)
15g (½oz) cloud ears, reconstituted (see page 39)
25g (1oz) golden needles, reconstituted (see page 39)
2 cakes bean curd, drained
30ml (2tbsp) potato flour
60ml (4tbsp) water
1.5 litres (2½ pints) prime or clear stock (see page 225)
2 eggs, lightly beaten with 10ml (2tsp) oil and pinch salt
25-50g (1-2oz) fresh coriander leaves, torn into pieces

FOR THE MARINADE
0.75ml (⅛tsp) salt
5ml (1tsp) thick soy sauce
3 turns black pepper mill
5ml (1tsp) Shaohsing wine or medium dry sherry
5ml (1tsp) potato flour
15-30ml (1-2tbsp) water
5ml (1tsp) sesame oil

FOR THE SEASONING
7.5ml (1½tsp) salt
4ml (¾tsp) sugar
15ml (1tbsp) thin soy sauce
15ml (1tbsp) thick soy sauce
45-60 (3-4tbsp) rice or white wine vinegar
5-7.5ml (1-1½tsp) ground black pepper
dashes of sesame oil (optional)

Serves 6-8

1 Slice the pork into matchstick-sized strips. Put into a bowl.

2 *Prepare the marinade:* add the salt, soy sauce, pepper and wine or sherry to the pork. Sprinkle with the potato flour and stir in the water in the same direction to coat the meat. Leave to marinate for 15-30 minutes or longer. Blend in the sesame oil.

3 Drain and squeeze out excess water from the mushrooms, cloud ears and golden needles but leave damp. Slice the mushrooms into the thinnest possible slivers. Cut the golden needles into 6-cm (2-inch) sections. Break up or cut the cloud ears into similarly-sized pieces.

4 Slice the bean curd cakes into 6-mm (¼-inch) thick pieces and then carefully slice again into strips 2.5cm x 6mm (1x¼ inch).

5 In a small bowl, dissolve the potato flour in the water.

6 In a large saucepan add the mushroom, cloud ears and golden needles to the stock and season with the salt, sugar and soy sauces. Bring to the boil and add the pork, separating with a pair of chopsticks or a fork. Then add the bean curd and as soon as the soup returns to the boil, slowly stir in the well-stirred dissolved potato flour. Slowly bring to the boil again.

7 Stream in the beaten egg through the gap of a pair of chopsticks or along the back of a fork, moving the chopsticks or fork in a circular motion at the same time. Remove from the heat and cover the pan for 45 seconds to allow the egg to set in tender flakes.

8 Add the coriander and stir to mix.

9 Stir in the vinegar and then the black pepper for seasoning.

10 Serve piping hot. Stir in dashes of sesame oil, if desired, just before serving. Put extra vinegar and black pepper on the table for those who like it really hot and pungent.

Note: left-over soup can be reheated but a little more vinegar and pepper may have to be added to renew the sharp taste.

Fish Fragrant Shredded Pork

Another Szechwan dish that uses the special fish fragrant sauce (see page 150).

INGREDIENTS
450g (1lb) lean pork, loin or leg
15g (½oz) cloud ears, reconstituted (see page 39)
6 water chestnuts, peeled fresh or drained canned
50-75g (2-3oz) canned bamboo shoots
75-90ml (5-6tbsp) groundnut or corn oil
5-6 cloves garlic, peeled and finely chopped
6mm (¼ inch) fresh ginger root, peeled and finely chopped
4-5 spring onions, cut into small rounds, white and green parts separated
15-30ml (1-2tbsp) Szechwan chilli paste (see page 226)
15ml (1tbsp) Shaohsing wine or medium dry sherry
10-15ml (2-3tsp) rice or white wine vinegar

FOR THE MARINADE
1.25ml (¼tsp) salt
5ml (1tsp) potato flour
15ml (1tbsp) water
5ml (1tsp) groundnut or corn oil
5ml (1tsp) sesame oil

FOR THE SAUCE
4ml (¾tsp) potato flour dissolved in 60ml (4tbsp) clear stock or water
22.5ml (1½tbsp) thin soy sauce
7.5ml (1½tsp) sugar

Serves 4 with 2 other dishes

1 Slice the pork into thread-like strips about 5-6cm (2-2½ inches) long and 4mm (⅙ inch) thick. Put into a bowl.

2 *Prepare the marinade:* add the salt, potato flour and water to the meat. Stir to coat then leave to marinate for 20-30 minutes. Blend in the two oils.

3 Cut the drained cloud ears, water chestnuts and bamboo shoots into narrow strips.

4 *Prepare the sauce:* mix together the dissolved potato flour, soy sauce and sugar. When ready to cook, add the green spring onion.

5 Heat a wok over a high heat until smoke rises. Add the oil and swirl it around. Add the garlic which will sizzle and take on colour instantly. Add the ginger and white spring onion; stir a few times. Stir in the chilli paste and then add the pork, cloud ears, water chestnuts and bamboo shoots. Sliding the wok scoop or metal spatula to the bottom of the wok, flip and toss for 1 minute, separating the pork strips. Splash in the wine or sherry around the side of the wok, stirring as it sizzles. Continue to stir for about 1½-2 minutes or until the pork, having turned white, is cooked. Add the well-stirred sauce, stirring as it thickens.

6 Remove from the heat, add the vinegar and stir to mix. Put on a warm plate and serve immediately.

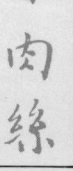

Dry-fried Four Seasonal Beans

A typical Szechwan dish in that it contains a variety of tastes to surprise the palate. Traditionally stir-fried first, the beans here are deep-fried for speed.

INGREDIENTS
450-550g (1-1¼lb) French beans, topped and tailed
30ml (2tbsp) dried shrimps, rinsed
25g (1oz) Szechwan preserved vegetable, rinsed
groundnut or corn oil for deep-frying
3-4 cloves garlic, peeled and finely chopped
1cm (½ inch) fresh ginger root, peeled and finely chopped
2.5ml (½tsp) salt
15ml (1tbsp) thin soy sauce
10ml (2tsp) sugar
30ml (2tbsp) shrimp water
10ml (2tsp) rice or white wine vinegar
5ml (1tsp) sesame oil
2 spring onions, cut into small rounds
Serves 4-6 with 2-3 other dishes

1 Soak the shrimps for 15 minutes in just enough boiling water to cover them. Drain them, reserving the soaking liquid. Chop into the size of matchstick heads (see page 38).

2 Chop the preserved vegetable by hand (it does not work with a food processor) into the same size as the shrimps.

3 Half fill a wok or deep-fryer with oil. Heat to a temperature of 190°C (375°F) or until a cube of stale bread browns in 50 seconds. Add the beans and deep-fry for about 4-5 minutes or until they wrinkle. Remove with a large hand strainer and drain on kitchen paper. Pour all but 30-45ml (2-3tbsp) oil into a container and save it for future use.

4 Reheat the oil until smoke rises. Add the garlic, let it sizzle, then add the ginger and stir a couple of

times. Add the shrimps and stir continuously. As the aroma rises, add the preserved vegetable and continue to stir, lowering the heat if they jump about too much.

5 Add the salt, soy sauce, sugar and shrimp water. Return the beans to the wok. Turn up the heat again and, sliding the wok scoop or metal spatula to the bottom of the wok, turn and toss the beans until the water has been absorbed.

6 Sprinkle in the vinegar and sesame oil. Add the spring onion and remove to a warm serving plate.

Note: as the taste of this dish actually improves if left standing, it can be cooked several hours or even a day in advance and then heated up just before serving. If there is any left over, the beans are also delicious eaten cold.

Pang Pang Chicken

Interestingly enough, this dish derives its name, not from the peppery hot and intriguing dressing as may be expected, but from the wooden stick (Pang in Mandarin) that is used to beat the chicken in order to loosen the fibres. To many people, this Szechwan dish is also known as Bon bon chicken.

INGREDIENTS
275g (10oz) cucumber, peeled
5ml (1tsp) salt
2 chicken breasts, 450-500g (1-1lb 2oz) boned, but with skin left on
600ml (1 pint) clear stock or water
8 spring onions, white parts only, cut into silken threads (see page 34)

30ml (2tbsp) thin soy sauce
5ml (1tsp) rice or white wine vinegar
7.5ml (1½tsp) sugar
20ml (4tsp) hot chilli oil with flakes (see page 225)
2.5ml (½tsp) ground roasted Szechwan peppercorns (see page 21)
5ml (1tsp) sesame oil

FOR THE DRESSING
20ml (4tsp) sesame paste

Serves 4-5 as first course

1 Halve the cucumber lengthwise and scoop out the seedy pulp in the centre. Cut the cucumber into thin pieces.

2 Sprinkle the salt over the cucumber and mix well. Put aside so that water will ooze out.

3 Put the stock in a saucepan and bring to the boil. Add the chicken and poach for about 15 minutes or until cooked. Remove the chicken breasts and leave to cool.

4 *Prepare the dressing:* put the sesame paste, well-stirred first in the jar, in a bowl and stir in the soy sauce, vinegar, sugar, hot chilli oil, peppercorns and sesame oil.

5 Rinse the cucumber in cold water to rid it of the salt, then squeeze out excess water. Arrange attractively on a serving plate.

6 When the chicken breasts are cool enough to handle, beat lightly on the skin side with a wooden rolling pin to loosen the fibres. Peel off the skin and tear the meat into long strips with your fingers. If you like the skin, cut it up into longish strips as well. Arrange them in the centre of the plate.

7 Place the spring onion on top of the chicken.

8 When ready to eat, pour the well-stirred dressing over the ingredients and mix to coat. Serve cold.

Note: this dish can be prepared hours in advance and refrigerated, covered, until ready to serve. It keeps quite well until the following day, though the dressing inevitably becomes a little watery.

CANTONESE MENU

Clear-steamed Sea Bass

The sea bass and the striped bass are arguably the most popular fish for Chinese living in Europe and America. Not surprisingly, they serve them steamed.

INGREDIENTS

1 sea bass, 700g-1.2kg (1½-2½lb), cleaned with head left on
1.25ml (¼tsp) salt
1.25ml (¼tsp) sugar
1-2cm (½-¾ inch) fresh ginger root, peeled and cut into silken threads (see page 35)
5-7 spring onions, cut into 5-cm (2-inch) sections and then silken threads (see page 34), green and white parts separated
60-75ml (4-5tbsp) groundnut or corn oil
30-45ml (2-3tbsp) thin soy sauce

Serves 2 as a main course; 4-6 with 2-3 other dishes

1 Pat the fish dry. Make 2-3 diagonal slashes on both sides of the fish. Lay it on a heatproof serving dish with slightly raised sides. If your wok or steamer is rather small, the fish can be halved.

2 Steam in a wok or steamer over a high heat for about 8 minutes until the fish is cooked and the flesh flakes easily (see page 45). Remove the cover, reduce the heat or turn it off. If too much water from the steam has collected on the dish, use kitchen paper to absorb some of it.

3 Sprinkle with the salt and sugar. Spread the ginger, then the green, and finally the white spring onion on the fish.

4 Heat the oil in a small saucepan over a high heat until smoke rises. Pour it, little by little, over the spring onion and ginger. The sizzling oil partially cooks them, enhancing the flavour.

5 Remove the dish from the wok or steamer. Add the soy sauce and serve immediately.

Asparagus with Crabmeat

Crabmeat adds rather than detracts from the natural sweetness of asparagus and the sight of the red and white meat on a bed of green makes this dish especially appealing.

INGREDIENTS

700g (1½lb) asparagus, cleaned and trimmed
75ml (5tbsp) groundnut or corn oil
4 thin slices fresh ginger root, peeled
15ml (1tbsp) Shaohsing wine or medium dry sherry
2.5ml (½tsp) salt
90ml (3fl oz) prime stock (see page 225)
1-2 cloves garlic, peeled and finely chopped
6mm (¼ inch) fresh ginger root, peeled and cut into silken threads (see page 35)
2-3 spring onions, white parts only, cut into small rounds
225g (8oz) cooked crabmeat

FOR THE SAUCE

4ml (¾tsp) potato flour
75ml (5tbsp) clear stock or water
30ml (2tbsp) oyster sauce
salt to taste

Serves 6 with 3-4 other dishes

1 Cut the asparagus into sections, the tips about 6cm (2¼ inches) long, the remainder about 3cm (1¼ inches) long.

2 *Prepare the sauce:* mix together the potato flour, stock or water, oyster sauce and salt.

3 Heat a wok over a high heat until smoke rises. Add 45ml (3tbsp) oil and swirl it around. Add the ginger and let it sizzle for a few seconds. Add the asparagus and turn and toss with the wok scoop or metal spatula. When hot, splash in 7.5ml (½tbsp) of the wine or sherry around the side of the wok. When the sizzling dies down, reduce the heat, add the salt and stock. Bring to the boil, cover and simmer fast for 4-5 minutes if the asparagus is thin, 6-7 minutes if medium-sized, longer if extra thick. The asparagus should be tender but crisp. Remove and keep warm.

4 Wash and dry the wok. Reheat over a high heat until smoke rises. Add the remaining oil and swirl it around. Add the garlic, ginger and spring onion, stir and let sizzle, releasing their aroma. Add the crabmeat and stir to mix. As soon as it is very hot, splash in the remaining wine or sherry. Pour in the well-stirred sauce and continue to stir as it thickens. Spoon over the asparagus and serve.

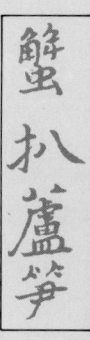

Golden Prawn Balls

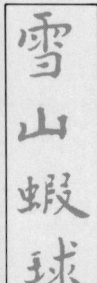

Crunchy to the bite, the prawn paste inside these deep-fried balls is firm but tender in texture. To achieve this, salt and egg white are essential ingredients.

INGREDIENTS

6-8 slices white bread, crusts removed
6 water chestnuts, fresh peeled or canned drained
50g (2oz) pork fat
450g (1lb) medium raw prawns without heads (about 350g [12oz]), shelled

groundnut or corn oil for deep-frying

FOR THE MARINADE
5ml (1tsp) salt
2.5ml (½tsp) sugar
5ml (1tsp) cornflour
1 egg white, lightly beaten

Serves 6 as a starter; makes about 24 balls

1 The bread is best if left out for 2-3 hours. Dice into small cubes, about 6mm (¼inch) square.

2 Finely chop or mince the water chestnuts.

3 Finely chop or mince the pork fat. Remove to a large, deep bowl.

4 Shell and devein the prawns (see page 39).

5 Crush the prawns with the flat side of a cleaver and then chop about 100 times. Alternatively, coarsely mince. Transfer to the bowl with the pork.

6 *Prepare the marinade:* add the salt and sugar to the prawns. Sprinkle with the cornflour and stir vigorously in the same direction for 1 minute.

7 Stir in the water chestnuts.

8 Add the egg white and stir again vigorously in the same direction for 1-2 more minutes. This gives the paste a firm, elastic texture.

9 Refrigerate for about 30 minutes. The paste can be prepared well ahead of time and left, covered, in the refrigerator until ready for use.

10 Spread the bread cubes on a clean tray.

11 Roll about 15ml (1tbsp) of the paste between your palms into a ball. Then roll it on the bread cubes until more or less covered. Put aside. Repeat until the paste is used up.

12 Half fill a wok or a deep-fryer with oil. Heat to a temperature of 180°C (350°F) or until a cube of stale bread browns in 60 seconds. Add the balls, 8-10 at a time or as many as can float freely, and deep-fry for about 2-3 minutes or until the bread cubes are golden in colour. The paste should be cooked by now. Remove with a hand strainer or perforated disc and drain on kitchen paper. Remove to a warm serving plate and serve immediately.

Dry-fried Prawns

This dish traditionally calls for large prawns, but I have adapted it to medium-sized ones.

INGREDIENTS

700g (1½lb) fresh or frozen medium raw prawns in the shell, without heads
4ml (¾tsp) sea salt
groundnut or corn oil
4 cloves garlic, peeled and finely chopped
1-2cm (½-¾ inch) fresh ginger root, peeled and finely chopped
2 fresh green chillies, seeded and chopped
4 large spring onions, cut into small rounds,

white and green parts separated

FOR THE SAUCE
1.25ml (¼tsp) potato flour
30ml (2tbsp) thin soy sauce
10ml (2tsp) sugar
15ml (1tbsp) Shaohsing wine or medium dry sherry
15ml (1tbsp) ketchup

Serves 6-8 with 3-4 other dishes

1 If frozen prawns are used, defrost thoroughly. Wash the shells well and remove the legs. Devein (see page 90), if preferred, although there is no harm in not doing so. Pat dry with kitchen paper. Put into a large bowl.

2 Sprinkle with the salt and mix well. Leave to stand for about 20 minutes.

3 *Prepare the sauce:* mix together the potato flour, soy sauce, sugar, wine or sherry and ketchup.

4 Half fill a wok or deep-fryer with oil. Heat to a temperature of 180°C (350°F) or until a cube of stale bread browns in 60 seconds. Tip in all the prawns "to go through the oil" for about 20 seconds, moving them gently with either long bamboo chopsticks or a wooden spoon. Turn off the heat, remove immediately with a large hand strainer and drain on kitchen paper. The prawns,

having turned pinkish, will be almost cooked.

5 Empty all but 30-45ml (2-3tbsp) oil into another container and keep for future use.

6 Reheat the oil in a wok until smoke rises. Add the garlic, stir a couple of times, then the ginger, stir, then the chilli, stir, and then the white spring onion and stir a few more times. Return the prawns to the wok and spread them out into a single layer, if possible. Lower the heat and sauté the prawns for about 30 seconds, letting them absorb the aroma of the garlic and ginger. Turn them over and sauté for another 30 seconds; take care not to burn the prawns.

7 Pour the well-stirred sauce over the prawns. As you do so, turn and toss the prawns with a wok scoop or metal spatula until most of the sauce has been absorbed. Add the green spring onion, remove to a warm serving platter and serve immediately.

8 To eat, pick up one prawn with a pair of chopsticks, bite into it and shell it with your front teeth whilst savouring the sauce on the shell. Neatly spit out the shell on to a side plate and eat the prawn meat in the normal way. If you want an easier way of eating the prawns, I suggest you use your fingers.

Stir-fried Fillet of Beef with Mango

This sophisticated modern dish is especially popular in the South of China where mangoes are greatly enjoyed. The combination of the sharpness of the ginger, the natural sweetness of the mango and the savoury sauce makes the beef an intriguing proposition to the palate.

INGREDIENTS
450g (1lb) beef fillet, trimmed
1 large mango, not too ripe
groundnut or corn oil for deep-frying
4 cloves garlic, peeled and finely chopped
4 spring onions, cut into 2.5-cm (1-inch) sections, white and green parts separated
2cm (¾ inch) fresh ginger root, cut into silken threads (see page 35)
15ml (1tbsp) Shaohsing wine or medium dry sherry.

FOR THE MARINADE
1.25ml (¼tsp) salt
2.5ml (½tsp) sugar
5ml (1tsp) thin soy sauce
5ml (1tsp) thick soy sauce
5ml (1tsp) Shaohsing wine or medium dry sherry
4 turns black pepper mill
7.5ml (1½tsp) potato flour
30ml (2tbsp) water

FOR THE SAUCE
2.5ml (½tsp) potato flour
10ml (2tsp) oyster sauce
5ml (1tsp) thin soy sauce
45ml (3tbsp) water

Serves 4 with 2 other dishes

1 Cut the fillet across the grain into chunky strips, about 5cm (2 inches) long and 1cm (½ inch) thick. Beat the beef strips with the broad side of a cleaver to loosen the fibres. Put into a bowl.

2 *Prepare the marinade:* add the salt, sugar, soy sauces, wine or sherry and pepper to the beef. Sprinkle with the potato flour, add the water, 15ml (1tbsp) at a time, and stir vigorously in the same direction to coat the pieces well. Leave to marinate in the refrigerator for 20-30 minutes.

3 Peel the mango, slice the flesh from the stone and then cut into strips.

4 *Prepare the sauce:* mix together the potato flour, oyster sauce, soy sauce and water in a cup and put aside.

5 Half fill a wok or deep-fryer with oil. Heat to a temperature of 180°C (350°F) or until a cube of stale bread browns in 60 seconds. Tip the beef into the oil and, using a long pair of chopsticks or a wooden spoon, stir gently to make sure that all the pieces "go through the oil" for about 30 seconds to have their juices sealed in. Remove them at once to a warm plate with a large hand strainer.

6 Empty all but 45ml (3tbsp) of the oil into a container and reserve for other use.

7 Reheat the oil over a high heat until smoke rises. Add the garlic, which will sizzle and take on colour. Add the white spring onion, stirring, and then add the ginger. Now return the beef to the wok and turn and toss with the wok scoop or metal spatula for about 30 seconds. Splash in the wine or sherry around the side of the wok. If you like your beef underdone remove once the sizzling has died down. If you prefer your beef well done, leave to cook a little longer, stirring until done. Keep warm.

8 Add up to 15ml (1tbsp) oil to the wok, swirl it around and add the mango. Cover and fry over a gentle heat for about 1 minute.

9 Add the well-stirred sauce to the wok. When it thickens and bubbles, add the green spring onion. Attractively arrange the mango, green spring onion and sauce with the beef. Serve immediately.

香芒牛肉

Red Bean Fool

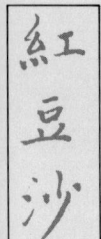

It is not the Chinese custom to serve a dessert after each meal; fruit is served instead. However, this inexpensive pudding is very popular with the Cantonese; it has a thickish consistency and is not overly sweet. They serve it hot, without cream.

INGREDIENTS

225g (8oz) red beans (azuki beans), washed and drained
20ml (4tsp) glutinous rice, washed and drained
1.7 litres (3 pints) cold water

1 piece dried tangerine peel, washed
15ml (3tsp) groundnut or corn oil
175g (6oz) sugar
double cream to serve, if desired

Serves 6

1 Soak the beans and rice for half a day or overnight in 1.1 litres (2 pints) of cold water. Do not drain. (This step may be omitted.)

2 Put the beans, rice and peel into a large saucepan, add the oil and the remaining cold water. If step 1 has been omitted, add all the cold water. Bring to the boil. (If boiling water is poured on to the tangerine peel, it will taste bitter.) Reduce the heat, cover and simmer for 2 hours, stirring occasionally and checking the water level. The volume should be reduced to 900ml-1 litre (1½-1¾ pints) for the right consistency – gluey – with water just covering the beans.

3 Add the sugar and simmer until completely dissolved. Remove and discard the tangerine peel. Leave uncovered to cool.

4 Liquidize the bean mixture. Chill the fool in the refrigerator. Serve with double cream at the table.

Note: for those who like a more pronounced flavour of the tangerine peel, it can be liquidized together with the cooked red beans. If desired, try the fool served hot with cream.

PEKING MENU

Peking Duck

This famous duck dish was introduced to Europe and America during the latter half of the 19th century: one source gives a definite date of 1875. In the well-established restaurants in Peking, the ducks used are raised for the express purpose of being roasted in a specially-constructed oven. Paradoxically, this duck can be made as in this recipe in a simple way, with remarkably good results. The duck will be very crisp with a rich dark red skin; the meat perfectly cooked and juicy. Traditionally, only the skin was presented to eat with the pancakes. The meat, cut up in the kitchen and stir-fried with bean sprouts, was served as a second course. These days, however, in both Peking and the West, the meat is carved to be served with the skin.

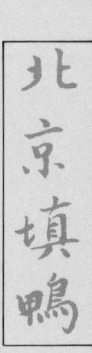

INGREDIENTS

1 plump oven-ready duck 2-2.3kg (4½-5lb)	into matchstick-sized pieces
30ml (2tbsp) honey	hoisin sauce or sweet bean sauce
300ml (½ pint) hot water	25-30 Mandarin pancakes (see page 210)
1.7 litres (3 pints) boiling water	
12 spring onions, white parts only	
1 large cucumber, cut	*Serves 4 as main course, 6-7 with 3-4 other dishes*

1 Melt the honey in the hot water in a cup or jug. Keep warm.

2 Put the duck in a colander. Scald it with the boiling water from a kettle, turning over several times to ensure even scalding. As the water is poured from the kettle on to the duck, the skin shrinks at once, becoming shiny. Wipe off excess water but leave damp. Put into a large bowl.

3 Pour the honey mixture all over the skin, including the wings, neck and tail. Return the liquid to the cup and repeat the process once more. To ensure even distribution, dip a brush into the liquid and smear over less accessible spots as well.

4 Hang the duck on either a special Chinese 3-pronged duck hook or on 2 butcher's "S" meat hooks, 1 each securing the shoulder joint and wing. Hang in a windy place for 10-24 hours until the skin is parchment dry. Do *not* prick the skin.

5 Place the duck breast side up on a wire rack in the middle of the oven with a tray of hot water underneath to catch the cooking juices. Roast in a preheated oven at 180°C (350°F) mark 4 for 20 minutes, at the end of which the skin will have turned golden brown. With a wooden spoon or spatula held in one hand and another spoon put inside the cavity, turn the duck over and roast the other side for 25-30 minutes. Turn over once more, breast side up again, and roast for another 20 minutes. If the skin is becoming too dark a red, lower the heat to 170°C (325°F) mark 3; if too pale, raise to 190°C (375°F) mark 5 for part of the rest of the roasting time. Do *not* prick the skin during the roasting; the oil which would ooze would spoil both the colour and the crispness of the skin. Remove from the oven and put on a wire rack to cool for a few minutes before carving.

6 While the duck is being roasted, cut the spring onion into 5-cm (2-inch) sections. Slice each section lengthwise into strips. Arrange on 1 or 2 dishes. Arrange the cucumber on 1 or 2 dishes.

7 Put 1-2 tablespoons of hoisin or sweet bean sauce into individual saucers for each person.

8 Steam the Mandarin pancakes for 10 minutes and remove to warm serving plates.

9 Just before carving, pour all the juice in the cavity into a container. Carve the skin into pieces about 5cm (2inches) square or into irregular shapes of approximate size. Carve the meat in a similar manner. Place the skin and meat on warm serving plates.

10 To eat, put a pancake on a plate (rather than in a bowl), smear on some sauce and top with 1 or 2 pieces of skin, either on their own or with meat as well. Add 1 or 2 pieces of cucumber and spring onion before rolling it up and eating.

Variation: Cantonese roast duck
Follow steps 1-4, above (the hanging time can be shortened to 6-10 hours). Smear a marinade of 20ml (4tsp) salt, 20ml (4tsp) sugar, 7.5ml (1½tsp) five-spice powder and 10ml (2tsp) Mei-kuei-lu wine or gin all over and in the cavity of the duck, then roast it as in step 5. Serve with a thick soy sauce.

Mandarin Pancakes

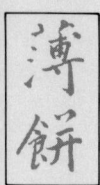

While Mandarin pancakes are a must with Peking duck, they are also traditionally served with dishes such as Mu-shu pork (see page 139). The Northern Chinese like these pancakes to be slightly on the firm side; the little bit of cold water added to the dough does the trick.

INGREDIENTS

450g (1lb) plain white flour
350-375ml (12-13fl oz) boiling water
15ml (1tbsp) cold water
little extra flour
10ml (2tsp) sesame oil

Serves 6 with Peking duck

1 Sift the flour into a mixing bowl. Pour in the boiling water gradually, stirring vigorously with a wooden spoon or a pair of chopsticks until well mixed. Then stir in the cold water. As soon as your hands can withstand the heat, form the mixture into a dough and knead lightly either in the bowl or on a lightly floured board or work surface for 3-4 minutes or until soft and smooth. Allow to stand in the bowl for 20-30 minutes covered with a cloth.

2 Transfer the dough on to a lightly floured board or work surface. Divide into 2 equal portions and knead a few more times until smooth again. Use as little extra flour on the board as possible or the pancakes will taste floury.

3 Using both hands, roll each portion of dough into a 40-cm (16-inches) long roll. Then, using a ruler as a guide, divide each roll into 16 x 2.5-cm (1-inch) pieces (a), making a total of 32.

4 One by one, stand each piece upright on the heel of your hand, slightly round off the dough, then flatten with the other hand (b), into a circle of about 5-6cm (2-2½ inches) diameter.

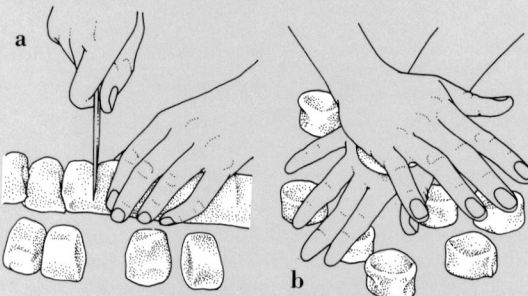

5 Using a brush, paint the surface of half of the pieces (16) with sesame oil (c). Place the remaining pieces on the oiled surfaces (d), making 16 pairs. Shape each pair of circles as evenly as possible.

6 Using a lightly floured rolling pin, roll out each pair into thin pancakes about 15-16cm (6-6½ inches) in diameter (e). To ensure even thickness and roundness, rotate the circles quite frequently, turning them over as well.

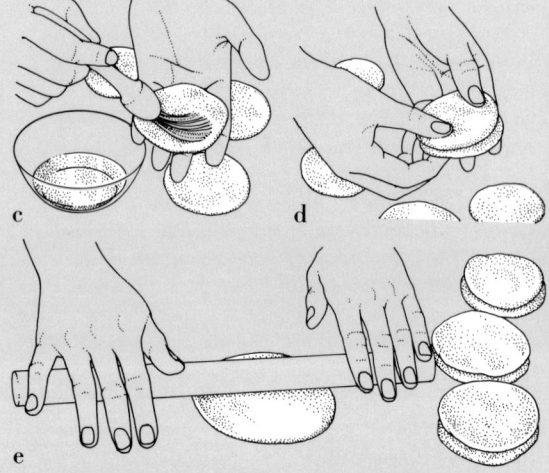

7 Heat an unoiled, flat heavy frying pan or griddle over a medium-to-low heat. Put in 1 pair of cakes at a time and fry for 1-2 minutes or until light brown spots appear (f). Turn over to fry the other side. In less than 1 minute part of the surface will puff up, indicating that they are done.

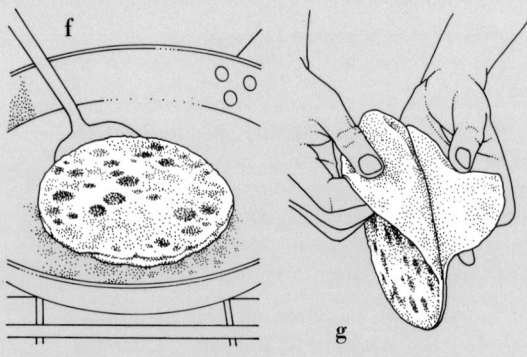

8 Remove from the frying pan and, while they are still hot, separate the 2 thin pancakes with the fingers (g). Put on a plate and cover with a cloth to prevent from drying up. Repeat until all are done.

9 Steam all the pancakes (in 2 batches if necessary) in a wok or steamer for 5-10 minutes before serving (see page 45).

Fish in a wine sauce

This is a Peking-style fish dish which is very delicate in taste and appearance. It is traditional to use cloud ears to complement the fish.

INGREDIENTS

450-700g (1-1½lb) lemon sole, Dover sole or flounder fillet, skinned
30ml (2tbsp) cloud ears, reconstituted (see page 39)
groundnut or corn oil for deep-frying
4 cloves garlic, peeled and finely chopped
1cm (½ inch) fresh ginger root, peeled and finely chopped

1.25ml (¼tsp) sugar
6 turns white pepper mill
1 egg white, beaten with 15ml (1tbsp) cornflour until well blended

FOR THE SAUCE
4-5ml (¾-1tsp) salt
15ml (1tbsp) cornflour
150ml (¼ pint) Shaohsing wine or semi-sweet white wine
150ml (¼ pint) clear stock

FOR THE MARINADE
2.5ml (½tsp) salt

Serves 4 with 2 other dishes

1 Pat the fish dry. Halve each side lengthwise and then slice each half crosswise into about 5-cm (2-inch) pieces. Put into a bowl.

2 *Prepare the marinade:* add the salt, sugar, pepper and the egg and cornflour mixture to the fish. Coat the fish well. Cover and leave to marinate in the refrigerator for about 1 hour.

3 *Prepare the sauce:* mix together the salt, cornflour, wine and stock.

4 Drain the excess water from the cloud ears but leave damp.

5 Fill a wok or deep-fryer with oil. Heat to a temperature of about 100-110°C (200-225°F) or barely hot. Put the fish in very gently and let it "go through the oil" for 1-2 minutes, stirring 2-3 times to separate the pieces. When the fish turns opaque, turn off the heat and remove with a perforated disc or spoon, handling gently so that the pieces do not crumble. Pour the oil into a container, leaving about 30-45ml (2-3tbsp) in the wok.

6 Reheat the oil until smoke rises. Add the garlic, stir, then the ginger, stir, and the cloud ears. Stir a few more times, then add the well-stirred sauce. Slowly bring to the boil, then return the fish to the wok and cook gently in the sauce until thoroughly hot. Remove to a warm serving dish. Serve immediately.

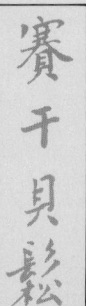

"Seaweed"

This Northern dish uses a special kind of seaweed which is not available elsewhere. However, the adapted ingredients used below do produce the desired delicious result.

INGREDIENTS

450g (1lb) spring greens or green leaves of cabbage, washed and dried
groundnut or corn oil for deep-frying

25g (1oz) blanched, flaked almonds
1.25ml (¼tsp) salt
10ml (2tsp) caster sugar

Serves 6

1 Remove and discard the tough stalks from the spring greens. Lay them out on a large tray to dry thoroughly.

2 Fold 6-7 leaves, or however many you can handle at a time, into a neat roll and, using a sharp knife, slice crosswise into the thinnest thread-like strips possible. Lay out on the tray again to air, for the drier the spring greens at this stage the easier it is to achieve the desired crispness, without their losing their vivid colour when deep-fried. (They can be prepared up to this point 6-8 hours ahead.)

3 Half fill a wok or deep-fryer with oil. Heat the oil to a temperature of 200°C (400°F), or until a cube of stale bread browns in 40 seconds. Add half the spring greens gently and deep-fry for about 2 minutes or until crisp; they will turn a slightly deeper green colour. Remove with a large hand strainer or perforated disc and drain on kitchen paper. Deep-fry the remainder.

4 Leave to cool then transfer to a serving dish. Sprinkle with the salt and mix thoroughly. Sprinkle with the sugar and again mix thoroughly. Garnish with the almonds.

5 Serve at room temperature. The "seaweed" will stay crisp overnight. Do not refrigerate.

Chinese Celery Cabbage in Cream Sauce

奶油津白

It is a well-known fact that, traditionally, the Chinese do not use dairy products for their cooking. However, in this classic modern dish from the Northern and Eastern areas a small amount of either evaporated milk or cream is used. In Peking and Shanghai, evaporated milk would be used, but when single cream is available it is just as good.

INGREDIENTS	FOR THE SAUCE
700-800g (1½-1¾lb) Chinese celery cabbage	15ml (1tbsp) potato flour
9ml (1¾tsp) salt	90ml (3fl oz) clear stock
60ml (4tbsp) groundnut or corn oil	150ml (¼ pint) evaporated milk or single cream
25g (1oz) cooked ham, Chinhua, Virginia or York is best, chopped	*Serves 6*

1 Discard the tough outer leaves of the cabbage. Wash the remaining leaves, halve each one lengthways, then slice them across into strips about 6cm (2½ inches) long.

2 Bring 1.4 litres (2½ pints) water to the boil in a large saucepan. Add 5ml (1tsp) of the salt and 15ml (1tbsp) of the oil (this will make the cabbage glisten)

and add the cabbage. Boil for about 1 minute then pour the cabbage into a colander. Refresh under cold running water and leave to drain until all the excess water has run out.

3 *Prepare the sauce:* dissolve the potato flour in 30ml (2tbsp) of the stock, then stir in the rest. Stir in the milk or cream and add the remaining salt.

4 Heat a wok over a moderate heat until moderately hot. Add the remaining oil and swirl it around. Add the cabbage and stir and turn with a wok scoop or metal spatula until thoroughly hot, taking care not to burn it. Push the cabbage to the sides of the wok, making a well in the centre.

5 Pour the well-stirred sauce into the centre of the wok. Stir the sauce continually until it thickens, then fold in the cabbage. Remove to a warm serving plate.

6 Arrange the cabbage attractively, sprinkle the chopped ham on top and serve.

Variation: Cauliflower in cream sauce. Use 2 cauliflowers, cut the florets into bite-sized pieces and cook in the same way as the celery cabbage.

Pickled Cabbage Peking Style

北京泡菜

Served cold as an hors d'oeuvre, salad or side dish, this dish keeps well in the refrigerator for at least two weeks. Avoid eating the Szechwan peppercorns.

INGREDIENTS	groundnut or corn oil
900g (2lb) white cabbage, quartered and cored	37.5ml (2½tbsp) sesame oil
30ml (2tbsp) salt	3 dried red chillies, seeded and chopped
1-2cm (½-¾ inch) fresh ginger root, peeled and cut into silken threads (see page 35)	5ml (1tsp) Szechwan peppercorns
75ml (5tbsp) sugar	75ml (5tbsp) rice vinegar
37.5ml (2½tbsp)	*Serves 6-8*

1 Shred the cabbage as finely as possible either in a food processor or with a knife. Put into a very large mixing bowl.

2 Sprinkle with the salt and mix. Leave to stand at

room temperature for 2-3 hours; the cabbage will decrease in bulk having released some of its water content. Take a handful at a time and, using both hands, squeeze out the excess water but leave damp. Transfer to a clean bowl.

3 Place the ginger in a bunch on top of the cabbage in the centre of the bowl.

4 Sprinkle on the sugar, taking care not to put it over the ginger.

5 Heat the oil and sesame oil in a small saucepan over a high heat until smoke rises. Remove from the heat and then add the chilli and peppercorns. Pour the mixture over the ginger first and then the surrounding cabbage in the bowl. The sizzling oil partially cooks the ginger, enhancing the flavour.

6 Add the vinegar and mix well. Leave to stand at room temperature for 2-3 hours before serving.

SHANGHAI MENU

Red-in-snow Soup with Pork

Crisp, pickled red-in-snow (labelled pickled cabbage on the can), although quite salty on its own, lends a delicious flavour to the other ingredients of this dish, making a really tasty soup.

INGREDIENTS
50g (2oz) cellophane
  noodles
100g (4oz) lean pork
1 small can red-in-snow
  or 200g (7oz), chopped
45ml (3tbsp) groundnut
  or corn oil
4-6 spring onions, cut
  into 2.5-cm (1-inch)
  sections, white and
  green parts separated

FOR THE MARINADE
10ml (2tsp) thin soy sauce
2.5ml (½tsp) sugar
5ml (1tsp) Shaohsing
  wine or medium dry
  sherry
4-6 turns white pepper mill
7.5ml (1½tsp) potato
  flour
15ml (1tbsp) water
5-10ml (1-2tsp) sesame oil

Serves 5-6

1 With a pair of scissors, cut the cellophane noodles into shorter lengths, about 7.5cm (3 inches), for easier handling when cooked. Soak in about 900ml (1½ pints) boiling water for about 30 minutes. Drain.

2 Cut the pork into matchstick-sized pieces (see page 38). Put into a bowl.

3 *Prepare the marinade:* add the soy sauce, sugar, wine or sherry, pepper, potato flour and water to the pork. Leave to marinate for about 15 minutes. Blend in the sesame oil.

4 Place 1.1 litres (2 pints) water in a large saucepan and bring to the boil. Add the oil, white spring onion and cellophane noodles. Pour in the red-in-snow and return to a gentle simmer.

5 Add the pork to the saucepan and, using a pair of chopsticks or a fork, separate the strips. Continue to simmer until the pork has cooked and turned opaque; this should not take more than 1 minute. Transfer to a warm soup tureen and serve.

Fu-yung Egg Slices

Fu-yung is Chinese for lotus. In poetry it is used to describe the pretty face of a young woman, and it is indeed a fitting adjective for this Eastern dish.

INGREDIENTS
50g (2oz) frozen petits
  pois
1-2 medium red tomatoes
6 large egg whites
4ml (¾tsp) salt
10ml (2tsp) cornflour
groundnut or corn oil for
  deep-frying

22.5ml (1½tbsp) potato
  flour
600ml (1 pint) clear stock
25g (1oz) ham, Chinhua,
  York or Virginia is
  best, finely chopped

*Serves 4 with 3 other
  dishes*

1 Blanch the petits pois in boiling water for 2-3 minutes. Drain.

2 Plunge the tomato in a bowl of boiling water for 1-2 minutes, then peel the skin. Halve lengthwise and seed. Slice each half lengthwise into 4-6 pieces.

3 Beat the egg whites lightly, add 2.5ml (½tsp) of salt and the cornflour and beat until homogenized. If there are too many bubbles skim them off.

4 Half fill a wok or deep-fryer with oil. Heat until barely hot, about 105-110°C (210-225°F). Pour in the egg white mixture, about 30ml (2tbsp) at a time, and let it come slowly to the surface. Lift at once with a perforated disc and put into a bowl. Repeat until all the mixture is used up, always adjusting the heat to make sure the oil is not too hot so that the velvety tenderness of the egg is maintained.

5 Dissolve the potato flour in 15-30ml (1-2tbsp) of the stock, then blend well into the remaining stock. Add the remaining salt.

6 Place the stock in a saucepan and bring slowly to the boil, stirring as it thickens. Add the petits pois, cook for a few seconds until hot, then add the tomato. Now add the fu-yung egg slices and cook for a few more seconds until piping hot. Remove from the heat and gently scoop all the ingredients on to a warm deep serving plate.

7 Arrange the petits pois and tomato attractively to give the best visual effect. Sprinkle on the ham likewise and serve immediately.

213

"Smoked" Fish Shanghai Style

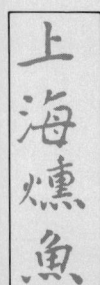

A favourite cold starter in Shanghai and Northern restaurants. "Smoked" fish has always been known by this mock title, for the fish is not smoked but marinated, then deep-fried and steeped in a spiced sauce with a special vinegar.

INGREDIENTS
1kg (2lb) hake or
   haddock steaks,
   ideally from the tail of
   the fish, cut 2cm (¾
   inch) thick
groundnut or corn oil for
   deep-frying

FOR THE MARINADE
4cm (1½ inches) fresh
   ginger root, peeled and
   chopped
45ml (3tbsp) thin soy
   sauce
15ml (1tbsp) Shaohsing
   wine or medium dry
   sherry

FOR THE SAUCE
700ml (1¼ pints) cold
   water
1 whole star anise or 8
   segments
2.5cm (1 inch) cinnamon
   stick
1 piece preserved
   tangerine peel, quarter
   of whole
5ml (1tsp) black
   peppercorns
2 large spring onions
4 slices fresh ginger root,
   3mm (⅛ inch) thick
45ml (3tbsp) Chinkiang
   or red wine vinegar
60-75ml (4-5tbsp) sugar

Serves 8

1 Pat the fish dry with kitchen paper, pierce the flesh in several places with a fork for better absorption of the marinade, and place on a large plate.

2 *Prepare the marinade:* using a garlic press, squeeze the juice from the chopped ginger on to the fish and discard the pulp. Add the soy sauce and wine or sherry. Turn the fish over several times so the steaks are coated with the marinade. Leave to marinate for 2 hours, turning the fish over from time to time.

3 *Prepare the sauce:* put the water, star anise, cinnamon stick, tangerine peel, peppercorns, spring onion and the ginger into a large saucepan. Bring to the boil, then lower the heat and simmer, uncovered, for 25-30 minutes to reduce the liquid to about 450ml (¾ pint). Strain the liquid into a bowl and discard the solids. Return the liquid to the saucepan and add the vinegar and sugar. Leave on one side while deep-frying the fish.

4 Put the fish on to a wire rack to drain for several minutes before deep-frying.

5 Half fill a wok or deep-fryer with oil. Heat to a temperature of 200°C (400°F) or until a cube of stale bread browns in 40 seconds. Carefully add half the fish and deep-fry for about 15 minutes until brown and firm but not hard. Remove with a hand strainer or perforated disc and drain on kitchen paper. Repeat with the rest of the fish.

6 Bring the sauce to the boil, stirring to dissolve the sugar. Add the fish and ladle the boiling liquid over it for 3-4 minutes, using a large spoon. Remove the fish to a large dish.

7 Continue to boil the sauce until it thickens and reduces to a syrupy glaze. Pour over the fish. Cool, cover and refrigerate for a few hours, or overnight, before serving cold.

Crystal Sugar Pork Knuckle

Eastern Chinese cooks specialize in dishes such as this, where the rind as well as the meat is so tender that only a pair of chopsticks (or a fork and spoon) is necessary to break it up.

INGREDIENTS
1 pork hand knuckle,
   about 1.4-1.6kg
   (3-3½lb)
4 thickish slices fresh
   ginger root, peeled
2-3 spring onions, halved
90ml (6tbsp) thick soy
   sauce

45ml (3tbsp) Shaohsing
   wine or medium dry
   sherry
25g (1oz) rock sugar (or
   granulated sugar if
   unobtainable)

*Serves 6 with 2 other
   dishes*

1 Pluck any hair off the skin of the hand knuckle. On the side where the skin is most tender, cut through to, and along the length of, the bone. This helps to keep the knuckle in shape, as well as absorbing the sauce better as it cooks.

2 Put the knuckle in a heavy saucepan or flameproof casserole and cover with cold water. Bring the water to the boil and boil, uncovered, for 4-5 minutes so that the scum collects on the surface. Pour off the water and if necessary, rinse the skin free of scum.

3 Return the knuckle to the saucepan or casserole. (If possible, place on a thin latticed bamboo mat

which will prevent the rind from sticking to the pot.)

4 Add the ginger, spring onions, soy sauce, wine or sherry and sugar to the pot. Pour in 1 litre (1¾ pints) water, bring to the boil, reduce the heat and simmer fast, tightly covered, for 1 hour, loosening the knuckle skin from the bottom of the pot once during cooking.

5 Turn the pork over, checking the water level to make sure it is about one-third of the way up the pork. Replace the lid and continue to cook for

another 1¼-1½ hours, moving the knuckle 2-3 times to make sure the skin is not sticking to the pot. The juice should by now be reduced to about 250ml (8 fl oz) or a little less.

6 Increase the heat and boil to reduce the sauce for a few minutes or until it is thick and glossy, continually spooning the sauce over the knuckle with a long spoon.

7 Transfer the knuckle to a warm serving dish. Discard the ginger and spring onion and pour the sauce over the pork.

Eight-treasure Bean Curd

The 18th century poet and official, Yüan Mei, wrote a cookery book called Sui-yüan Recipes, *a unique legacy of his times from a Chinese man of letters. In the recipe called Prefect Wang's Eight-treasure Bean Curd, Yüan Mei briefly outlined how the dish traced its origin to the Imperial kitchen. This dish consists of many hidden ingredients which, whilst they melt in the mouth, give just the hint of a nutty bite.*

王太守八寶豆腐

INGREDIENTS

4 medium dried Chinese mushrooms, reconstituted (see page 39)
2 cakes bean curd, drained
3 egg whites
4-5ml (¾-1tsp) salt
15g (½oz) solid lard
22.5ml (1½tbsp) potato flour
30ml (2tbsp) double cream
30ml (2tbsp) melted lard or 45ml (3tbsp) groundnut or corn oil
175ml (6fl oz) prime stock (see page 225)

50g (2oz) cooked chicken breast, finely chopped
25g (1oz) blanched walnuts, finely chopped
25g (1oz) blanched almonds, finely chopped
50g (2oz) ham, finely chopped, Chinhua, York or Virginia is best
10ml (2tsp) melted chicken fat or sesame oil

Serves 6 with 3-4 other dishes

1 Drain and squeeze out excess water from the mushrooms but leave damp. Finely chop.

2 Blend or mash the bean curd. The smoother the purée, the smoother the texture of the cooked dish. Put into a large bowl.

3 Add half the egg whites and salt to the bean curd and beat until well amalgamated. Add the remaining egg whites, the solid lard, cornflour and double cream. Beat the mixture until stiff; the volume will have increased. Stir in half the stock.

4 Heat a wok over a high heat until smoke rises. Add the melted lard or oil and swirl it around. Pour the bean curd mixture and the remaining stock simultaneously into the wok. Stir with the wok scoop or a large wooden spoon for about 1 minute or until the mixture turns ivory in colour. Lower the heat if the mixture begins to brown. Stir in the mushroom, chicken, walnut, almond and half the ham. When well mixed, bring to simmering point and pour the mixture into a warm deep serving bowl.

5 Add the chicken fat or sesame oil and garnish with the remaining ham sprinkled on top before serving.

Yangchow Fried Rice

揚
州
炒
飯

Originating from Yangchow in Eastern China, this dish has become just as much of a favourite with the Cantonese. In fact, it is one of the most well-known and popular rice dishes both inside and outside China. Prawns or small shrimps are always used; in the South, char-siu or Cantonese roast pork (see page 134) is used instead of ham.

INGREDIENTS

225g (8oz) fresh or frozen raw peeled prawns
120ml (8tbsp) groundnut or corn oil
2 cloves garlic, peeled and finely chopped
15ml (1tbsp) Shaohsing wine or medium dry sherry
2 large eggs
salt and pepper
about 800g (1¾lb) or 5-6 cups boiled rice, cooked at least 3-4 hours in advance (see page 170)

4 spring onions, cut into thin rounds, white and green parts separated
225g (8oz) cooked ham, diced
225g (8oz) frozen petits pois or peas
22.5ml (1½tbsp) thick soy sauce
30-45ml (2-3tbsp) clear stock

FOR THE MARINADE

2ml (scant ½tsp) salt
7.5ml (1½tsp) cornflour
½ egg white

Serves 4 as a main course

1 If frozen prawns are used, defrost thoroughly. Devein the prawns (see page 39) and cut into 2-cm (¾-inch) pieces. Pat dry with kitchen paper. Put into a bowl.

2 *Prepare the marinade:* mix together the salt, cornflour and egg white. Stir into the prawns, making sure they are evenly coated. Refrigerate, covered, for a minimum of 3 hours or overnight.

3 Heat a wok over a high heat until smoke rises. Add 30ml (2tbsp) of the oil and swirl it around.

Add the garlic and, as soon as it takes on colour, tip in the prawns. Separate them, stirring and tossing with a wok scoop or metal spatula for about 30-45 seconds or until almost cooked and turning pinkish. Splash in the wine or sherry around the side of the wok; as soon as the sizzling dies down, remove the prawns and put aside. Wash and dry the wok.

4 Beat the eggs lightly with 15ml (1tbsp) of the oil and a little salt. Heat a large frying pan until moderately hot, add 15ml (1tbsp) of the oil and swirl it around to cover the whole surface.

5 Pour in half of the beaten egg and tip the pan to spread the egg evenly to the edges. When firm, turn the crêpe over and fry the other side for a few seconds. Remove the crêpe to a plate and slice into thin strips.

6 Separate the rice grains as much as possible. Blanch the petits pois or peas in boiling salted water for 3 minutes and drain well.

7 Reheat the wok over a high heat until smoke rises. Add the remaining oil and swirl it around. Stir in the white spring onion. Pour in the remaining beaten egg, then immediately tip in all the rice. Sliding the wok scoop or spatula to the bottom of the wok where the runny egg is, turn and toss the rice, separating any lumps.

8 When thoroughly hot, add the ham, stir, then the petits pois or peas, stir, and then the prawns. Still stirring, add the soy sauce and stock.

9 Finally, put in half of the egg strips and the green spring onion. Remove to a warm serving platter and arrange the remaining egg strips on top for garnish.

VEGETARIAN MENU

Rainbow Salad

This multi-coloured plate of lightly stir-fried vegetables is made all the more delectable by the subtle dressing of sesame paste and vinegar. This dish can be prepared ahead of time and, if refrigerated, will keep overnight without losing much of its crunchiness.

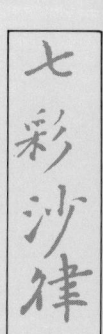

INGREDIENTS
6 large dried Chinese mushrooms, reconstituted (see page 39)
350g (12oz) cucumber, halved lengthwise and seeded
7.5ml (1½tsp) salt
225g (8oz) carrots, peeled
1 medium red pepper, halved lengthwise and seeded
75ml (5tbsp) groundnut or corn oil
7 spring onions, halved lengthwise, cut into 5-cm (2-inch) sections, white and green parts separated
225g (8oz) bean sprouts
1 large egg, lightly beaten

FOR THE DRESSING
30ml (2tbsp) sesame paste
10ml (2tsp) water
20-25ml (4-5tsp) rice or white wine vinegar
2.5ml (½tsp) salt
10 turns pepper mill

Serves 4-6 with 2-3 other dishes

1 Drain and squeeze out excess water from the mushrooms but leave damp. Slice into the thinnest possible slivers.

2 Cut the cucumber into very thin slices. Put into a bowl, sprinkle with 2.5ml (½tsp) of the salt to draw out excess water. Leave for 15-30 minutes, then drain thoroughly.

3 Shred the carrots into very thin slices. Put into a bowl, sprinkle with 5ml (1tsp) salt to draw out excess water. Leave for 15-30 minutes, then drain thoroughly.

4 Slice the red pepper into thin strips.

5 *Prepare the dressing:* mix the sesame paste with half of the water first and stir in the same direction; the paste will thicken. Add the rest of the water and continue to stir; the paste will become thinner. Now add the vinegar, little by little, stirring to blend. Stir in the salt and pepper.

6 Heat a wok over a high heat until smoke rises. Add 60ml (4tbsp) of the oil and swirl it around. Add the white spring onion and stir a couple of times. Stir in the mushroom, then the red pepper and stir some more. Now add the carrots and bean sprouts. Sliding the wok scoop or metal spatula to the bottom of the wok, flip and turn vigorously over a high heat for about 2 minutes or until the vegetables are barely cooked and still very crunchy. Add the green spring onion, stir a few more times and remove to a serving plate to cool. If water starts to ooze, drain.

7 Heat a large frying pan over a moderate heat. Add 15ml (1tbsp) oil, tipping the pan to ensure even spreading. When the oil is moderately hot, pour in the lightly beaten egg and quickly tip the pan to let the egg reach evenly to the edges. When cooked on one side, loosen the edges with a spatula and flip the crêpe over to cook the other side quickly until firm but not hard. Remove to a plate and cut into strips about 4cm (1½ inches) long and 5mm (⅕ inch) wide.

8 When the stir-fried vegetables are cool, mix in the cucumber. Stir in the dressing and toss well. Arrange the egg strips on top.

9 Chill, covered, in the refrigerator before serving. It can, however, also be served at room temperature if preferred.

Lohan's Delight: Buddhist Vegetarian Dish

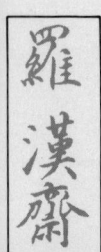

Lohan (Arahat), following general Buddhist principles, were also known as "destroyers of the passions". Fittingly, this dish does not use any of the usual condiments of ginger, garlic and spring onion, for in Buddhist belief they arouse human passions which, in turn, impede one's hopes of achieving Nirvana, the state of absolute peace and blessedness.

INGREDIENTS

9g (⅓oz) cloud ears, reconstituted (see page 39)

15g (½oz) golden needles, reconstituted (see page 39)

12 medium dried Chinese mushrooms, reconstituted in 350ml (12fl oz) boiling water (see page 39)

15g (½oz) hair algae

45ml (3tbsp) groundnut or corn oil

100g (4oz) canned bamboo shoots, thinly sliced

75-100g (3-4oz) canned ginkgo nuts

20 pieces deep-fried gluten (see page 156)

2.5ml (½tsp) salt

5-7.5ml (1-1½tsp) sugar

45ml (3tbsp) thin soy sauce

10ml (2tsp) sesame oil

FOR CURING HAIR ALGAE

450ml (16fl oz) water

2 thickish slices fresh ginger root, peeled

10ml (2tsp) Shaohsing wine or medium dry sherry

10ml (2tsp) groundnut or corn oil

Serves 4 with 2 other dishes

1 Drain the cloud ears and golden needles and squeeze out excess water from the mushrooms, but leave damp. Reserve the mushroom soaking liquid.

2 Soak the hair algae in plenty of cold or tepid water for about 10 minutes so that it will become pliable. Then rinse in many changes of water, picking over it, removing impurities and discarding the fine sand which settles at the bottom of the bowl.

3 *To cure:* put the water, ginger, wine or sherry and oil in a wok or saucepan and bring to the boil. Submerge the algae and boil for about 5 minutes. Drain through a fine sieve and discard the ginger.

4 Heat a wok over a high heat until smoke rises. Add 15ml (1tbsp) of the oil and swirl it around. Add the cloud ears and golden needles and toss and turn for about 30 seconds, adjusting the heat if the cloud ears make a loud explosive noise. Remove to a warm dish nearby.

5 Add the remaining oil and swirl it around. Add the mushrooms and bamboo shoots and turn and stir for about 30 seconds or until very hot.

6 Return the cloud ears and golden needles to the wok, and add the hair algae, ginkgo nuts and gluten pieces. Pour in the mushroom water, add the salt, sugar and soy sauce and bring to the boil. Cover, lower the heat and simmer fast for 10-15 minutes or until most of the water has been absorbed.

7 Remove to a warm serving plate. Sprinkle on the sesame oil and serve.

Stir-fried Bean Sprouts

Rich in protein, these ubiquitous sprouts which come from mung beans, can be eaten cooked or in a salad. The Chinese always cook them, but only slightly to preserve their crunchiness.

INGREDIENTS
225-450g (8oz-1lb) bean sprouts
30-45ml (2-3tbsp) groundnut or corn oil
2-4 spring onions, cut into 2.5-cm (1-inch) sections, white and green parts separated
2-3 very thin slices fresh ginger root, peeled
salt to taste or about 2.5-4ml (½-¾tsp)
10-15ml (2-3tsp) thin soy sauce or 15-30ml (1-2 heaped tbsp) oyster sauce

Serves 2-3 with 2 other dishes

1 Do not wash the bean sprouts. Instead, refrigerate them until they are to be cooked. If they have to be washed, make sure to drain them well and shake off any remaining water before refrigerating them.

2 Heat a wok over a high heat until smoke rises. Add the oil and swirl it around. Add the white spring onion and as soon as it sizzles, add the ginger. Tip in the bean sprouts and, leaving the heat on high all the time, slide the wok scoop or metal spatula to the bottom of the wok and then turn and vigorously toss the bean sprouts right and left and all over for about 2-3 minutes. Sprinkle with the salt and green spring onion towards the end. The bean sprouts will be cooked but still firm and crisp, having exuded only the minimum of water.

3 Remove to a warm serving plate and pour over the soy or oyster sauce. Serve immediately.

Note: take care not to overcook this dish. Since frozen bean sprouts are inevitably soggy, never freeze them. When reheated, they will have lost much of their crunchiness.

Variation: Stir-fried lettuce
Use 550-700g (1¼-1½lb) Webb, Cos or Iceberg lettuce, tearing large leaves into smaller pieces, instead of bean sprouts. Cook as above. Serves 4 with 2 other dishes.

Bean Curd in a Simple Sauce

Reddish bean curd cubes dotted with white and green; the first step of this dish is essential for a perfect result.

INGREDIENTS
4 cakes bean curd
30-45ml (2-3tbsp) groundnut or corn oil
5-6 spring onions, cut into small rounds, white and green parts separated

FOR THE SAUCE
1.25ml (¼tsp) salt
1.25ml (¼tsp) sugar
15ml (1tbsp) thick soy sauce or optional oyster sauce
15ml (1tbsp) thin soy sauce
5ml (1tsp) Shaohsing wine or medium dry sherry

Serves 4 with 2 other dishes

1 Cover the bean curd cakes in hot water and steep for 15 minutes in order to firm them up, making handling easier.

2 Lift them from the water and slice each cake into 32 cubes: divide one cake lengthwise into 4, then crosswise into 4, and then halve the thickness of each piece, making 32 in all. Handling gently, put them into a sieve to drain excess water.

3 *Prepare the sauce:* mix together the salt, sugar, soy sauces and wine or sherry.

4 Heat a wok over a high heat until smoke rises. Add the oil and swirl it around. Add the white spring onion, stir and let it sizzle. Then add the bean curd. Sliding the wok scoop or metal spatula to the bottom of the wok, gently turn and fold the cubes to blend with the oil and spring onion for about 1 minute.

5 Add the sauce to the wok, continuing to fold and turn gently a few more times to let the cubes take on colour. Lower the heat, cover and cook for another minute.

6 Add the green spring onion. Carefully remove the bean curd mixture to a warm serving plate. Serve immediately.

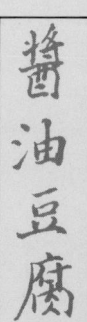

Stir-fried Spinach in Bean Curd "Cheese" Sauce

If you do not use white bean curd "cheese", which gives the dish an exotic taste, you will still find that the spinach is delicious simply stir-fried in garlic and seasoned with salt.

INGREDIENTS

450g (1lb) fresh spinach, washed
1.4 litres (2½ pints) water
5ml (1tsp) salt
75ml (5tbsp) groundnut or corn oil
2½-3 cakes white bean curd "cheese" with chilli
4-5 cloves garlic, peeled and finely chopped
2.5ml (½tsp) sugar
½ fresh green or red chilli, seeded and sliced (optional)
10ml (2tsp) Shaohsing wine or medium dry sherry

Serves 3-4 with 2 other dishes

1 Remove any stringy roots and hard stalks from the spinach.

2 Place the water in a saucepan, bring to the boil and add the salt and 15ml (1tbsp) of the oil. Blanch the spinach for 1 minute. Drain and rinse with cold water immediately. Drain well and put aside. This can be done a few hours beforehand without the spinach losing its vivid colour and texture.

3 Mash the bean curd "cheese" in a small bowl with a small amount of the juice from the jar. Stir in the sugar.

4 Heat a wok over a high heat until smoke rises. Add 60ml (4tbsp) oil and swirl it around. Add the garlic, bean curd "cheese" and chilli and stir. Splash in the wine or sherry around the side of the wok. Add the spinach and stir and turn continuously with the wok scoop or metal spatula for 1-2 minutes to incorporate the sauce. Lower the heat if the sauce is being absorbed too quickly. Remove to a warm serving plate. Serve immediately.

Stir-fried Broccoli and Chinese Mushrooms

For the non-vegetarian, this dish is excellent if 30ml (2 heaped tbsp) oyster sauce is used instead of the soy sauce.

INGREDIENTS

12 dried Chinese mushrooms, the thick floral ones are best, reconstituted (see page 39)
350g (12oz) broccoli, preferably spears
45ml (3tbsp) groundnut or corn oil
4 very thin slices fresh ginger root, peeled
4 spring onions, cut into 2.5-cm (1-inch) sections, white and green parts separated
2.5ml (½tsp) salt
1.25ml (¼tsp) sugar

FOR THE SAUCE
5ml (1tsp) potato flour
90ml (6tbsp) mushroom water
15ml (1tbsp) thick soy sauce or 30ml (2tbsp) oyster sauce

Serves 4 with 2 other dishes

1 Wash the mushrooms and simmer in about 450ml (¾ pint) of water for about 30 minutes. When cool, clip off the stems and discard. Squeeze out excess water but leave damp. Reserve the soaking liquid.

2 Peel off the hard outer layer of the broccoli stalks, if necessary. Leave whole or cut into large bite-sized pieces.

3 *Prepare the sauce:* dissolve the potato flour in the mushroom water. Stir in soy or oyster sauce.

4 Heat a wok until hot. Add the oil and swirl it around. Add the ginger and white spring onion. Stir a few times and then tip in the mushrooms. Stir a few more times and add the broccoli. Sliding the wok scoop or metal spatula to the bottom of the wok, flip and toss for about 30 seconds. Add about 105ml (7tbsp) mushroom water and sprinkle with the salt and sugar. Cover and cook over a moderate heat for about 6 minutes.

5 Remove the cover. Taste to see if the broccoli is ready: it should be tender yet still firm and crisp.

6 Pour the well-stirred sauce over the broccoli and mushrooms, stirring continuously as it thickens. Add the green spring onion, stir to mix, then remove to a warm serving plate.

7 Attractively arrange the mushrooms, cap side up, on top of the broccoli. Serve immediately.

MIXED MENU

Dried Oysters and Hair Algae

The Chinese are very fond of puns, and the Chinese language lends itself particularly to this play on words for it is very rich in tones. Mandarin, the official language, has four tones to each sound while Cantonese, the lingua franca *in the South, has at least seven. This often allows two, or even three, meanings to a term, each with a slightly different pronunciation. This dish, beloved of the Cantonese, is a classic example of this point. Dried oyster and hair algae sounds similar to the Chinese New Year greeting of either "Good deeds and prosperity", or "Good business and prosperity". For this reason, Southern Chinese make sure they eat this dish during the first fortnight of the Chinese New Year when much food and many different dishes are consumed.*

INGREDIENTS
24 dried oysters
15g (½oz) hair algae
16 medium dried Chinese mushrooms, reconsistuted in 350ml (12fl oz) boiling water (see page 39)
350g (12oz) roast belly pork (see page 146)
30-45ml (2-3tbsp) groundnut or corn oil
1-2 cloves garlic, peeled and cut diagonally into thin slices
4-6 thin slices fresh ginger root, peeled
6 spring onions, white parts only, cut into 2.5-cm (1-inch) sections
15ml (1tbsp) Shaohsing wine or medium dry sherry
600ml (1 pint) liquid, made up of oyster water, mushroom water and clear stock
30ml (2tbsp) oyster sauce
15ml (1tbsp) thin soy sauce
2.5ml (½tsp) sugar
30ml (2tbsp) potato flour, dissolved in 120ml (4fl oz) water

FOR CURING HAIR ALGAE
450ml (16fl oz) water
2 thickish slices fresh ginger root, peeled
10ml (2tsp) Shaohsing wine or medium dry sherry
10ml (2tsp) groundnut or corn oil

Serves 8 with 4-5 other dishes

1 Rinse the dried oysters thoroughly, rubbing gently with the fingers to get rid of any impurity. Put into a bowl and pour over sufficient boiling water to just cover. Soak for about 3-4 hours or even overnight until quite soft again. Remove and discard the hard muscles. Reserve soaking liquid.

2 Soak the hair algae in plenty of cold or tepid water for about 10 minutes so that it will become pliable. Then squeeze and rinse in many changes of water, picking over it, removing impurities and discarding the fine sand which settles at the bottom of the bowl.

3 *Cure the hair algae:* put the water, ginger slices, wine or sherry and oil in a wok and bring to the boil. Submerge the algae and boil for about 5 minutes. Drain through a fine sieve and discard the ginger.

4 Drain, squeeze out excess water from the mushrooms but leave damp. Reserve the soaking liquid.

5 Cut the belly pork into rectangular pieces of more or less the same size as the dried oysters.

6 Heat a wok over a high heat until smoke rises. Add the oil and swirl it around. Add the garlic, stir, then the ginger, stir, and the white spring onion and stir. Add the pork, oysters and mushrooms and, sliding the wok scoop or metal spatula to the bottom of the wok, turn and toss gently for about 1 minute or until very hot. Splash in the wine or medium dry sherry around the side of the wok. When the sizzling dies down, add the liquid, oyster sauce, soy sauce and sugar. Bring to the boil, reduce the heat and simmer fast, covered, for about 30-45 minutes.

7 Make a well in the middle of the wok contents, add the algae and continue to simmer fast for another 15 minutes. Add more liquid if necessary – at the end of the cooking time there should be about 175-250ml (6-8fl oz) liquid still unabsorbed.

8 Leaving the liquid in the wok, remove the pork, oysters and mushrooms and arrange them attractively on a warm serving plate or bowl. Place the whole bunch of algae on top in the centre so that your family or guests recognize the symbolic greeting of prosperity immediately.

9 Return the liquid in the wok to simmering point. Mix in sufficient well-stirred dissolved potato flour, until the sauce has thickened enough to coat the back of a spoon. Pour over the ingredients and serve hot.

Lion's Head

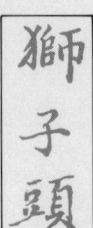

Originating from Yangchow in Kiangsu Province, this dish is so called because each pork meatball is supposed to resemble a lion's head, and the cabbage its mane.

INGREDIENTS

450g (1lb) Chinese celery cabbage
8 water chestnuts, fresh peeled or canned drained
450g (1lb) pork, about 50-75g (2-3oz) of which is fat
scant 45ml (3tbsp) water
2.5ml (½tsp) salt
30ml (2tbsp) thick soy sauce
15ml (1tbsp) Shaohsing wine or medium dry sherry
5ml (1tsp) brown sugar

15ml (1tbsp) cornflour
45ml (3tbsp) groundnut or corn oil
300ml (½ pint) clear stock
10-15ml (2-3tsp) potato flour

Serves 6 with 3 other dishes

1 Cut each cabbage leaf crosswise into 5-cm (2-inch) pieces, separating the stalk from the leafy top pieces.

2 Chop the water chestnuts by hand or mince coarsely.

3 Chop the pork by hand or mince coarsely. Put into a large bowl. Stir in the water, 15ml (1tbsp) at a time, and continue to stir in the same direction for 1-2 minutes or until smooth and almost gelatinous. Pick up the pork mixture and throw it back into the bowl about 20-30 times. This stirring and throwing action makes the pork light and tender, producing the desired effect when cooked.

4 Add the salt, soy sauce, wine or sherry and sugar and mix well. Stir in the water chestnuts. Add the cornflour and stir vigorously to mix. Divide the mixture into 4 equal portions, shaping them into thick round cakes – each a lion's head.

5 Heat a wok over a moderate heat. Add the oil and when smoke rises, put in the lions' heads to brown, 2 at a time, for about 2 minutes each side or until golden in colour. Remove to a plate, leaving the oil in the wok.

6 Add the stalk pieces of the cabbage and stir-fry for about 30 seconds, then add the leafy pieces and continue to stir-fry for another minute to partially cook and reduce their bulk.

7 Transfer half of this cabbage to line the bottom of a large flameproof or ovenproof casserole. Place the lions' heads on top, then cover them with the remaining cabbage, adding the oil from the wok as well. Add the stock.

8 To cook, either:
bring the casserole to the boil on top of a cooker. Lower the heat and simmer, covered, for 2 hours. This traditional way produces the best result.
Or: cook in a preheated oven at 180°C (350°F) mark 4 for 20 minutes, reduce the heat to 170°C (325°F) mark 3 and continue to cook for a further 2 hours.

9 To serve, arrange the cabbage underneath and around the meatballs on a warm plate so as to give the illusion of a lion's head and mane. Thicken the sauce with the potato flour mixed with a little water and pour over the meatballs.

Plain-boiled Vegetables

In the South, where green vegetables grow in abundance, boiling is as popular a method of cooking as stir-frying. Chinese flowering cabbage and broccoli are especially suitable.

INGREDIENTS

5ml (1tsp) salt
60ml (4tbsp) groundnut or corn oil
30ml (2tbsp) oyster sauce

or 22.5ml (1½tbsp) soy sauce
450g (1lb) Chinese flower cabbage, trimmed

Serves 6 with 3 other dishes

1 Put 1.4 litres (2½ pints) water into a saucepan and bring to the boil. Add the salt and 22.5ml (1½tbsp) of the oil.

2 Place the cabbage in the water and return to the boil. Boil for about 30-60 seconds. It should be tender but still have a bite. Drain well in a colander.

3 Remove the cabbage to a warm serving plate. Pour the rest of the oil over evenly and then the oyster or soy sauce. Serve hot.

Paper-thin Lamb with Spring Onions

This is one of the famous Peking dishes. The spring onion is an indispensable ingredient because it adds so much flavour to the lamb, not to mention increasing the overall fragrance of the dish.

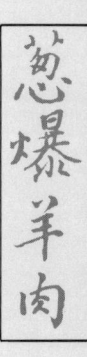

INGREDIENTS
350g (12oz) lamb fillet, trimmed
45-60ml (3-4tbsp) groundnut or corn oil
2 cloves garlic, peeled and thinly sliced
225g (8oz) spring onions, sliced into long slivers
dashes of sesame oil to taste

FOR THE MARINADE
10ml (2tsp) thin soy sauce
10ml (2tsp) Shaohsing wine or medium dry sherry

FOR THE SAUCE
1.25ml (¼tsp) salt
2.5ml (½tsp) sugar
10ml (2tsp) thick soy sauce
10ml (2tsp) Shaohsing wine or medium dry sherry
5ml (1tsp) sesame oil

Serves 4 with 2 other dishes

1 Slice the lamb into paper-thin pieces (chilling the meat in the freezer beforehand for 1-2 hours will make slicing easier). Pat dry afterwards if necessary. Put into a bowl.

2 *Prepare the marinade:* add the soy sauce and wine or sherry to the lamb. Leave to marinate for 15-30 minutes.

3 *Prepare the sauce:* mix together the salt, sugar, soy sauce, wine or sherry and oil in a small bowl and put aside.

4 Heat a wok over a high heat until smoke rises. Add the oil and swirl it around. Add the garlic, let it sizzle and take on colour. Put in the lamb and, sliding the wok scoop or metal spatula to the bottom of the wok, turn and toss for 20-30 seconds or until partially cooked. Pour in the sauce, stirring to incorporate, and add the spring onion. Flip and toss until the lamb is cooked and the mixture has absorbed most of the sauce. The dish should be slightly dry in appearance.

5 Remove to a warm serving plate and sprinkle with sesame oil to enhance the flavour. Serve immediately.

Yu-ling's Hot and Numbing Chicken

Chiang Yu-ling, my Mandarin teacher and friend, herself an excellent cook of Northern cuisine, has contributed much interest and information to this book. She has kindly given me this recipe.

INGREDIENTS
2 chicken breasts, about 500-550g (1lb 2oz-1lb 4 oz), skinned and boned
groundnut or corn oil
15ml (1tsp) Szechwan peppercorns
2 large cloves garlic, peeled and sliced
4 thin slices fresh ginger
1 large spring onion, cut into 4-cm (1½-inch) sections
2-3 fresh green chillies, each about 7.5cm (3 inches) long, seeded and sliced diagonally into long strips

15ml (1tbsp) Shaohsing wine or medium dry sherry
1.25ml (¼tsp) salt
1.25-2.5ml (¼-½tsp) sugar
2.5ml (½tsp) ground roasted Szechwan peppercorns
2.5ml (½tsp) cornflour dissolved in 30ml (2tbsp) water
5ml (1tsp) sesame oil

FOR THE MARINADE
2.5ml (½tsp) salt
6 turns white pepper mill
5ml (1tsp) cornflour
½ egg white, beaten

Serves 4 with 2 other dishes

1 Cut the chicken flesh into large cubes. Put into a bowl.

2 *Prepare the marinade:* add the salt, pepper, cornflour and egg white to the chicken. Stir in the same direction until well coated. Leave to marinate for 20-30 minutes.

3 Half fill a wok or deep-fryer with oil. Heat until it is just hot (about 110°C [225°F]). Add the chicken to "go through the oil" for about 60-75 seconds separating the pieces with a long pair of chopsticks. Remove with a large hand strainer or perforated disc and keep nearby. The chicken, having turned whitish, will be almost cooked.

4 Empty all but 30ml (2tbsp) of the oil into a container and save for other uses. Reheat the oil over a medium heat. Add the Szechwan peppercorns and fry for about 1 minute or until they have released their aroma and turned dark brown. Remove and discard.

5 Add the garlic, ginger and spring onion and fry over a high heat until the edges are brown and their aroma released. Remove and discard.

6 Lower the heat and add the chilli. Stir and turn for about 1 minute to release its peppery hot flavour, taking care not to burn it. Remove to a small dish and keep nearby.

7 Turn up the heat. Return the chicken to the wok and stir and turn in rapid succession for about 30 seconds, or until hot. Splash in the wine or sherry around the side of the wok, stirring continuously as it sizzles. Add the salt and sugar and sprinkle on the ground peppercorns. Trickle in the well-stirred, dissolved cornflour and continue to stir as it thickens. Return the chilli to the wok and stir to mix for about another 10 seconds. Sprinkle on the sesame oil, then remove to a warm serving plate. Serve immediately.

Eight-treasure Rice Pudding

This Northern pudding can be served anytime but more especially during Chinese New Year. "Eight-treasure" is a reference to the Buddhist eight treasures which guard and enrich one's life. The ingredients for decorating the pudding can be substituted by nuts or other dried fruits.

INGREDIENTS
350g (12oz) white
  glutinous rice
450ml (16fl oz) water
6 dried Chinese red dates
30ml (2tbsp) plain flour
275g (10oz) canned red
  bean paste
30ml (2tbsp) groundnut
  or corn oil
50g (2oz) lard
45ml (3tbsp) sugar
1 glacé cherry
18 small cubes candied
  orange peel

18 sultanas
18 raisins

FOR THE SYRUP
Either:
45ml (3tbsp) sugar
250ml (8fl oz) water
10ml (2tsp) cornflour,
  dissolved in 30ml
  (2tbsp) water
Or:
120ml (4fl oz) maple
  syrup

Serves 8

1 Wash the glutinous rice 3-4 times or until the water is no longer milky. Drain and put into a baking tin or a heatproof plate. Add the water. Steam in a wok or steamer for about 25 minutes (see page 45).

2 Meanwhile, soak the dates in hot water for 15 minutes, then slit open and remove the stones, leaving the dates whole.

3 *Prepare the red bean paste:* add the flour to the bean paste and blend well. Heat a wok or frying pan over a moderate heat, add the oil and then the bean paste. Cook for about 5 minutes, turning and stirring all the time to prevent it from sticking. This thickens it sufficiently to keep it from leaking through the rice during steaming. Remove and leave to cool.

4 Well grease a glass heatproof bowl, about 1.4 litres (2½ pint) capacity, with some of the lard.

5 Blend the remaining lard and the sugar into the cooked rice.

6 Form a decorative pattern in the base of the bowl with the dried fruits. Put the cherry in the centre. Dot a ring of 6 triangles round it with the orange peel, make 6 lines, alternating 1 sultana and 1 raisin, to go up the sides of the bowl between the orange peel and, lastly, place 1 red date between 2 lines of sultanas and raisins.

7 Gently but *firmly* press one fairly thick layer of rice on to the bottom and sides of the bowl to cover the dried fruits without disturbing the pattern. Put the red bean paste into the centre, then cover with the remaining rice, pressing down to make the surface flat and even. There should be about 2.5cm (1 inch) space between the rice level and the rim of the bowl so that the rice does not overflow when steamed.

8 Put the bowl inside the wok or steamer and steam for about 1¼ hours. Check the water level periodically, adding boiling water if necessary.

9 About 15 minutes before the rice pudding is ready, prepare the syrup. If the traditional syrup is used, put the sugar and water in a saucepan and slowly bring to the boil. When the sugar is completely dissolved, trickle in the dissolved cornflour, stirring as the mixture thickens. Pour into a warm bowl. Alternatively, bring the maple syrup to the boil and pour into a warm bowl. This syrup complements the pudding well.

10 Remove the bowl from the wok or steamer and invert the pudding on to a warm plate so that the decorative pattern is on top. The best way to do this is to put the bowl in the middle of a long towel. Cover the bowl with the plate. Pick up the towel, bowl and plate with both hands and turn upside down, then gently remove the bowl as the rice pudding slips onto the plate.

11 Pour the syrup over and serve hot.

SPECIAL RECIPES

Stock

There are many ways of making stock, but the Chinese believe that the most balanced result comes from a long simmering of chicken, pork and ham. Abalone was traditionally included but as this is now so expensive, most people are content to dispense with it. In the Chinese kitchen, a distinction is made between the first yield of this simmering, called the prime stock, and the second yield, called the clear or secondary stock.

A question often raised is whether or not you should use stock cubes: if you are desperate, by all means use them but I would suggest using them only in an emergency rather than on a regular basis. Stock keeps well in the refrigerator for up to a week but will keep longer if brought to the boil every second day.

PRIME STOCK

INGREDIENTS	pork, without rind
700g (1½lb) chicken thighs, drumsticks and necks	700g (1½lb) ham or mild gammon, without rind
700g (1½lb) mostly lean	*Makes 1.7 litres (3 pints)*

1 Put the chicken, pork and ham or gammon into a deep stockpot or saucepan and add 2.8 litres (5 pints) water. Bring to the boil and skim off the scum that surfaces until the water is clear.

2 Partially cover with a lid. Lower the heat to maintain a fast simmer and cook for about 3 hours. The liquid, which should have reduced to about 1.7 litres (3 pints), is the prime stock. Pour through a sieve into a storage container.

Note: the meat in the stockpot is still tasty enough to serve as a meal if clear or secondary stock is not to be made. Dip the chicken or pork in thin soy sauce and eat the ham as it is.

CLEAR STOCK

INGREDIENTS	salt to taste.
left-over ingredients from prime stock	*Makes about 1 litre (1¾ pints)*

1 Refill the stockpot or saucepan with 1.7-2.3 litres (3-4 pints) water. Bring to the boil, reduce the heat to maintain a fast simmer and cook, partially covered, for 1½-2 hours, reducing the liquid to 900ml-1.1 litres (1½-2 pints). This is the clear stock.

2 Pour through a sieve into a storage container. Discard the meat. Keep in the refrigerator as for prime stock. Season with salt to taste.

Variation

Another way of making prime and clear stock is to use about 2kg (4½lb) of pork or ham bones, spare ribs, chicken or duck carcass, giblets and stalks from dried Chinese mushrooms. Simmer them in about 4 litres (7 pints) water, reducing the liquid to about 2.5 litres (4½ pints) for prime stock. Add water again to make more or less the same amount for clear or secondary stock.

Hot Chilli Oil

This is sometimes sold in a bottle under the name of Chilli oil, although I personally prefer the taste of this home-made version.

INGREDIENTS	250ml (8fl oz) groundnut or corn oil
12 dried red chillies, each about 7.5cm (3 inches) long, or 24 small ones	

1 Slit open the dried chillies. Remove and discard the seeds. Chop into flakes and put into a glass jar.

2 Heat the oil in a saucepan until it smokes. Remove at once from the heat. Leave to cool for 3-4 minutes.

3 Pour into the jar. The chilli flakes will rise to the surface but will sink to the bottom gradually. The oil becomes spicy hot almost immediately but will become more so in a few days time. It keeps for months in a cool place.

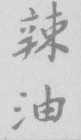

Szechwan Chilli Paste

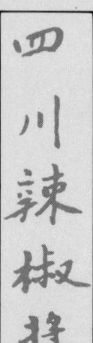

INGREDIENTS

dried red chillies ground yellow bean sauce

1 Grind sufficient red chillies in a food processor or use a mortar and pestle.

2 In a bowl, mix the chilli and the yellow bean sauce, in the proportion of 15ml (1tbsp) ground

chilli to 30ml (2tbsp) ground yellow bean sauce. (Natives of Szechwan will no doubt find this proportion too mild, while people unused to spicy foods will find it almost too hot. Use your judgement to suit your own taste.) The chilli paste will keep for months in a jar stored in a cool place.

Sweet Bean Sauce

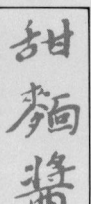

INGREDIENTS

15ml (1tbsp) water
135ml (9tbsp) sugar
135ml (9tbsp) ground
   yellow bean sauce
15ml (1tbsp) groundnut
   or corn oil

1 Put the water, sugar, yellow bean sauce and oil in a wok or saucepan. Heat over a low heat for 3-4 minutes or until the sugar has completely dissolved, stirring all the time to mix into a smooth sauce.

2 Leave to cool and serve at room temperature.

Flavour-Potting

Flavour-potting is a cooking technique popular in every Chinese region whereby meat, poultry or offal are cooked and then steeped in a specially prepared sauce. The idea is that the flavour of the sauce should permeate the meat and that the sauce should in turn be enriched by the taste of the meat and its fat. The spices used in the sauce vary from area to area and from cook to cook, but the ones most frequently used are: star anise, Szechwan peppercorns, fennel seeds, cinnamon, ginger and liquorice. In China, flavour-potting spices are generally bought ready-made from a herbal pharmacy, and these mixtures, labelled mixed spices, are now exported and sold in Chinese shops. In this recipe I have also added preserved tangerine peel.

The flavour-potting sauce, if properly kept and periodically re-heated, should go on indefinitely. Indeed, many families pride themselves on keeping the same one for months if not years!

INGREDIENTS
FOR THE SAUCE

100g (4oz) bag of mixed
   flavour potting spices
   or 12 whole star anise
12.5g (½oz) cinnamon
1 cardomom (t'sao kuo)
5ml (1tsp) cloves
45ml (3tbsp) fennel seeds
60ml (4tbsp) Szechwan
   peppercorns
5g (⅕oz) liquorice
25g (1oz) dried ginger root
2.8-3 litres (5-5½ pints)
   water
50g (2oz) fresh ginger
root, unpeeled and
bruised
2-3 large pieces
   preserved tangerine
   peel
30ml (2tbsp) sea salt
450ml (16fl oz) thick soy
   sauce
50ml (2fl oz) thin soy sauce
150g (5oz) rock sugar or
   granulated sugar
175ml (6fl oz) Shaohsing
   wine or medium dry
   sherry
30ml (2tbsp) mei-kuei-lu
   wine or gin

1 Put the mixed spices in a bag made from 3 layers of cheesecloth or muslin and tie the opening with cotton or string. Put into a large, deep stockpot.

2 Add the water, fresh ginger and tangerine peel. Bring to the boil, reduce the heat and simmer for about 15 minutes to release the aromatic flavours.

3 Add the sea salt, soy sauces, sugar and wine or sherry, continuing to simmer until the sugar has completely dissolved. Check the taste of the sauce: it should be quite salty, rich and aromatic. It is now ready for other ingredients to be cooked in it.

GLOSSARY

Beans and Bean Products

Bean curd, fresh
White, custard-like product made from ground soy beans and used extensively in Chinese cooking – its rôle is equivalent to that of dairy products in Western cuisine. Bean curd is made from soy beans which have been finely ground with water then strained through a cloth. The resulting "milk" is brought to the boil before gypsum is added to set it into a curd. The curd is then put into boxes and weights are applied to squeeze out the remaining whey. As it is impractical to make at home, bean curd is usually sold in Chinese stores in cakes about 2.5cm (1 inch) thick and 6.5cm (2½ inches) square. Bean curd keeps for up to 3 days in the refrigerator if the water in which it stands is changed every day.

Bean curd "cheese", red fermented
Brick red in colour, very strong and cheesy in taste, this type of bean curd is fermented with salt, red rice and rice wine. It is used for flavouring meat, poultry and vegetarian dishes and is usually stored in jars or earthenware pots in 2.5-5cm (1-2 inch) square cakes. After a jar has been opened, the bean curd "cheese" will keep for months if refrigerated.

Bean curd "cheese", white fermented
Ivory in colour, sold in 2.5cm (1 inch) cakes, this fermented bean curd sometimes has chilli added to it. It is used to flavour certain vegetables, or is served as a side dish with rice or congee. It is sold in jars and keeps for months if refrigerated.

Bean curd, puffed
Fresh bean curd cubes, deep-fried until golden in colour and airy inside (see p.152). They keep well in the refrigerator for about a week.

Bean curd sheets
Thin, dried bean curd sheets, about 15 x 45cm (6 x 18 inches), usually sold with about one third of their length folded in. To make them pliable, either soak them or spray them with water. Store them in a cool, dry place.

Black beans, fermented
Whole soy beans preserved in salt and ginger. Although pungent in taste, when combined with garlic and cooked in oil they lend a delicious flavour to any other ingredients. Some black beans are canned in brine but the dried ones are by far the best. They keep for months if stored in a cool, dry place.

Crushed (ground) yellow bean sauce
Nut brown purée of fermented yellow soy beans, wheat flour, salt and water. Usually sold in cans labelled "Crushed yellow bean sauce" or "Ground yellow bean sauce", this is a major seasoning in Chinese cooking of all regions. Once opened, store in a covered jar in the larder or refrigerator.

Red beans (*Phaseolus angularis*), **azuki beans**
Native to China, but now also grown in America and Europe, these small red beans are the seeds of the plant *vigna angularis*. In Chinese cuisine they are eaten mostly as a dessert.

Red bean paste
Thick, reddish-brown paste made from puréed, sweetened red beans or azuki beans; a very popular filling for sweet dishes.

Soy bean paste, hot
Very hot and spicy paste of soy beans crushed with chilli, sugar and salt; an indispensable ingredient for making the Szechwan twice-cooked pork (see p.126). Usually sold in jars, it keeps for a long time.

Sweet bean sauce
Made of crushed yellow bean sauce sweetened with sugar. This is the traditional dipping sauce for the famous Peking duck, although the readily available hoisin sauce is more widely used in the West.

Szechwan chilli paste, chilli paste
Hot paste of dried red chilli peppers and ground yellow bean sauce (left) which forms the basis of the famous Szechwan fish fragrant sauce. When stored in a covered jar topped with a little oil to prevent it from drying out, it keeps for months in a cool place.

Yellow beans in salted sauce
Whole yellow soy beans fermented with salt, wheat flour and sugar. Although not as widely used as fermented black beans, they too are used as a seasoning when cooking meat or vegetables. Sold in cans, they should be refrigerated in a covered jar once opened.

Cereals, Grains and Noodles

Buckwheat noodles
Very thin, beige-coloured noodle strips made of buckwheat flour and wheat flour with water. They are a great favourite of the Northern Chinese and are available as dry noodles in some Chinese and Japanese stores.

Cellophane noodles, transparent vermicelli, bean thread
Made from ground mung beans, these noodles are usually sold in a bundle tied by a thin thread. Wiry and hard in their dry state, they have to be soaked in water and then drained before use. They are eaten not so much as a staple but more as a vegetable which absorbs tastes from other ingredients and provides a slippery texture. They keep indefinitely in a cool place.

Egg noodles, fresh or dry
Made of wheat flour, egg and water, these are the most common all-purpose Chinese noodles. They are usually sold in two widths: thin, thread-like noodles and broad, strip noodles. Fresh, soft noodles are sold packed in plastic bags; dry noodles are sold in compressed rounds (often called noodle cakes) and are sometimes pre-cooked by steaming. Fresh noodle cakes keep well in a sealed bag in the refrigerator for up to a week or they can be frozen, each wrapped individually. Dried noodles, if kept in a covered tin or jar, will keep for months. Egg noodles are seldom made at home but are bought in Chinese grocery stores. Noodles from other countries can be used as a substitute; the only difference is that Chinese noodles are more elastic in texture.

Long-grain rice (*Oryza sativa, spp.*)
The white grains of this versatile rice are husked and polished. It is known that the Chinese grew and ate this rice as early as the 12th century BC in the Chou dynasty, and indeed, it remains the staple food for the Chinese today. Rice will keep for months in a covered container.

Rice noodles, rice sticks
Wiry, white noodles made from rice flour. Although slender like cellophane noodles, they do not look translucent like the latter. They are sold, dried, in tightly folded bundles and will keep for months in a covered tin or jar. Only a brief soaking and cooking time are required.

River rice noodles
Made from rice ground with water which has been steamed in thin sheets then rolled and cut up into strips about 1cm (½ inch) wide, these noodles are sold both dry and fresh. The dry noodles have to be boiled and drained before use. Despite the fact that the dry variety will last for months in a covered tin or jar, the fresh ones are by far superior, especially for stir-frying. However, they must be used within 1 or 2 days after buying or they will lose their tender quality.

Spring roll wrappers
Two types: Cantonese, which are smooth like a noodle dough and Shanghai which are transparent, like rice paper. Sold frozen in packets, they are easily pulled apart when defrosted. The Shanghai type is used in this book.

Tientsin fen pi
Dry, transparent, brittle round sheets about 22.5cm (9 inches) in diameter, made from ground mung beans. When soaked in boiling water, they have a slippery texture and are eaten as a cross between rice noodles and cellophane noodles. Sold in packets, they keep for a long time in a cool place.

U-dong noodles
Off-white noodle strips about 3mm (⅛ inch) wide, made of wheat flour and water. These Japanese and Korean noodles are similar in texture to Northern Chinese noodles and are available as dry noodles in Oriental stores.

White glutinous rice (*Oryza sativa spp.*)
More rounded in shape than long-grain rice, white glutinous rice is sticky when boiled. It is eaten by the Chinese both as a savoury (see Stir-fried glutinous rice) and as a pudding (see Eight-treasure rice pudding); it is also used as a stuffing (see Duck stuffed with glutinous rice). It will keep for months in a covered container.

Wonton wrappers
Made of the same dough as egg noodles (wheat flour, egg and water), and sold in 7.5cm- (3-inch) sized squares. Like noodles, they are not usually made at home but are bought fresh from Chinese stores. They can be frozen.

Yi noodles, yifu noodles
Egg noodles woven into a round cake, already deep-fried when sold in Chinese stores. They keep well in a cool place for about 2 weeks. If left for too long, they may become rancid.

Dried products

Abalone *(Haliotis tuberculata)*
For most people, this shelled mollusc is available only in canned form, with its ivory-coloured flesh already cooked. Even so, it is delicious eaten cold or hot, on its own or with other ingredients. If eaten hot, it must be cooked very briefly, for over-cooking will make it rubbery. The juice in the can is valuable as a basis for sauces or soups.

Agar-agar
Processed gelatin extracted from dried seaweed, it is usually sold in bundles of long, narrow crinkly strips. Used as a thickener, it is extremely heat-resistant and can only be dissolved slowly in boiling water. Store in a sealed plastic bag in a cool place, but *not* in the refrigerator.

Bird's nest
Nests made by swallows of the Collocalia genus which live on the cliffs of the South-East Asian islands. What makes these nests unique is that the birds line them with a gelatinous mixture of predigested seaweed which hardens to form a transparent layer. There are many grades of bird's nest but since the whole nests are extremely expensive and hardly available in the West, it is advisable to use the broken ones. The whiter the colour and the fewer specks of feathers there are, the better the quality of the nest. The packets sold in Chinese stores are usually pre-processed, so the cleaning job is not too laborious.

Chinese black mushrooms
(Lentinus edodes)
Edible tree fungus which adds both flavour and texture to a dish. They vary in quality, size and price but the best and most expensive are the floral mushrooms (*fa gu* in Cantonese, *hua ku* in Mandarin). These have floral patterns on the surface of the caps, which curl under. Second in quality come the thick mushrooms whose relatively thick caps also curl slightly inwards along the edges. The lowest quality are the flat mushrooms which have thin and flat caps. What is usually available in Chinese stores are packets of mixed quality and size. They keep for a long time in a covered container.

Chinese sausages
Wind-dried pork, or pork and duck liver sausages, usually sold in pairs about 15cm (6 inches) long. The pork sausages should look pinkish with white pork fat showing through the casing; the liver sausages should look dark brown. Both types must be cooked before eating. They will keep well in a covered jar and will keep for months in the refrigerator.

Cloud ears *(Auricularia auricula)*
Edible tree fungus grown in large quantities in the western provinces of Szechwan, Hunan and Yunnan. Thin and brittle when dry, they expand to form thick brown clusters when soaked for about twenty minutes. More delicate and refined than wood ears, they are used in stir-fried dishes to absorb flavours from other seasonings but, above all, to provide a slimy but crunchy texture. They should be well rinsed to remove sand, and the hard knobs of the mushroom should be removed if necessary. Store in a covered container.

Cornflour, cornstarch
Fine, white starch extracted from maize, used to thicken sauces or marinades.

Creamed coconut
Milky white in colour and solid in form like a bar of soap, concentrated coconut milk can be kept in the refrigerator for months.

Dried red dates *(Ziziphus jujuba)*
Dried red jujub with sweet, prune-like taste.

Edible jellyfish *(Rhopilema esculenta)*
Beige in colour and rubbery to the touch, this jellyfish is sold in round sheets about 37.5-40cm (15-16 inches) in diameter, dried, folded and packaged in a plastic bag with large grains of salt between the folds. The salt must be shaken off and the jellyfish soaked in water for 1-2 days before use. Packages of jellyfish already cut up in strips are also available but it is more economical to buy the former. Jellyfish will keep indefinitely in a sealed bag.

Golden needles *(Hemerocallis fulva)*, **tiger-lily buds**
Dried buds of the tiger-lily flower which grows in abundance in Northern China. Usually about 7.5cm (3 inches) long, they are called golden needles because of their colour and shape. They absorb the tastes of other ingredients that they are cooked with and also provide a subtle lightness of texture. They will keep indefinitely if stored in a covered jar or in a sealed plastic bag.

Oysters *(Crassostrea gigas)*
Brown, rectangular and quite firm to the touch, these oysters have been salted and dried in the sun. Considered an epicurean delicacy, they add a "smoky" taste to meat and bland ingredients. Because they are expensive, make sure that they are not mouldy when you buy them. If refrigerated they will keep for a long time.

Potato flour
Flour ground from cooked potatoes. As a thickening agent, it is more gelatinous than cornflour and gives a more subtle and glossy finish to a sauce. In thickening the same amount of liquid, use about two-thirds the amount of potato flour to cornflour. Tapioca starch and arrowroot are also popular thickening agents.

Rock sugar, crystal sugar
This crystallized, pale topaz-coloured cane sugar comes in lumps and has a "pure" taste. Demerara sugar comes closest to it in taste but white granulated sugar can also be used as a substitute. It will keep indefinitely in a dry container.

Scallops (*Amusium pleuronectes*)
Golden and round, with the large ones weighing between 10-15g ($\frac{1}{3}$-$\frac{1}{2}$oz) each, these are white scallops which have been dried in the sun. Inherently sweet, they are used to add a sweet flavour to other ingredients; they are also used as the main ingredient in sophisticated dishes such as Dried scallop soup (see page 59). They keep for a long time in a covered jar in a cool place.

Shark's fin
The fins from more than one species of shark that have been cured and dried in the sun. Many countries in Asia, Europe and South America produce shark's fin, but the product from Manila, the "Manila yellow", is the best. Such fins are, however, extremely expensive and take about four days to prepare. The fin used in this book had already been processed, partially cooked and dried again and it consisted of the cartilage with some "fin needles". On its own, shark's fin has no taste but when combined with other ingredients in a prime stock, it is without peer. Besides being highly nutritious, the Chinese regard shark's fin, whether served as a soup or a red-braised dish, as the pinnacle of gastronomy. Store in a covered jar in a cool place.

Shrimps
Small, shelled shrimps of various sizes, salted and dried in the sun. They are used as a seasoning for vegetables and meat and are very often used in stuffings. Choose those with a fresh, pinkish colour. To store, put in a covered jar in a cool place.

Straw mushrooms (*Volvariella volvacea*)**, padi-straw mushrooms**
Small mushrooms with cone-shaped black caps, cultivated on rice straws in paddy fields. The canned product, mostly from Taiwan, is most popular but should be drained and rinsed before use. They add texture more than taste to other ingredients. (The dried straw mushrooms with their stronger smell are used to lend taste to bland vegetables or in soups.) Store in the refrigerator.

Tangerine peel
Dark brown, hard and brittle dried peel of tangerines, often used in combination with star anise and Szechwan peppercorns. It should keep indefinitely in a cool place.

Water chestnut flour
Flour with a greyish tinge, ground from water chestnuts, used as a thickener in certain savoury and sweet dishes when a light and subtle effect is called for.

Wood ears (*Auricularia polytricha*)
Like cloud ears, this edible fungus is cultivated in large quantities in Western China. However, they are larger in size than cloud ears, coarser in texture, often black on the surface and white underneath, and need to be cooked for a longer period of time. They are used more in soups than in stir-fried dishes. Store in a covered tin.

Oil and Fat

Chicken fat
Rendered by slowly frying the solid fat removed from near the tail and other parts of the chicken, it is used by the Chinese for stir-frying certain vegetables to enhance their flavour.

Corn oil
Light, odourless, polyunsaturated oil processed from the sweetcorn plant. Even though it lacks the special nutty flavour of groundnut oil, it is a very satisfactory substitute because it is less expensive and more easily available.

Groundnut oil, peanut oil
Before the introduction of groundnuts or peanuts to China from America in the 16th century, vegetable oils, in particular rapeseed oil, were commonly used for cooking. Since the intensive cultivation of groundnuts in succeeding centuries, groundnut oil, with its rich and nutty flavour, has become the most important cooking oil in China. Corn oil, which is much more easily available and less expensive in other parts of the world, can be used as a satisfactory substitute. (For deep-frying, however, other vegetable oils will do equally well.)

Hot chilli oil, chilli pepper oil
Easily made from steeping dried red chilli flakes in hot oil (see p. 225), this oil is used to add extra spiciness to food. It can be bought in bottles but the homemade product is generally superior.

Lard
Fat rendered from pork, this used to be considered the aristocratic fat for cooking in China because of the flavour and richness it added to food. Even today cookbooks published in China call for the use of lard in stir-frying and deep-frying. However, lard is heavy and high in saturated fats, and most Chinese people do not use it for daily home cooking; they use groundnut oil, corn oil or other vegetable oils instead. Lard keeps well in the refrigerator for several months.

Sesame oil, sesame seed oil
Thick, aromatic, and light brown in colour, this oil is pressed from roasted white sesame seeds. As such, it is quite different from the cold-pressed Middle Eastern sesame oil, which should not be used as a substitute. Chinese sesame oil is not used for general cooking; rather, because of its heavenly aroma, it is used for marinating ingredients or for sprinkling on food just before it is served. It will keep indefinitely in a cool place.

Sauces

Chilli sauce
This tangy, orange-red sauce is made of crushed fresh chilli peppers, vinegar, salt and plums. It is used both as a spicy hot seasoning and as a dip for crisp food. Store in a cool place.

Fish sauce
Golden brown, transparent sauce made from fish, salt and water. It adds more fragrance and taste to other ingredients or sauces than a sniff of it on its own might suggest. Stored in a cool place, it keeps for a long time.

Hoisin sauce
Reddish brown and thick, sweet yet slightly hot, this sauce is made from soy beans, wheat flour, salt, sugar, vinegar, garlic, chilli and sesame oil. It is used as a dip as well as in cooking and marinating. It keeps in a covered jar for a long time and, if refrigerated, will keep indefinitely.

Oyster sauce
Nut brown in colour, this sauce is made from extracts of oysters, wheat flour, cornflour and glutinous rice, salt and sugar. Not as strong as soy sauce, the sweet and "meaty" taste it lends to other ingredients, whether as part of a sauce mixture or as a dip for meat, poultry and vegetables, makes it a special favourite with the Cantonese. Bottled oyster sauce can be kept in a cool place while canned oyster sauce, once opened, should be transferred to a covered jar or bottle.

Sesame sauce, sesame paste
Thick, aromatic paste of pulverised sesame seeds. The paste has to be thoroughly incorporated with the oil covering it and then thinned with oil or water before use. Tahini paste should *not* be used as a substitute; rather, use peanut butter which has a similar fragrance.

Shrimp paste, shrimp sauce
Made from ground shrimps fermented in brine, this paste is available in two forms: a pinkish purée and a more solid, slightly saltier paté. The purée form is used in this book. Both kinds have to be diluted with water before being used, very often to enhance the taste of bland seafood, such as squid. Usually sold in a jar, it keeps almost indefinitely in a cool place.

Soy sauce
Made from fermented soy beans with wheat or barley, salt, sugar and yeast, this sauce is one of the most ancient seasonings in Chinese cookery. It is at once the most basic and the most versatile condiment for all Chinese cuisines, whatever the regional differences. There are two main kinds of soy sauce: the thick, also called dark soy sauce and the thin, also called light soy sauce. Both are used in general cooking, for marinating and as dips. Very often they are used together with salt. It is the mark of a good cook to know how much of each to use, thereby achieving the delicious end result. *Thick soy sauce* is thicker in consistency than thin soy sauce, darker brown in colour and sweeter in taste. Since it gives a reddish brown hue to food, it is the predominant sauce in red-braised dishes and in flavour-potting. Because of its sweetness, it is preferred by many as a dip at the table.
Thin soy sauce is thinner in consistency, lighter brown in colour and more salty in taste.

Wines and vinegars

Chinkiang vinegar
Thick, dark brown product of Chinkiang in Chekiang province, this has a low vinegar content and a special fragrance and flavour. It is used in cooking or as a dip. It comes in bottles and keeps indefinitely in a cool place. If red wine vinegar is used as a substitute, either use less of it, or add more sugar.

Kao-liang liqueur
A clear spirit made from sorgham (kao-liang in Chinese) grown in north-east China. This very strong liqueur, which the Chinese drink with food, is produced in the distillery founded in Harbin in 1930. Vodka can be used as a substitute.

Mei-kuei-lu wine
Made from Kao-liang spirit and the petals of a special species of rose, this is a very strong liqueur with a unique aroma. It is used in the master sauce for flavour-potting, and is used to add fragrance to marinades. Gin or vodka can be used as a substitute.

Moutai wine
Production of this spirit began in 1704 in a small town called Moutai in Kweichow province, Western China. Made from wheat and sorgham, it is as much these ingredients as the local spring water that give this spirit its distinctive bouquet. It is drunk in small quantities with food.

Red vinegar
Red in colour, this vinegar is also low in vinegar content. It is usually used as a dip to go with fried noodles or Shark's fin soup because the Chinese believe that it makes these foods more easily digestable.

Rice vinegar
Clear in colour and used in cooking or pickling vegetables, this vinegar is neither as sharp nor as pungent as malt vinegar; it keeps indefinitely. Use cider or white wine vinegar as a substitute.

Shaohsing wine
Named after the town in the eastern province of Chekiang, this yellow wine, with its golden sheen, is one of the oldest wines ever produced in China. Fermented from glutinous rice with yeast, this wine owes its fame as much to these ingredients as to the water from the Chien Lake. Between 15-20% proof, there are numerous brands of Shaohsing wine, differing in age and quality, although the one most commonly available in Chinese stores abroad is simply labelled Shaohsing wine. The Chinese drink it warmed up with food, because it tastes much better that way. It is also used in small quantities in marinades or in cooking to enhance the flavour and the taste of the food. Medium dry sherry can be used as a substitute.

Herbs and Spices

Cassia (*Cinnamomum cassia*), **Chinese cinnamon**
Dried bark of the cassia tree. It is used in the master sauce for flavour-potting and is one of the ingredients of five-spice powder. Cinnamon sticks can be used as an alternative.

Coriander (*Coriandrum sativum*), **Chinese parsley, cilantro**
Fresh, green herb with a long stalk branching into flat, serrated leaves; usually sold by the bunch. Pungent, acidic and aromatic, it is used both as a garnish and as a seasoning, especially in Northern China. It will remain fresh for up to a week if refrigerated in an open plastic bag.

Dried red chilli (*Capsicum frutescens*), **chilli peppers**
Crimson red, very often simply called dried chillies, they are sold in two sizes: small, up to 4cm (1½ inches) long and large, about 7.5cm (3 inches) or longer. They are an indispensable ingredient in Szechwan/Hunan cuisine as they provide the fiery spiciness. For the uninitiated, it is perhaps advisable to remove the seeds and the white internal walls, since they are the hottest part of a chilli. They can keep indefinitely in a covered container.

Five-spice powder
Golden brown powder consisting of five and sometimes six ground spices with a liquorice-like flavour. The four basic spices are: star anise, cassia or Chinese cinnamon, cloves and fennel seeds. The remainder are often Szechwan peppercorns and sometimes ginger and cardamom. Five-spice powder is mostly used in marinades for meat, poultry or fish, but it must be used sparingly. It is sold in small packets and can be kept indefinitely in a covered jar.

Flavour-potting mixed spices
Labelled Mixed Spices, these ready-mixed packets are specially sold in Chinese stores for use in flavour-potting. Each packet contains the most commonly used spices in flavour-potting: star anise, Szechwan peppercorns (fagara), cinnamon, ginger, fennel seeds, cloves, liquorice and cardamom.

Garlic (*Allium sativum*)
The bulb of a perennial plant.

Like ginger root and spring onion, it is indispensable in Chinese cooking.

Ginger powder
Dried ginger root ground into a powder. Used as a seasoning, it cannot be used as a substitute for fresh ginger root.

Ginger root, fresh *(Zingiber officinale)*
The knobbly, yellowish green root stalk of the ginger plant. Spicy hot in taste, it is used to provide flavour and to counter rank odour, especially fishiness. Like garlic and spring onion, it is an essential ingredient in Chinese cooking, dating back to the Han times. Choose firm ginger with smooth skin and it will keep well if refrigerated in a plastic bag.

Ground roasted Szechwan peppercorns
Szechwan peppercorns roasted in a dry wok and then ground up into a powder. Used to add aroma to other ingredients, they can be made at home.

Shallot *(Allium ascalonicum)*
Small, firm onion with a milder flavour than Spanish onions.

Spring onion *(Allium cepa)*, **scallion**
A young onion with a long, white bulb topped with tubular green leaves. "White" refers to the firm, essentially white, section which makes up most of the onion; "green" refers to the leaves. The roots attached to the white end must be chopped off and discarded before use. Dating back to the Han times, spring onion forms one of the three basic condiments in Chinese cooking, the other two being garlic and ginger. It keeps fresh in the refrigerator for a few days.

Star anise *(Illicium verum)*
Shaped like a star with eight segments and reddish brown in colour, this hard spice is widely used in Chinese cooking to flavour meat and poultry; it has a distinctive liquorice taste and aroma. It keeps indefinitely in a covered jar.

Szechwan peppercorns *(Xanthoxylum piperitum)*
Tiny, reddish-brown peppercorns which have a stronger aroma than black peppercorns and produce a numbing rather than a burning effect. Available both whole and seeded, the seeded variety have a better aroma and flavour.

White sesame seeds *(Sesamum indicum)*
Tiny, flat seeds from the sesame plant; they keep for a long time in a covered container. (See also sesame oil and sesame paste.)

Vegetables

Bamboo shoots *(Dendrocalamus latiflorus)*
The young shoots of several species of bamboo cultivated for consumption in China. Those available from November to January are called winter shoots and those available from January to April are called spring shoots. Fresh bamboo shoots are only occasionally available in the West; what are available, however, are canned bamboo shoots in chunks or in slices; they should be rinsed before use. If they are not all used at once, the remainder must be transferred to another container, covered with water and refrigerated. If the water is changed every other day, they will keep well for 2-3 weeks.

Bean sprouts *(Phaseolus aureus)*
Tender sprouts from small green mung beans, about 5-10cm (2-4 inches) long. When choosing these sprouts, which are high in protein, look for those which are white and plump and avoid any which are limp and yellow. While bean sprouts can be eaten raw in salads, the Chinese prefer to eat them slightly cooked so that they retain their light and crisp qualities. Fresh bean sprouts can be kept refrigerated in a plastic bag for up to 3 days. Do not buy canned bean sprouts which are just a soggy mass.

Chinese broccoli, *(Brassica alboglabra)* **Chinese kale, gaai-laan**
Chinese broccoli is distinguished by its oval-shaped leaves which have a bluish-green sheen, and the white flowers in the middle of the plant. The stalk is like that of broccoli but the taste is more pronounced, reminiscent of asparagus. It keeps in the refrigerator for about 3 days.

Chinese cabbage *(Brassica chinensis)*, **Chinese white cabbage, bok-choy, bai-tsai**
Thick, white-skinned cabbage with tender dark green leaves. It is similar in appearance to Swiss chard, but it is sweeter and juicier.

Chinese celery cabbage *(Brassica pekinensis)*, **Tientsin cabbage, Peking cabbage, Chinese leaves, wong nga baak**
A tight head of cylindrical white stalks extending into yellowish-white crinkled leaves. This Northern Chinese vegetable is popular among most Chinese because of its sweet, mild flavour and its versatility: it can be stir-fried, braised and put into soups. In recent years, it has become popular in the West and is therefore available in supermarkets. Choose firm heads and see that the leaves are not shrivelled. If refrigerated, it will keep for about 2-3 weeks.

Chinese chives *(Allium tuberosum)*
Similar to chives in appearance, they are, however, darker green in

colour, more fibrous in texture, stronger in taste and have flat not tubular leaves. They are only available in Chinese supermarkets and will keep well in a plastic bag in the refrigerator.

Chinese flowering cabbage (*Brassica parachinensis*), **choi-sum**
This vegetable is distinguished by its yellow flowers and long stems of about 15-20cm (6-8 inches). Because of its subtle taste, it is a great favourite of Southern Chinese, served either stir-fried or simply blanched; the stems need not be peeled. It keeps well in the refrigerator for about 3 days.

Ginkgo nuts (*Ginkgo biloba*), **silver apricot**
The ginkgo tree was originally a sacred Chinese tree but it now grows in Japan and other parts of the world. The nuts, pits of the ginkgo fruit, have to be cracked and peeled. Unfortunately, the flesh inside the beige shell seems to dry up easily with the result that exported nuts are often rotten and hard inside. It is therefore advisable to use canned ginkgo nuts. Mild and tender, they are a favourite of vegetarians. Any left-over nuts should be transferred to a container, covered with water and put in the refrigerator.

Hair algae (*Nematonostoc flagelliforme*), **fa-t'sai**
Black, hair-like algae, this product of the Tsinghai and Sinkiang provinces is sold in a dried form and it must be reconstituted by soaking. Totally tasteless on its own, it absorbs other flavours and provides a slippery and bouncy texture to the dish. Stored in a covered container, it will keep indefinitely.

Mange tout (*Pisum sativum*), **snow peas**
Tender green peapods containing flat, barely formed peas. Valued for their crisp texture and sweet,

subtle flavour, they are best stir-fried. When choosing, look for the flat, tender green ones. If refrigerated in a plastic bag, they will keep for more than 1 week.

Mustard green (*Brassica juncea*), **mustard cabbage, gaai-choi**
There are many varieties of mustard green and some, with their bitter tangy taste, are more suitable for pickling than cooking. A common variety, whose green stalks extend into single, large oval, ribbed leaves, has a distinctive taste when simply blanched or put into soup. It is only sold in Chinese supermarkets. Choose firm green plants and avoid those with limp yellow leaves. It keeps well for a few days in a plastic bag in the refrigerator.

Red-in-snow (*Brassica juncea var. multiceps*), **pickled cabbage**
A red-rooted variety of mustard plant grown in Chekiang province which, being very resistant to cold, can be seen sprouting up through the spring snows, hence the name. This crisp green vegetable is cut and preserved in salt. Available in cans and soaked in brine, it is mostly used as an accompaniment to pork or in soup.

Szechwan preserved vegetable (*Brassica juncea var. tsatsai*), **cha-t'sai, ja-choi**
Made from the swollen nodules on the stems of a species of mustard plant grown in Szechwan province which have been preserved in salt, pressed to squeeze out much of their liquid content and then pickled with a fine red chilli pepper powder. The chilli has to be rinsed off before use. Spicy hot and salty, it gives both a crisp texture and a peppery flavour to other ingredients. Sold in cans, they keep for a long time if stored in a covered jar once opened.

Taro (*colocasia antiquorum*)
Root vegetable which, whether small, like potatoes, or long and fat like yams, has dark brown skin, often with earth-encrusted

root hairs, and a grey or purple flesh. When choosing, press the skin to make sure that it is firm rather than soft, rotten or dried up. When cooked, it is slimy and it is often cooked with duck or fatty pork. Taro keeps well in a cool place for more than a week.

Water chestnuts (*Eleocharis tuberosa*)
Fresh water chestnuts are the walnut-sized bulbs of a sedge cultivated in swampy paddy fields or in muddy ponds. As a result, their mahogany-coloured skin is often encrusted with mud but when washed and peeled, the flesh is white, very crisp and subtly sweet; they can be eaten raw. Canned water chestnuts, although less crisp and sweet will provide a crunchy texture to vegetables and meat dishes. Press fresh water chestnuts to make sure they are not rotten or dried up. They can be kept in the refrigerator for up to a week. Canned ones last up to 1 week if covered with water.

Winter melon (*Benincasa hispida*)
Wax gourd with a white pulp which can weigh from a few pounds up to 100 pounds; it is often cut up and sold by weight in wedges. When buying a wedge, make sure that the pulp has not dried up or turned yellow. The flesh, which when cooked is almost transparent, is often used in soup with pork, chicken or duck. A whole winter melon keeps for 2-3 months in a cool place; a wedge will keep for up to a week if refrigerated in a plastic bag.

Young corn (*Zea mays*)
Tender, miniature corn on the cob, usually sold in cans. They are either put into vegetarian dishes or used as an ingredient with meat.

INDEX

The Author

Yan-kit So is a well-known Chinese cookery expert who has successfully demonstrated her special techniques and recipes at Leith's School of Food and Wine, at Betsy's Kitchen and at la Petite Cuisine School of Cooking. Born in Chungshan, China, raised and educated in Hong Kong, and later in London, she has also lived in India and the USA. Yan-kit So is the author of numerous articles on Chinese cuisine – she contributed recipes and features on regional cooking to *Robert Carrier's Kitchen* – and is currently working on two other cookbooks.

Yan-kit So holds a PhD in history from London University and has translated several Chinese short stories for publication by the Chinese University of Hong Kong. She lives with her son in London.

Acknowledgments

Dorling Kindersley would like to thank the following for their help in the production of this book: Barbara Croxford for initial work on the recipes; Chiang Yu-ling and Charlene Stolper for assisting Yan-kit in photographic sessions: Chiang Hsueh-lien and Kuo Kang Chen for their art services and the stylist Penny Markham.

Photography
Paul Williams

Typesetting
Rowland Phototypesetting (London) Limited

Reproduction
Arnoldo Mondadori, Italy

Illustrators
Jim Robins   Eugene Fleury

I would like to thank the following for encouraging and helping me to embark on cookery professionally: Joanna Collingwood-Anstey, Felicity Bryan, Pamela Harlech, Nancy Royal, Alice Tessier and Caroline Waldegrave. Thanks are also due to those who have contributed ideas and materials, and to those with whom I have discussed various aspects of the book: Alan Davidson, Hilda Ho, Catherine Hwang, Kester Kong, May Kong, Charlene Stolper, So Yan-lap, Agnes Tang, Chef Lam Yi-ling and Chef Woo Kwun. I am especially grateful to Chiang Yu-ling for sharing with me her knowledge and skill on Peking and Szechwan cooking. Last, but not least, I wish to thank the editors, Barbara Crawford and Fiona MacIntyre, and the designer, Sue Storey, for their editorial and artistic effort in shaping the book.

Yan-kit So
1984